A FURTHER GUIDE TO FLY DRESSING

A FURTHER GUIDE TO
FLY DRESSING

John Veniard

A & C BLACK : LONDON

Second Edition 1972
Reprinted 1975, 1977, 1980, 1985
First published 1964

A. & C. BLACK (PUBLISHERS) LTD
35 BEDFORD ROW, LONDON WC1R 4JH

© 1972, 1964 A. & C. BLACK (PUBLISHERS) LTD

ISBN 0-7136-1247-9

Printed in Great Britain by
J. W. Arrowsmith Ltd, Bristol

ACKNOWLEDGEMENTS

This book, as was the *Fly Dressers' Guide*, is the result of a great deal of work by many others as well as myself, so I would therefore like to add the following names to those listed in the first "Guide", plus more thanks once again to Mr. Eric Cumberland Owen for his work in producing the coloured plates of flies, and Donald Downs for his help with some of the drawings.

Great Britain
Capt. The Hon. R. Coke, Col. D. G. Fraser, Mr. K. Stewart, Alec Iles, S. A. Shrimpton, Gordon Hay, John B. Price, The late Courtney Williams, the late Roger Woolley, Col. Joscelyn Lane, Dr. Bell, Col. Esmond Drury, Derek Moseley, T. C. Ivens, Mr. M. A. Wardle, John Goddard, Peter Deane, Frank Sawyer, R. H. Hughes, T. K. Wilson, Ian Wood, the late William Bannerman, G. O. Jones, H. Westmorland, Tony Leigh, J. J. Halpin, L. R. N. Gray, Richard Walker, David Jacques, H. A. J. Featherstonhaugh, A. J. Haytor, A. B. Bourne.

North America
W. R. Coffey, W. J. Golding, Lew Oatman, C. G. Joudry, Harry Darbee.

Australia and Tasmania
Elsa Lowry, J. M. Gillies, Rice Jackson, Canon D. M. Wallace, A. R. Peacock, A. R. Burk, the late Howard Joseland, M. E. McCausland.

New Zealand
Don Page, Mr. and Mrs. Arthur Brett, C. H. Kendrick, R. Sanderson, J. M. Gillies, A. M. McDonald, the late Michael Foster, R. H. Wigram.

South Africa
Q. E. Carter, Dr. McShane, E. V. Evans, Mrs. Helen B. Hilliard, Col. W. Park Gray, R. S. Crass, B.Sc., F. Bowker, H. G. Place, Alan Yates, Mr. Friel, W. W. Small, Dr. Drew, Chris. Hieber, G. B. Mackenzie, Derek Thorneville, Lionel M. Walker, Jack Blackman, the late J. Spranger Harrison.

CONTENTS

SECTION 4
A list of British trout fly patterns

SECTION 5
Additional list of British patterns

SECTION 6
The introduction of new patterns

SECTION 7
Australian, New Zealand and South African patterns

SECTION 8
Canadian and U.S.A. patterns

SECTION 9
Scandinavian patterns

SECTION 10

ILLUSTRATIONS

Plates between pages 80 and 81

ILLUSTRATIONS

Drawings

PREFACE

It was that noted exponent of the art of tying flies for salmon, Dr. T. E. Pryce-Tannatt, who said that one hour's practical demonstration by an expert was of more service to the fly tyer than volumes of written directions.

But Dr. Pryce-Tannatt wrote those words long before John Veniard came out with his remarkable volume—the *Fly Dressers' Guide*—and he surely could not have imagined that printed instructions, with the copious use of illustrations, as were contained in Mr. Veniard's book, could so simplify the art of general fly dressing that the veriest novice could understand them without the help of practical demonstrations.

John Veniard has, of course, a distinct advantage over Dr. Pryce-Tannatt and all the rest of us who have written about fly dressing; he is a member of a firm that is a by-word among fly-tyers as suppliers of fly dressing materials.

In this capacity Mr. Veniard has been able to draw from a great storehouse of information about flies of all types that he (and the firm of Veniards) has gathered in the process of ministering to the material needs of the world's fly dressers over a long period of years.

But this new book by John Veniard, which is complementary to his first work and rejoices in the title of *A Further Guide to Fly Dressing*, is not in any sense a reshuffled version of the earlier volume, which still stands on its own feet as the best standard work on fly dressing ever to come off the printing presses.

No, in this latest book, Mr. Veniard makes a distinctly new approach to the subject. Understandably, in a guide of this kind he still provides many items of practical advice for the fly dressing beginner, but, in addition, there are new ideas on techniques, materials, etc., including, I am pleased to see, instructions about and dressings of tube flies, which will be of incalculable value to the expert as well as the novice.

As one who has written quite extensively on the subject of artificial flies, their dressings, and their histories, I am familiar with the difficulties that Mr. Veniard must have encountered in the process of collecting material for the section in his book which deals with new fly patterns, their origins, and their inventors.

But Mr. Veniard has done the job well, and has found time to provide what is, in effect, an exposition of every useful type of artificial fly for every conceivable kind of fish in waters in every part of the world.

I have no hesitation whatever in recommending this new book to those who find pleasure and profit in tying flies. It is delightfully illustrated with diagrams and magnificent coloured plates by Mr. Eric Cumberland Owen, who collaborated so successfully with Mr. Veniard in his earlier work.

Once, when reviewing Mr. Veniard's previous book, I said that it was the type of volume that I was loth to leave down after sampling its excellence. The new one is built to a similar pattern and deserves to find a prominent niche in the library of every angler who ties flies as an amateur or professional.

TOM STEWART

INTRODUCTION

When the first "Guide" was published I was under the impression that I had covered most territory as far as patterns and procedure were concerned, but the amount of material I gathered subsequently goes to prove that the development of the artificial fly and the methods of making it, never ceases.

This, therefore, is not another general instructional book on fly tying, but has been produced in an effort to keep all interested fly tyers up to date with modern patterns and procedures.

I do not doubt that in another ten years another mass of information will have been collected, for experience has taught me that the interest in the development of the artificial fly remains constant.

It has been my pleasure in the past, and I hope it will be for some time to come, to assist with advice on materials, many of those who are trying to improve on present patterns or introduce new ones. It is this particular aspect of fly fishing which convinces me that the fly fisherman who ties his own flies, must derive more pleasure and satisfaction from angling than anyone else who indulges in it. Not only is there the close study of nature in the medium that gives the contentment for which angling is noted, there is also the satisfaction derived from trying to beat nature at her own game, with concoctions of his own devising, put together with his own hands.

JOHN VENIARD

INTRODUCTION TO THE SECOND EDITION

I can now qualify the remarks I made in the introduction to the first edition, as it became necessary to produce another book in 1970 to categorise the mass of information I had collected on Reservoir fishing. The result was *Reservoir and Lake Flies* published in February of that year.

Much of the material I collected, however, was more relevant to this book, but rather than upset its rather pleasing format, Mr Archie Black very kindly consented to my putting an addendum at the back, and by this means I have been able to add considerably to its usefulness, not only in this edition but also in the future. I have no doubt that the development of the fly for fishing will continue its interesting evolution just as much in the future as it has in the past.

1971   JOHN VENIARD

FLY TYING PROBLEMS AND THEIR ANSWERS

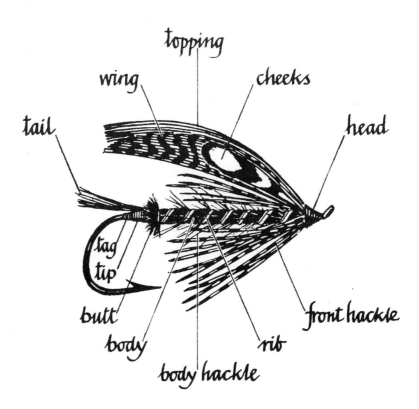

topping

wing

cheeks

head

tail

tag
tip

butt

body

body hackle

rib

front hackle

Parts of the fly

PREFACE

"Fly Tying Problems and Their Answers" was originally published in a series of articles in the *Fishing Gazette*, between October 1956 and February 1957. It was published in booklet form in 1959, and is brought up to date here.

Many of the suggestions and ideas were given to me by a number of fly tying enthusiasts, and I have named them in the chapters concerned. Much credit must be given to their ideas and ingenuity, and I am sure that they will be very pleased to know that these in conjunction with any good fly tying manual, should enable anyone to tie flies without recourse to individual tuition.

My personal advice to anyone who ties flies, regardless of the stage of proficiency he or she may have reached, is: If ever you come up against any difficulty, concentrate on that difficulty until it is overcome. In other words, the particularly difficult problem should be practised until it no longer presents any difficulty. It is not necessary to follow slavishly any instructions, written or otherwise, that purport to show how it is done. A little careful thought, several attempts by trial and error, and above all a little patience, will soon simplify every problem you are likely to come up against.

I would also like to express my appreciation of the late Mr. Marston, who was editor of the *Fishing Gazette* at the time the articles were published, for his co-operation in the publication of the articles concerned.

In conclusion I would like to quote some words from one of the many letters I received from Captain the Hon. R. Coke during the publication of the articles, and who made a considerable contribution to the ideas and suggestions:

"I welcome any endeavour to persuade fishermen to tie their own flies, not only for reasons of economy, as it is a great hobby and one that could do something to halt universal spinning, especially for trout, which I consider an outrage."

PREFACE TO FLY TYING PROBLEMS AND THEIR ANSWERS
SECOND EDITION

As a result of my fortunate meeting with Donald Downs in 1969, "Fly Tying Problems" in its book form was published by Messrs. A. & C. Black in a de-luxe edition. The reason for this was Donald's ability to illustrate my written text in a manner hitherto unknown in books of fly-tying instruction. As most of "Fly Tying Problems and Their Answers" in this volume has been re-illustrated by him, I need enlarge no further on this, and leave my readers to form their own conclusions.

John Veniard.

INTRODUCTION

THERE MUST BE MANY FISHERMEN who are in the habit of reading angling periodicals who have not failed to notice the increased interest in, and practice of, fly fishing in this country. This post-war upsurge is due to several reasons, not the least being that the old idea that fly fishing is a rich man's hobby is fast dying a long overdue death.

Increased travel facilities, and hotels which cater for fishermen only, in areas where fly fishing is, in the main, all that is allowed, have all helped to spread the cult. Moreover, having once tried this delightful method of angling, most fishermen are keen to continue. Nor is fly fishing confined to game fish as it used to be, now that so many coarse-fish anglers have discovered how they can increase the range of their angling methods.

This increase in the numbers of fly fishermen has brought one factor to light which never bothered earlier devotees, namely, the shortage of well-made flies. I am not saying that good flies are not made any more, as this is definitely not true, but the fact is that although the demand for flies has considerably increased, the number of tyers making them is less than before the last war. Many were lost to other industries during the war, and there have been few replacements. It is therefore impossible for present-day tyers to cope with the demand the new interest has created, and also fulfil their export commitments. The demand for British-made flies is still world wide, even though many countries which never had tyers of their own are now building up this trade.

To my mind, the fly is a more important part of the "team" than the rod, reel, line or cast, for without it these expensive items might just as well be left at home for all the effect they can have on one's catch. I know that the fly cannot be presented to the fish without them also, that is why I used the word "team", but the big difference is that they cost many pounds collectively, whereas the fly is comparatively cheap. Even with today's inflated prices and Purchase Tax, it is still possible for the amateur, after he has bought his fly tying equipment, of course, to sit down and make a fly for a very reasonable sum. It would be difficult to state an exact figure, as this must vary with the type of fly being tied, the range being from a simple hackled fly like the "Blue Upright", for instance, to a complex salmon fly such as the "Jock Scott".

It is this fact which is the point of this preamble. There is only one answer if one cannot buy the fly one wants—"do it yourself". There is not a fly in the book the amateur cannot tie once the necessary know-how has been acquired, and there are many books on the market devoted solely to imparting this knowledge.

In spite of this vast storehouse of knowledge, however, there always seems to be one or other part of the craft which eludes the would-be fly tyer, and this results in many giving up before they really even got started. With myself it was the putting on of wings, a stage in fly tying which causes most of us trouble in the early stages. Others have difficulty with other aspects, of course, as I know from the correspondence I receive from old hands and new ones, who want to know some little thing or other.

It is these few minor difficulties which have probably built up the old prejudice that fly tying is too difficult for the non-professional, but it is amazing how easy the whole business becomes once one has got over one's personal hurdle.

I know for a fact that some beginners are put off by the appearance of their early efforts, which is quite ridiculous, for no matter how expert one may become, the first flies one ties usually look terrible. A single lesson from an expert can be of more value than all the books, but I do maintain that it is possible to teach fly tying by the written word and clear illustration, provided it is done properly.

There is also the question of knowing the right materials to use, as some dressings given in books can be very vague on this subject. For instance, if the wing of the fly calls for a mallard feather, this could be any one of five different feathers from the mallard which are used for winging purposes.

I have always felt that if fly tyers had some means of having their questions answered, it would be of great help not only to the questioner, but to many who have been put off merely because there was some small stage in the procedure they could not master, or did not know what material to use. I do not mean that they should have another series of fly tying articles inflicted upon them, but I do think that there must be many, beginners and old hands, who would be pleased to take advantage of some book or part of a book devoted solely to the detailed description of the more tricky points of fly tying, descriptions of materials to be used, and suggestions as to what materials can be used as substitutes for those that are scarce or unobtainable.

The answers to these questions may result in many doubtful starters becoming proficient enthusiasts, which would be doing them a favour, as there is no doubt that fly tying is one of the most interesting and pleasurable hobbies allied to the gentle art.

FLY TYING TERMINOLOGY

Bi-visible Flies. These are designed to improve the visibility of flies to both angler and fish, particularly when using dark flies in poor light. It merely entails the adding of a white or light-coloured hackle to the front of the hackle called for in the dressing. In other words, if a white hackle was wound in front of the hackle used on the "Red Palmer" the fly would then be called a "Red Palmer Bi-visible".

Bobbin Holder. A tool for holding a whole reel of silk during tying, dispensing the silk as required.

Detached Body. The body of an artificial fly, complete in itself, tied on to the hook shank, but separate from it.

Dry Fly. A fly so dressed that it will remain afloat when in contact with the water.

Dubbing. See Fur Bodies.

Dubbing Needle. Used to pick out fur fibres on a "dubbed" body, to simulate legs, feelers, etc.

Fluorescence. Some fly-tying materials are now treated so as to have this property—the ability to reflect light rays during the hours of daylight—useful during dull days and heavy water conditions. It is not possible to get dark shades—such as black, only pastel shades of the primary colours, or variations of them, can be achieved. Manufactured fibres such as nylon react very well to this treatment, but natural materials such as hackles can be quite effective.

Fur Bodies. These are formed by twisting or "dubbing" furs on to the tying silk, and then winding them round the hook-shank to form the body of the fly.

Hackle. Feather wound round the hook-shank to represent the legs or wings of a fly.

Hackle Pliers. Used to grip the tip of the hackle to facilitate its winding.

Herls. Short fibres or "flue" which stand out from individual feather fibres or quills. When these fibres or quills are wound round the hook-shank, the "flue" stands out at right-angles, imparting a certain amount of translucence to the solid body. Peacock and ostrich tail feather fibres are the two best examples of herls, but fibres from wing quills and tail feathers of many other birds are also used, heron, condor, goose and swan being very popular.

Irons. This is the Old Scottish name for Salmon Fly Hooks and has now become general idiom for any type of hook.

Low-Water Flies. Very lightly dressed salmon flies, the wing-tips of which are dressed well forward of the bend of the hook. They are used in summer or low-water conditions by means of the "Greased Line" method. So called because the whole of the line and the cast—to within 18 in. of the fly—is greased so that the fly does not sink very far below the surface.

Mallard Feathers for Wings. One often comes upon this term in the dressing of a fly, but as the mallard supplies so many feathers for wings, some difficulty may be experienced in deciding which one to choose. The best thing I can do here is give the names of the best known flies which use different types of mallard feathers.

Bronze Mallard Shoulder Feathers. "Mallard and Claret" and all the other "Mallard" series of flies. "Connemara Black", "Golden Olive", "Fiery Brown", "Thunder and Lightning", "Blue Charm", and nearly all other salmon flies which have mixed wings.

Grey Mallard Flank Feathers. This is a grey speckled feather similar to teal flank, but with much lighter markings. It is used for "John Spencer", "Queen of Waters", "Grizzly King", "Professor", and as a substitute for teal and pintail feathers in many salmon flies.

Grey Mallard Quill Feathers. These are the wing primary feathers, and can be used for nearly any fly which calls for a grey wing, particularly in the larger sizes, i.e. "Silver Saltoun", "Wickham's Fancy", "Blae and Black", etc.

Blue/White Tipped Mallard Quill Feathers. These also come from the wing, the blue part of the quill being used for one of the best known of all flies—the "Butcher". Strips taken from the white tip of the feather are used for "Heckham and Red", and all the others of the "Heckham" series, "McGinty", "Jock", and, in fact, any fly which has a wing with a white tip. This includes small and low-water salmon flies where a white-tipped turkey tail feather would be too large.

Married Fibres. Fibres taken from different feathers and then joined together to form one whole wing section. Used mainly for mixed and built wing salmon flies.

Palmer Fly. Any fly which has the hackle wound from shoulder to tail. A fly so dressed is usually referred to as "tied Palmer".

Parachute Fly. This term is used for flies with the hackle wound in a horizontal plane instead of round the hook-shank.

Quill. Body: Usually formed by one of the fibres from a peacock's tail, after the flue has been stripped from it. Strips cut from the centre quill of tail or wing quill feathers with a knife can also be used. Wings: When a dressing calls for a wing from a "quill" this means that the feather fibres from the quill are used for the wing.

Ribs. These can be formed of silk, herls or tinsels. On trout flies they are usually meant to simulate the segmentations of insect bodies, whereas on salmon flies their function is to strengthen the body material and protect any body hackle if used.

Silk Bodies. Strands of silk, usually floss, wound directly on to the hook-shank to form the body.

Tail. See Whisks.

Tail Feather. When a dressing calls for a wing or part of a wing from a tail feather, this means that the feather fibres from the tail are used. "Grouse and Green" uses feather fibres from the grouse tail.

Teal Feathers for Wings. As with the mallard, the teal supplies several feathers for wings. When a fly has a black and white barred feather for the wings, it is the breast or flank feather of the teal which is used. Such flies are "Peter Ross", "Teal and Green", "Teal and Blue" and all the others of the "Teal" series. The grey feathers of the wing can be used for such patterns as "Wickham's Fancy" or any other largish pattern requiring a grey wing.

Tandem Hooks. Two or more hooks whipped to gut, nylon monofilament, or wire, in line with each other. Used mostly for sea and lake trout lures sometimes referred to as "Demons" and "Terrors". The now very popular "Worm Fly" is usually tied on a two-hook tandem.

Tinsel. Strips of flat metal and strands of silk covered with metal. Used for whole bodies or just for ribbing. When in doubt use a flat tinsel for a whole body, and the covered silk tinsel for ribbing.

Tinsel Bodies. Bodies made of metal strip wound the length of the hook-shank, used to impart "flash" to a fly, particularly those flies which are supposed to resemble a small fish.

Tube Flies. Flies which have the body hackle and wings (if any) tied on to a length of plastic or metal tubing. The hook is supplied by tying a double or treble hook to a length of gut, and passing it through the tube.

Tying Silk. Fine natural silk, by which all materials are tied to the hook.

Wax. This enables the tying silk to grip the materials firmly while the fly is being tied. Solid or liquid types can be used.

Wet Fly. A fly so dressed that it will sink when cast.

Whip Finish. The best method of finishing off a fly. It consists of two or three turns of the tying silk laid over the end of the silk before it is pulled tight.

Whip Finisher. A tool so designed to simplify the application of the whip finish of the fly. It is only suitable for this purpose and cannot apply whip finishes to rods, hooks to gut or any other article which has a projection beyond the actual whip finish.

Whisks. Fibres of feathers used to form the tail. If material such as wool or silk is used, they are more often referred to as a "tag" instead of a tail.

Wings. Here is a list of the various types of wings used on trout and salmon flies.

Wet Fly. A flat wing sloping back over the body of the fly.

Double Split Wing Dry Fly. Formed of two sections each, taken from a pair of matched wing quills and tied in so that the tips point outwards.

Fan Wings. Formed of two small breast feathers, usually from the mallard drake, tied in to curve outwards.

Advanced Wing. Term used when the wing slopes over the eye of the fly instead of the body. Can be a flat wing or a double split wing.

Down Wing. Used for dry flies which simulate the Sedge group, Stone flies and Alder flies.

Rolled Wing. These consist of a roll of feather fibres taken from a wing quill or tail. They are used for the down wing types mentioned above, and for some well-known types of North Country upright winged dry flies.

Upright Wing. Any wing that stands upright from the body of the fly. They can be double split wings, fan wings, rolled wings, hackle point wings, etc. etc.

Bunch Wings. Wings formed by a bunch of fibres cut from any feather. They can be tied upright, low over the body, advanced or split.

Split Wings. Any wings that have their points separated.

Hackle Point Wings. Almost self-explanatory. The tips of hackles are used to form the wings, two for most patterns, four for mayflies.

Spent Wings. Wings tied so that they lie flat on the water when cast—imitating the spent fly. Hackle points or hackle fibres are the most popular of this type.

Hackle Fibre Wings. Similar to "bunch wings" in so far that a bunch of hackle fibres is used for the wings.

Shaving Brush Wings. Hair or feather fibres tied in so that they point forward over the eye of the hook in line with the shank. Down-eyed hooks should be used to facilitate the tying on of the cast, or the tying silk should be so wound so as to form a slight split down the centre of the wing.

Hair Wings. Wings formed of animal fur fibres. Invariably down wings or wings of the "shaving brush" type.

Streamer Wings. Wings formed of whole hackles or long strips of other feathers, the tips of which project well beyond the bend of the hook.

Strip Wings. A term used for salmon-fly wings which are made of strips taken from one type of feather only.

Whole Feather Wings. Term used when a whole feather or two whole feathers back to back, form the wing of the fly.

Mixed Wings. Wings that are formed from the fibres of several different feathers, "married" together to form single whole sections.

Herl Wings. Wings that are formed with the feathers normally used for herl bodies. The "Alexandra" is the best-known example.

Wing Cases. The "hump" incorporated in the dressings of nymphs and beetle imitations to simulate the wing housing. They are usually formed of feather fibres tied in at one point, folded down on to the body and then tied in at another point. If fur or silk is used for the body, this should be thickened between these two points so as to accentuate the "hump".

Varnish. This is applied to the final turns or whip finish of the fly, to prevent the silk unravelling during use. Clear varnish is usually used for dry flies, while spirit and coloured varnishes are used for wet flies and salmon flies.

It is as well to have some method of ensuring that bottles of varnish are not knocked over whilst actually tying. An accident of this nature could ruin many hours of work, or make valuable items of material unusable. A simple stand capable of taking a selection of varnishes and thinners etc., was designed by Peter Deane and is illustrated below. Further contributions to this book by Mr. Deane are given on pages 162-165.

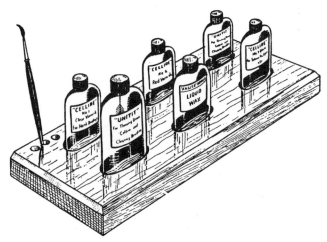

The "Peter Deane" fly tyers' bottle stand

CHAPTER ONE

WINGS AND WINGING

THE TYING-ON OF WINGS is usually the first difficulty encountered by the amateur fly tyer.

Like many other apparently involved processes, once one knows how, it is simplicity itself. The main difficulty appears to be how to impart this knowledge by the written word and illustration, so that the beginner is left in no doubt as to how it is done. There are several books of instruction which do this quite well, so all I can do is endeavour to make the explanation simpler still.

Tools for winging are obtainable, and although I prefer to use my fingers, mainly for reasons of speed, these tools can put a well-shaped wing on to the hook and are ideal in demonstrating the technique required to do so.

The secret, if secret it be, of a well-tied wing, is to bring each fibre of the slips of feathers used down on top of the fibre beneath it, without any divergence from the vertical. This is achieved by forming a loop of the tying silk over the wing, gripping the hook, silk and wing firmly, and then drawing the tying silk tight. Three tight turns should be made in this manner, before removing the fingers. Do not pull the silk tighter after removing the fingers, as this tends to pull the wing over to the far side of the hook.

The position of the fingers for this operation is shown in Fig. 1.

The procedure when using winging pliers is as follows. Prepare the left and right wings and place them in the tool, the spring tension of which will keep them in position. Place the tool near the hook and then pass at least two turns of the tying silk through the eye of the tool. Place the tool on top of the hook-shank where the wing is to be tied in and then draw this silk tight. Now comes what to my mind is the most important part of the instruction. Hold the tool by the jaws which grip the wing, and not by its top. Not too tightly or you will find it impossible to draw the wing down. This will ensure that each fibre comes down one on top of the other, and also demonstrates what you would do if you were not using the winging tool. Also most important—put another turn of silk round the hook-shank to ensure that the wing will not move when the tool is removed.

If it is a wet-fly or a salmon fly being tied, the surplus end of the wing can now be cut off and several turns of silk taken over the remaining butt to form the head.

If a dry-fly is being tied, the wing slips will have been placed so that the points turn outwards. When the tool is removed the wings must be again gripped firmly (not including the hook this time), raised to the vertical, a couple of turns put

25

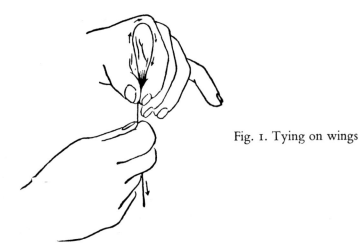

Fig. 1. Tying on wings

round their base, and then another round the hook-shank. This will keep them in the upright position, and another figure-of-eight turn between them will keep them separated. At all times keep the tying silk taut, and make all turns of silk as tightly as the strength of tying silk will allow. Slackness at any time is fatal.

Fig. 2. Winging pliers

When I make my own dry-flies I prefer to tie the wings in the forward position. That is, with the wings pointing over the eye of the hook and not to the rear when they are tied in. The procedure for tying them in is exactly the same, except that the wings are tied in before the body and tail, etc., instead of last, as is the usual method. This means that the wing can be tied in nearer the eye, and the butt can be covered by the body material. It is also only necessary to wind the hackle at the back of the wing instead of the back and the front, which makes a much neater job in my opinion. It is, however, even more essential that the wings be fixed firmly in the upright position, as there are no hackle fibres in front of the wings to assist in keeping them upright.

Before starting to tie his winged flies the beginner will do well to practise the winging procedure on its own. To do this I advocate a largish hook, and a wing material consisting of fibres which stay well together. The best one I know is the primary feather from the wild duck (mallard) wing, and with the help of the foregoing the absolute tiro should be able to form a reasonable wing after several attempts.

With regard to the softer materials used for winging some sea-trout and salmon flies, such as teal flank and mallard shoulder feathers, the procedure with these is exactly the same, except that the firm approach is even more essential. It also helps if double thicknesses of these feathers are used, i.e. two slips from a left-hand feather for one side of the wing, and two slips from a right-hand feather for the other, as this prevents that "wispy" effect one often gets when using these feathers I have not given any details of how one should prepare the slips for one's wings, as this is not very difficult, and is well covered in all the books of instruction I have seen.

The natural shape of the feathers one uses for wings can also be utilised to give the desired shape to the wings. If the top edge of the wing slips is left at the top when the wing is tied in, the resulting wing will be as Fig. 3. If put on upside down the result is as Fig. 4.

(See "Wonderwing" photograph between pages 80 and 81.)

3 (*left*) Wing slip tied in with top edge left at the top.

4 (*right*) Wing slip tied in upside down

Shaping the wings

The following method of winging was given to me by Col. D. G. Fraser, and although he states that he has used it for trout flies only, I found it worked just as successfully with salmon fly wings.

The idea is based on the fact that no matter how carefully wings are compressed and controlled whilst being tied in, there *must* be a tendency for the wing fibres to follow the tying silk over the hook-shank when the silk is drawn tight, and the waxier the tying silk is, the more pronounced becomes the tendency. (Fig. 2 shows the recognised method of tying in a wing.)

This is very true, and even in a less exaggerated form, it can result in a crease or "pleat" forming on the far side of the wing, although its basic shape may not be affected.

To overcome this one-sided pull, Col. Fraser uses an additional length of tying silk to that being used to tie the fly. This additional length is not waxed, and is used to form the loop over the wing with which we are all familiar, and as *both* its ends can be drawn down at once there is no irregular pull on one side.

To facilitate its introduction between the fingers and over the wing, a small weight is fixed to one end. A light wooden bead is suggested, and the device in use is described as follows:

Normal fly-tying procedure is carried out to the stage where the wings are placed on top of the hook-shank, being held by the forefinger and thumb. The actual tying silk is left hanging down in its holder or weighted with hackle pliers, at the point where the wing is to be tied in. The beaded end of the unwaxed piece of silk is then inserted plumb-bob-wise between the far side of the hook and the forefinger holding the wing. It is at this stage that the necessity for the weight on the end will be appreciated, as it would be difficult to introduce the silk without some form of weight to control it. A loop is then taken over the extended finger of the free hand, and the other end of the unwaxed silk is guided between the near side of the hook and the thumb holding the wings. The extended forefinger is extracted from the loop, and *both* ends of the unwaxed silk drawn down, compressing the wing fibres on to the top of the hook-shank. Fig. 1 shows an end-on view of the loop over the wings and the two "legs" of the unwaxed silk hanging down. After they have been pulled down, the two "legs" are pushed to the left out of the way, and the actual waxed tying silk is wound round the wings and hook in the normal way. The tips of the finger and thumb can be opened slightly at this stage to ensure that the turns of the tying silk are close up to the point where the loop is holding the wings on the hook-shank. These turns must be to the right of the loop, of course, otherwise the wings will be distorted in the manner described earlier.

Col. Fraser states that one turn of the tying silk is all that is necessary, and the unwaxed silk is then withdrawn by pulling straight downwards on the beaded

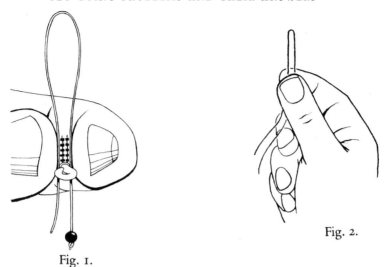

Fig. 1.

Fig. 2.

Winging device

end. The surplus wing material can now be cut off and the head of the fly formed. It is always advisable to hold the wings in position while doing this.

I think the idea is an excellent one, so much so that it occurred to me that it might even be improved upon. The most difficult part of the procedure (perhaps "least easy" would be a better description) is the introduction of the unwaxed silk loop between the finger and thumb and over the wing. If the loop could be made rigid, this introduction would be greatly simplified, so I tried replacing the unwaxed silk with a piece of fine, but stiffish wire about 6 in. long, and folded in half. It worked first time. The piece of folded wire is held about 1 in. from the bend, Fig. 2, and the introduction of the loop so formed is simplicity itself. The tips of the finger and thumb holding the wing in position are opened slightly, and the loop inserted to the position where the wing is to be drawn down. The finger and thumb are then compressed once again, and the piece of wire drawn down as was the beaded silk. The ends of the wire are then pushed to the left and the tying silk brought into play to fix the wing permanently. There is one slight difference in the procedure when using the wire, however. If it was removed, as was the silk, by pulling on one end, it might cut through some of the fibres of the wing. It is better, therefore, to push the loop up slightly from underneath the hook-shank, and then withdraw it from above.

Both these methods produced an absolutely flat wing, seated right on top of the hook-shank, and I hope the many who have had this difficulty with their fly tying, will find they are the answer to their problem.

During the course of the articles in the *Fishing Gazette*, a very considerable contribution was made by Captain the Hon. R. Coke, whom I have known for many years as a very keen and meticulous fly tyer.

The following tips of his are concerned with wings and winging, but others will be found in the chapters they concern.

Firstly, his method of winging: The procedure is to carry out the winging process in the usual way, but instead of pulling the loop *down*, the tying silk is taken round the hook-shank underneath, and back between the wing and thumb holding it. The end of the tying silk is then pulled up vertically instead of downwards, and as the wing and the hook-shank are totally encompassed by the tying silk, the compression of the wing fibres one on top of the other is assured. The process should be carried out twice, and throughout, the wing and hook-shank must be held firmly in the thumb and forefinger of the left hand, including a small portion of the butt end of the wing. This is most important.

His next tip has to do with our other old friends mallard and teal wings. As I have already mentioned, these feathers have more cohesion as wings when double strips of fibres are used for each side of the wing. Captain Coke's method incorporates the same principle, but it is only necessary to cut off a single strip from each side of the feathers being used, and this is done as follows.

Cut a left- and a right-hand strip from the required feathers, both *double* the width required for the wing, leaving the quills on. Stroke out the fibres to stand at right-angles to the quills. Now place the two strips one on top of the other, best side downmost. Now cut the quills off both strips and fold the double strip you now have exactly in half down the middle. A small "V" cut with the scissors at the base of the strips, and in the middle, will help the folding process.

Hold the wing in the forefinger and thumb of the left hand, and if any fibres are out of place they can be removed with a dubbing needle or stiletto. The result is a firm, well-shaped wing ready for tying in, less apt to disintegrate, and having much greater substance.

It is ideal for those flies which require a wing of either teal, mallard, or widgeon, etc., such as the "Teal Blue and Silver", or "Thunder and Lightning". It also eliminates the necessity of tying in an underwing of some other feather when tying a fairly large fly, but if an underwing is part of the dressing, as in a "Blue Charm", for instance, the underwing of mallard can be tied in the normal way, and the overwing of teal folded over it in the manner described in the foregoing. I hope I have made the instructions quite clear, especially as they are not the type which lend themselves easily to illustration.

PREPARING HEN PHEASANT TAILS FOR WINGS

The ease with which one can prepare materials for wings varies with the type of feather being used. Mallard wing quills are very amenable, whereas the bronze

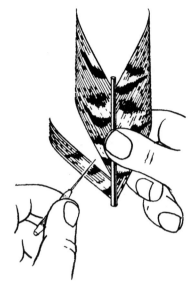

Fig. 1. Preparing the tail feathers of the hen pheasant

shoulder feathers can be more difficult. It will usually be found that the wing quill feathers of all birds are always easier to prepare than are the body feathers.

In between the two are the tail feathers used for wings, and of these the hen pheasant tail is about the most difficult to prepare. As they are used very extensively for such flies as the "Invicta" lake and sea trout fly, and the low-water salmon fly "March Brown", I think they deserve some special attention.

The usual trouble found is that no matter how wide a portion of these fibres are cut off, only a very fine tapered wing is produced.

This is because of the very acute angle at which the fibres of these tails are set in the quill, and when these fibres are drawn down to stand out at a more usable angle they have a strong tendency to spring back to their natural position. This makes it difficult to get a wide portion of fibres to tie in.

To overcome this, I handle the fibres as follows: instead of pulling the fibres right down, I merely separate the required width from the main body of the tail, as Fig. 1. I then grasp the fibres at a point that will make the wing slightly longer than I wish to tie, Fig. 2. I then pull down the fibres remaining on the left, very gently, as though the part I was holding with my right hand was the quill. This causes the fibres to take the shape shown in Fig. 3, and I then cut them off where shown and tie them in in the usual way.

I would point out that some of these tails are easier to handle than others, and a good, fresh, long-fibred tail from a mature bird will manipulate much better than a dried-up one, or one from an immature bird. I also find that they tie in much better in the horizontal position than when set upright, although this is not really an important factor.

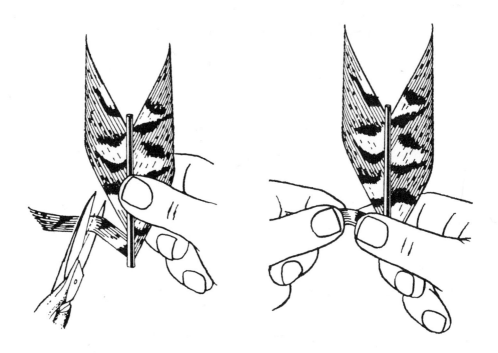

Fig. 2 *and* 3. Preparing the tail feather of the hen pheasant

While on the subject of difficult wing materials, a few words about the mallard shoulder feathers and teal flank feathers would not come amiss. The tips of these feathers have a strong tendency to fly apart when tied in, particularly on small flies.

What should always be remembered about these feathers is that not only are the main fibres very soft and delicate, but also that the intermediary hairs that hold the main fibres together, are also delicate in proportion. Consequently, once the fibres are moved or split, they never hold together again quite so well. Therefore, when cutting out the slips, the fibres should not be drawn down as are the fibres on wing quills, they should merely be cut straight off from the feather.

Also, as these soft fibres will compress into a very small space, it is better to make the wings of double thickness. In other words, two slips from a right-hand feather and two slips from a left-hand feather. If these double slips are tied in without disturbing the original shape of the fibres in any way, it will be found that the tendency for their tips to fly apart is greatly reduced. I would also stress once again that one's material should be as fresh as possible, as once the natural oils dry out of these feathers, it is almost impossible to keep their tips together when tying in as wings.

With larger flies, these difficulties are greatly reduced, the reason for this being that the nearer to the quill of the feather one gets, not only are the fibres much sturdier, they also marry together much better. In fact, an attempt to tie a small fly with the fibres from a large feather will invariably result in the tips flying apart. Unfortunately, it is not possible to get very small brown mallard feathers, as the brown speckling is not present in feathers below a certain size.

This tendency for the tips to fly apart when they are tied in is much less apparent when the method described on page 30 is used.

CHAPTER TWO

WINDING HACKLES

THE WINDING OF HACKLES is a frequent item of my correspondence.

Doubling them is dealt with in Chapter Three, and this chapter is concerned with the tying and winding of hackles for dry flies. The usual complaint is as follows:

"When tying hackle dry-flies I find that my flies seem sparse in hackle and untidy compared with shop flies. The hackle fibres seem to point over the eye, rather than give the straight frontal hackle of the professional tyer. Why is this?"

I am often asked this question, and the main answer is that as the professional is always tying flies, his finished product should look better than that of the amateur. This is only a generalisation, of course, as I have seen flies tied by amateurs that were perfect specimens of neatness and balance, and not all the flies one sees in the shops today would get a faultless pass! One result of tying flies continually, is the automatic knowledge which is acquired, of putting every turn of silk and material in its right place. This is the absolute essence of a well-tied fly.

To concentrate on hackles, however, there are several reasons why the fibres do not stay at an absolute right-angle to the hook-shank.

1. If the hackle is not drawn through the fingers so that all the fibres stand out at right-angles to the stem, those fibres which are on the side nearest the hook-shank when the hackle is being wound will be splayed out by the stem.

2. Tying in the hackle so that the fibres are not straight up and down, will result in their going off at different angles when the hackle is wound.

3. If the hackle stem should overlap itself at any time during the winding, the fibres will again be forced out of line.

4. If the hackle is not pulled tight all the time it is being wound, this will result in the stem twisting and sending out the fibres in all directions.

5. Careless winding of the silk through the fibres, if this method of finishing off is used, will also disturb them.

6. Tying in the front fibres when finishing off.

One other point, which you will observe I stress repeatedly in this book. The tying silk must be kept taut at all times when tying flies. Slackness at any time can only result in an untidy-looking fly, or even one that literally falls to pieces before it is removed from the vice.

My method of tying a simple hackle fly is as follows: form tail and body of fly, leaving ample room at the head for hackle. Select the hackle and draw it

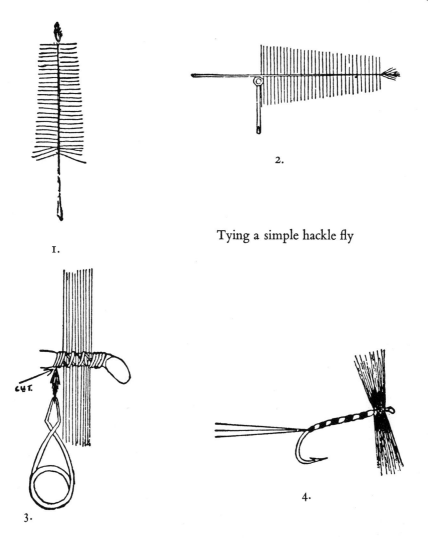

Tying a simple hackle fly

1.

2.

CUT.

3.

4.

through the fingers so that it looks like Fig. 1. Tie it in on top of the hook-shank (or underneath, whichever you prefer), holding it by the stem, close to the eye of the hook. The stem should now be at a right-angle to the hook-shank, the tip pointing away from you, and the fibres absolutely vertical, Fig. 2. Now wind the tying silk back to the body in close, even turns, tying in the stem of the hackle at the same time, which must, of course, be bent back towards the tail for this purpose. The turns of silk *must* be even, laid on as they appear on a new reel of silk. Uneven turns of silk will distort the hackle stem. Now grip the tip of the hackle in the hackle pliers and, keeping the hackle taut all the time, wind it up to the body.

When the body is reached, allow the hackle tip to hang down in the pliers, and take a turn of silk round it and the hook-shank. Continue winding the silk through the hackle to the eye of the hook, holding it as tightly as possible. These turns of silk will tie down the hackle stem, and if kept taut it will be observed that the silk hardly disturbs the hackle fibres. Extra care must be taken when the front fibres are reached, and then two turns are taken in front of them. The fibres should be brushed lightly to the rear before attempting the whip finish in the front, and the turns of this finish should just touch the front fibres, but not overlay them in any way, Fig. 3. I find a whip-finishing tool in invaluable for this, as one can lay the turns of silk in exactly the right place without disturbing the hackle fibres. A symmetrical fly should look like Fig. 4, and if the points I have stressed are fully observed, a result like this is fully guaranteed.

If you possess those very long-stemmed, short-fibred hackles which make the best dry-flies, they can be wound with one side stripped off. This would, of course, be the side nearest the hook-shank when the hackle is wound. Symmetry is assured if this is done, although it must be remembered that the hackle will not be as "full" as when both sides are retained. The foregoing procedure is the same for the stripped hackle also.

With regard to what I said about every turn of silk and material being in its proper place, until this is done automatically, it is as well to be able to observe one's flies clearly during the tying. I find the best way to do this is to have one's vice raised up so that the fly is as near to the level of the eyes as possible. It is far better than looking down on the fly. If this cannot be done with your vice, ensure that you have a suitable background so that the fly gives a sharp silhouette. This will show up any slack winding or divergence of the material.

CHAPTER THREE
DOUBLING HACKLES AND "FALSE" HACKLES

Now for "doubled" hackles. There are several methods of turning back the fibres of hackles, known to us all through various books of instruction, but I will keep to what I think is the most simple one. This entails the use of a spare hook and one's tying vice and hackle pliers.

The hackle to be doubled is tied on to the hook by its tip or butt, and then held vertically by the hackle pliers. The fibres are then stroked to the left, best side outside, until the necessary "V" sectional appearance is attained. It is as simple as that. I advocate doubling the hackles on a spare hook, as if one strokes the fibres a little too vigorously the hackle may be pulled from the hook, and that would be a calamity if it was a body hackle being doubled as the body of the fly would have to be unwound and the hackle tied in afresh. This is not so important, of course, if it is a throat hackle. Also by this method several hackles may be prepared and then put aside until they are required. The illustrations may be of some help: the first, Figs. 1, 2 and 3, showing how the hackle is tied in and treated.

Note that the hackle is tied in close to the body and then wound towards the eye of the hook (Fig. 4).

When winding a body hackle, it is important to ensure that the hackle stalk is not twisted in any way, otherwise the "doubling" is nullified. It also helps if the fibres are stroked back towards the tail during the winding. Make sure that every turn of the hackle is close up against its companion turn of the ribbing tinsel, as this not only protects that hackle stalk, but will also keep the doubled hackle fibres in position (Fig. 5). Fig. 6 shows both doubled body and throat hackles on fly which is now ready for winging.

Another method (Figs. A-C) of doubling was recently given to me by Jimmy Younger, whose family have been well known in Scottish fly tying and fly fishing for several generations. He uses hackle pliers held in the hand to hold the hackle to be doubled, and the illustration of this method should be clear enough without further explanation from me.

If doubling hackles still presents some difficulty to the reader, the following method of making "false" hackle may produce better results. It is another one of the ideas sent to me by Capt. the Hon. R. Coke, and although it is not a new idea, as he freely admits, he considers it to be one not used generally enough.

"False" hackles consist of a bunch of fibres torn from a feather and tied in at the throat in very much the same manner as one would tie in a wing. By this means,

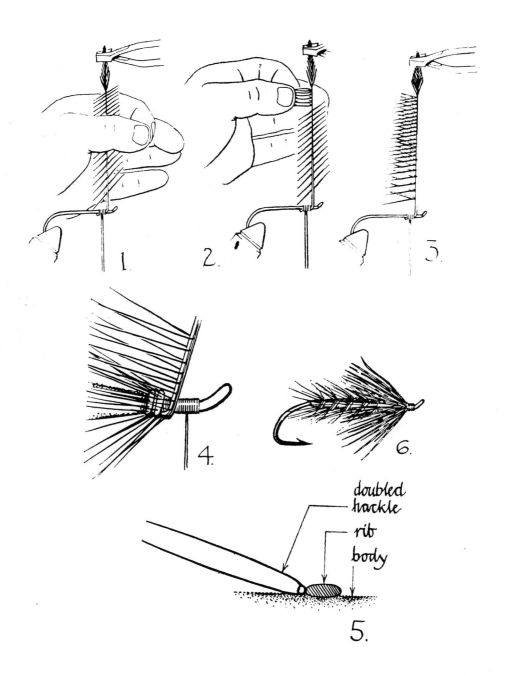

doubled
hackle
rib
body

such difficult feathers as blue jay can be used without the bother of splitting the quill and its subsequent breakages, resulting in greater economy and reducing bulk at the head of the fly. Ordinary poultry hackles which are too large for normal use may also be utilised on flies of any size. The procedure is as follows:

The fly is tied to the stage where it is necessary to add the throat hackle, and the tying silk anchored with a half-hitch. The hook is then taken from the vice and put back upside down. The feather to be used as a hackle is then selected, and its fibres pulled down to stand out at right-angles to the stem. Tear off a good bunch of the fibres, keeping their tips in line as much as possible. These fibres are now tied in on top of the hook-shank (this is underneath, of course, as the hook is upside down), using the normal winging procedure of the loop over the finger and thumb of the

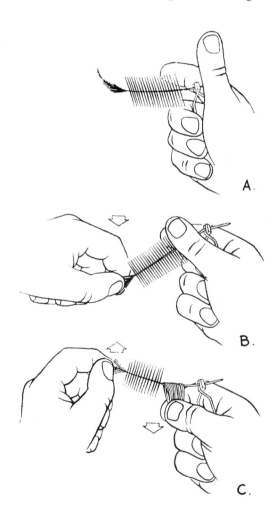

A.

B.

C.

left hand. To spread the fibres over the whole area of the throat it is better to place the fibres rather to the side of the hook facing you, so that when the silk is drawn tight the fibres are pulled over to the far side. In other words, although we are using the winging principle to tie in the fibres, we forget about all the principles we have learned for bringing feather fibres down one on top of the other, but endeavour to produce a split "wing".

After one turn of the tying silk has been taken, it should be put in the retaining button or hackle pliers (if not weighted with a bobbin holder), and the fibres separated and adjusted with a dubbing needle or stiletto. One bunch of fibres is usually enough, but on larger flies another two small bunches can be tied in, one on either side of the original one.

This process may sound involved, but in practice is very simple. Moreover, when the hook is once again reversed it will be found that there is practically no "hump" to be levelled off before the wings are tied in, which means that a small head results and the wings lie low over the body.

Many feathers can be tied in by this method to give pleasing results other than jay. Partridge body feathers, heron, guinea fowl (gallena) all lend themselves to it, and the necessity of doubling them is eliminated. It can only be applied to throat hackles, of course, as body hackles must still be wound on the stem.

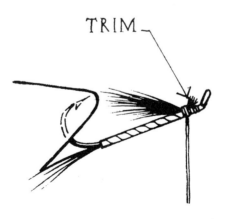

TRIM

"FALSE" HACKLE

CHAPTER FOUR
STIFFENING DRY-FLY HACKLES

STILL ON THE SUBJECT OF HACKLES, Captain Coke has the following method of stiffening his dry-fly hackles, an idea born of the scarcity of the good-quality hackles required to keep our flies afloat. It is this: after completing the fly to the stage where the hackle is required, select a large hackle of the same colour and cut off about 1 in. from the tip. This is the best part to use as any web which may be in the feather is much less apparent at its extreme tip. Stroke the fibres to right-angles to the stem and clip them to about $\frac{1}{8}$ in. in length either side of the stem. The length would vary according to the size of fly, of course, but in this instance we are left with a hackle 1 in. long with a width of $\frac{1}{4}$ in. along its entire length.

This hackle is now tied in at the shoulder of the fly, and one, or at the most two, turns taken round the hook-shank and finished off. The effective hackle is then selected and tied in and wound behind and in front of the cut hackle, and the fly finished off in the usual way.

The stiff, short fibres of the cut hackle act as stiffeners to the weaker fibres of the ordinary hackle, and are quite invisible if the job is done properly. A fly tied in this manner is most effective in rough water, where it is most important to have one which cocks and floats well.

Incidentally, this two-hackle principle is used for the Dr. Baigent "Refractra" dry-flies, the difference being that instead of the long-fibred hackle being cut short it is left long, the effective hackle forming the legs forming the centre of the hackle. By this means, Dr. Baigent claimed that the surface of the water was disturbed by the fibres of the long hackle, giving an altered refraction and thus a more natural look to the artificial from the fish's point of view.

There is also a method of waterproofing hackles before they are wound, by using a well-diluted solution of cellulose varnish on them. The procedure is as follows: Strip the soft fluffy fibres from the base of the hackle, and draw the remaining fibres down to right-angles to the stem, as per illustration No. 1 on page 35.

The solution is then applied to the thumb and forefinger used to draw down the hackle fibres, and the drawing-down process continued. This results in a fine film of the solution being applied to the fibres, which will dry into a waterproof "skin", which is far less liable to absorb moisture than an untreated hackle.

Any fibres that should adhere to each other can be separated by a dubbing needle, but this should only happen if the solution is too "tacky".

Hackles when treated should be clipped into a "Bulldog" paper clip by the stem, and hung up to dry. This does not take very long, as a thin solution of cellulose varnish dries very rapidly.

The experiments for the above were carried out with the "Cellire" brand of cellulose varnish, using "Unitit" thinners, and although it may sound rather messy, a practically unsinkable fly is the result.

CHAPTER FIVE
MAKING FLIES WITH "PARACHUTE" HACKLES

THE POPULARITY OF THE PARACHUTE FLY seems universal, as I have had requests from overseas as well as from the British Isles for the best method of making them up.

As most of you will already know, they differ from orthodox flies in that the hackle is wound on a horizontal plane, not on a vertical one, as is usual. To facilitate this, a short vertical projection on top of the hook-shank is required, but hooks made with this projection already fitted are not readily obtainable. It is possible, however, to overcome this by resorting to makeshifts, such as by whipping pieces of gut or bristle to the top of the hook-shank, with a projecting end bent upwards. It is better to have this projection fairly long at this stage, so as to make the winding of the hackle much easier. The surplus can be cut off afterwards. A small spot of varnish should be dropped on top of the projection when the fly is finished, so that the hackle will not slip off it.

An alternative method, and one which I use myself, is as follows.

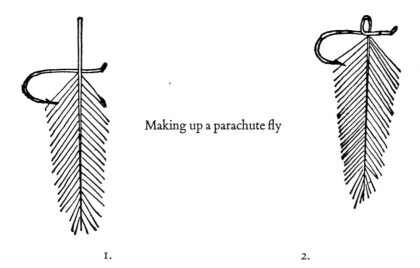

Making up a parachute fly

1.   2.

Put the hook in the vice, and tie in the hackle as shown in Fig. 1. The projecting hackle stalk is then looped over and tied to the hook-shank as shown in Fig. 2.

The body and tail of the fly are now formed, leaving the hackle stalk loop projecting above. The tying silk should be taken to the right of the hackle.

The hackle is now wound horizontally round the loop of hackle stalk, and to simplify this operation, it helps if a dubbing needle is pushed through the loop. The hackle can then be wound quite easily between the needle and the body of the fly.

When two or three turns have been made, tie down the tip of the hackle to the right of the loop. The tying silk is then threaded through the loop and pulled so that the loop is drawn towards the eye of the hook. It is tied down firmly, and the usual whip finish made at the eye.

It is customary to use a hackle with fairly long fibres when tying these flies, and the finished article should be as Fig. 3.

3. Finished parachute fly

If a winged fly is required, these can be tied in before the hackle is, and the procedure carried out *underneath* the hook-shank. This means, of course, that the hackle would be tied in the reverse way up. It can be done on top of the hook-shank, but the wings have to be flattened into the "spent" position to enable the hackle to be wound.

As all the hackle fibres come into contact with the water, instead of only a few as in conventional flies, it is not necessary to make as many turns of hackle. Two are usually enough, and three the maximum.

It is possible, if one is an adept fly tyer, to use the wings of the fly as the "axle" of the parachute hackle. The hackle is wound round the base of the wing, but it is very difficult to do this and still retain the good shape of the wings.

It has been proved many times that the extra trouble expended on making these flies is well worth while. Their universal appeal is based on results obtained, which are said to be due to the more lifelike appearance of the straddled hackle, and the natural way they drop on to the water when cast.

CHAPTER SIX
MAKING "SHAVING BRUSH" FLIES

THE MOST STRAIGHTFORWARD METHOD I have found for forming the wings of these flies is as follows: Hackle Wings: Use a very stiff hackle with good length to the fibres. Draw the hackle through the fingers so that the fibres stand out at right-angles to the stem as Fig. 1. Tear off about $\frac{1}{4}$ in. to $\frac{1}{2}$ in. of fibres as shown at the bottom of the illustration, and it is most important that the tips of the fibres be kept level. These should be tied in on top of the hook-shank as per Fig. 2, a layer of tying silk being put on first so that the fibres will not twist round the shank. This will not be sufficient for the "wings" and there should be two or three lots of fibres tied in. I advocate the tearing of only a few of the fibres at a time, otherwise it is difficult to keep the tips in line.

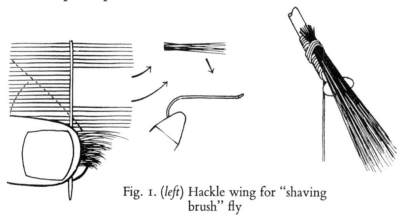

Fig. 1. (*left*) Hackle wing for "shaving
brush" fly

Fig. 2. (*above*) Tying in the fibres

Two or three turns of the tying silk must be put round the hook-shank and the fibres to ensure that they are well anchored, and then a half-hitch to fasten the silk. The fibres must now be parted in the centre and pressed to stand out at an angle on each side of the hook-shank, and turns of the tying silk taken between them and round the hook-shank as shown in enlarged form in Fig. 3. This also shows how the wings should appear as seen from above.

The tail body and rib are now formed, and the hackle wound over the base of the wings to cover the turns of silk used to fix them in position. The finished fly should now be as Fig. 4. Why it is called a "Shaving Brush" immediately becomes obvious.

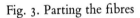

Fig. 3. Parting the fibres   Fig. 4. The finished "shaving brush" fly

Fur Wings: The method of tying in these wings is very similar, but it is even more important that a good bed of tying silk be wound on to the hook-shank before the fibres are tied in. Fur fibres are very prone to twist round the hook-shank when the silk is pulled tight, unless this is carried out.

To cut the fibres from the skin, raise up a bunch and twist them. If the diameter of the twisted fibres is about $\frac{1}{8}$ in., this will be sufficient for a May-fly, less being required for small flies. Cut the fibres off near to the skin, making sure that their tips remain in line as for the hackle fibres. The fur fibres are now tied in on top of the hook-shank, and fixed with a half-hitch as before. Now cut off the surplus ends of the fibres, as they will only get in the way at this stage. The fibres must now be lifted up and two turns of the tying silk put round them alone, and then a further two round them and the hook-shank as per Fig. 5. This will anchor them firmly,

Fig. 5. Making fur wings

as this springy material has a habit of working loose unless well tied in. It is as well to put a drop of Cellire varnish on the turns of silk at this stage to make them really secure. The fur fibres must now be separated and fixed in this position as were the hackle fibres, and the fly completed by adding the tail, body, rib and hackle.

The two main points to remember are:

1. A good bed of silk on which to tie the fibres, especially for the bucktail ones.

2. Leave plenty of room at the eye end of the hook for manipulation of the wings during tying, and also for when the time comes to attach the cast to the fly.

As a result of the article on the "Shaving Brush" type of fly, I received another method of forming these wings from Mr. K. Stewart, of Stevenston, Ayrshire.

By his method the wings are tied beforehand, to be affixed to the fly at the appropriate stage. His method is as follows:

Fig. 6. Another method of making the "shaving brush" fly

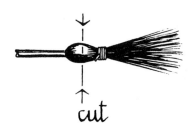

Fig. 7. The final stage in making the wings

A pin is bent to the shape of a hook and placed in the vice, and then two good-quality, stiff-fibred hackles are tied in and wound to the right as one would do on a normal fly. The fingers are then moistened and the fibres stroked to the right as shown in Fig. 6. They must be pulled firmly to get them into this position. Now take a separate piece of waxed tying silk and wind two or three turns at the point shown in Fig. 7. Tie them very tightly, and add a slight touch of clear varnish to the binding. The fibres are now cut through at the point shown in Fig. 7, and the completed "wing" slid off the end of the pin. It is now ready to be added to the fly being tied, after allowing sufficient time for the varnish to dry.

One good point about this method is that all the "wings" can be made up before starting to tie the flies.

CHAPTER SEVEN

MAKING HERL BODIES AND BUTTS

TO BE A GOOD FLY TYER one must not only know how to tie the materials on
to the hook, it is also necessary to know how to take advantage of their charac-
teristics. The natural curve of the fibres on a wing quill, for instance, can be utilised
to give a desired curve to the wing being made from them.

The herls used for bodies or butts also have a helpful characteristic in that the
fibres on the quills run along one edge only. If a quill is cut across, looking at the
two ends produced one sees the cross-sections as illustrated below. Fig. 1.

The peacock and ostrich herls which are used so extensively in fly tying have
this characteristic very markedly, and by taking advantage of this, a neat, well-
shaped tag can be put on a salmon fly, and a good, full body on a trout fly.

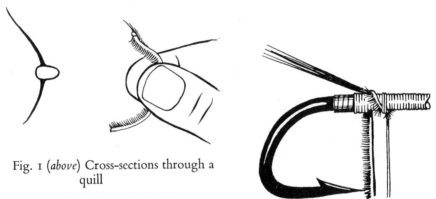

Fig. 1 (*above*) Cross-sections through a
quill

Fig. 2 (*right*) Making the herl butt

For the butt, the ostrich herl should be tied in underneath the hook-shank and
on the extreme right of the space devoted to the butt, with the fibres on the left-
hand side, Fig. 2. The herl is then wound once to the extreme left as per Fig. 3,
and the remaining turns made to the right so as to cover this first turn, as Fig. 4. I
do not think this requires further clarification, and you will find that it always
produces good results.

For a trout-fly body I always use two strands of peacock herl tied in together at

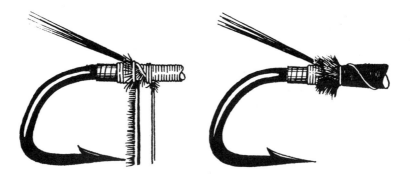

Figs. 3 *and* 4. Further stages in making the herl butt

the tail end of the fly, both having the fibres or "flue" on the left-hand side. The two quills are now wound one after the other, each turn of the rearmost quill being brought down on to the top of the foremost one, as shown in Fig. 5. This produces a much fuller body than if the two quills are twisted together as is advocated in some fly-tying books.

Fig. 5. Tying the herl body

I have also been asked how to avoid the gap which often appears between one of these herl bodies and its hackle. To do this, the hackle should be tied in at the eye of the hook, and not close up to the body. The tying silk is then wound back to the body, followed by the hackle which must be wound right up to the herl body. The tying silk is then wound back to the eye, through the hackle, and tied off. This method eliminates the gap, and also ensures a firm fixture of the hackle. See Chapter Two.

When selecting herls for tags or bodies it is, of course, necessary to choose those which have plenty of "flue" on them. This varies considerably, and the selection should be made according to the size of the fly being tied.

CHAPTER EIGHT

PREPARING AND TYING IN GOLDEN PHEASANT CRESTS FOR TOPPINGS AND TAILS

ALTHOUGH SALMON FLIES TAKE LONGER to tie than trout flies, in my opinion they are much easier, and they do not present so many difficulties to the amateur. The two main items of procedure that most beginners find difficult to overcome are: (1) putting on the final topping of golden pheasant crest; and (2) doubling the body and throat hackles.

It is these two items for which I get most requests for advice and assistance. Both have something in common in that if the feathers are prepared properly before they are tied in the difficulties are reduced. I will deal with the golden pheasant crest here, doubling hackles being dealt with in Chapter Three.

These feathers when on the living bird are a perfect shape for putting on a salmon fly, but during the drying and storing of the skins, many of the crests get twisted out of shape. It is logical to assume, therefore, that if one form of treatment will put the feathers out of shape, another will restore them to a useful contour once again.

Moistening them and placing them in the curve of wine glasses, etc., is one method frequently advocated, but this rather limits the shapes one can attain, and does not always remove the twist. The best method I know is to moisten them thoroughly and then lay them on their sides on a smooth surface in the shape you wish them to attain. I use a part of a linoleum work-bench myself, and, provided one knows that the feathers are clean, saliva is the best moistener.

The feathers must be made very wet, and the shape required is imparted by the finger-tips. Any shape can be achieved, from a dead straight line to a half-circle, or the end of the crest can be turned down sharply so that it curves down to meet the tail of the fly in a pleasing manner.

The crests should be left on the flat surface until they are quite dry, otherwise the desired shape is not maintained. On removal it will be observed that all the fibres of the crest are clinging together, and to bring it back to its natural state I use a stiffish fibred brush of the type normally used to clean typewriter keys. This brushing will not remove the imparted shape, especially if the crests are allowed to stand for a good length of time before being picked up. I like to leave mine for twenty-four hours.

The next step is to remove the unwanted fibres from the butt end of the crest, leaving it the required length of the fly to be tied. The stripped butt is then flattened between the thumbnail and the ball of the first finger, and one will find that its soaking has made the quill more amenable to this treatment.

One very good aspect of this method is the fact that as the crest has lain on its side during the shaping process, the curve is always in an exactly flat plane with all twist removed. Therefore, when it is placed over the wing, the flattened quill can be tied in at once without it being necessary to manipulate it so that the crest will envelope the wing properly.

It is always a good idea to select a crest about $\frac{1}{2}$ in. longer than the wing to be covered, as this makes it easier for the stripped and flattened butt to be tied in.

Crests for tails can also be treated in the same manner, again using a longer one than is strictly necessary so that only the butt is tied in and none of the fibres. This prevents the latter splaying out in all directions.

The foregoing instructions may seem rather long drawn out, but the actual procedure will be found to be very simple and will impart that extra "finish" which is the hall-mark of a well-tied fly.

CHAPTER NINE

MAKING "DUBBING" BODIES

ALTHOUGH I HAVE DEALT WITH "DUBBING" BODIES in the first *Fly Dressers' Guide*, this item of procedure seems to cause so much difficulty to newcomers to fly tying that I feel that it will not hurt to give it further emphasis here.

I was shown the following method by a professional tyer who gave me my first instruction in tying many years ago, and I have yet to see any superior method, either for quickness of application or durability in use.

You all must have seen illustrations of dubbing spiralled round the tying silk, but this is not good enough if the fur is to stay on during use. It must encompass the tying silk completely as does the rubber casing round a piece of electric wire.

Important points to remember during the spinning of the fur on to the silk are:

1. See that the tying silk is well waxed.

2. Only use a small amount of fur at a time, spread out to cover as large an area of the thumb as possible.

3. Do *not* roll the silk backwards and forwards on the thumb, but in *one* direction only.

4. Keep the tying silk taut all the time.

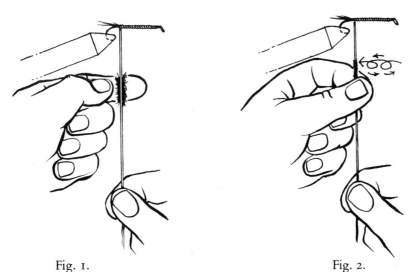

Fig. 1.   Fig. 2.

First stages in making "dubbing" bodies

The procedure is as follows: hold the tying silk taut in the right hand, at a right-angle to the hook and pulling it towards the body. Select a minute pinch of the necessary fur and spread it on the ball of the left thumb. If it looks more like an almost indiscernible mist rather than a bunch of fur fibres, so much the better, especially for small trout flies. Now bring the taut silk down on the thumb as Fig. 1. Lower the second finger of the left hand on to the thumb and roll the silk *and* the fur in a clockwise direction as per Fig. 2. This is the action which wraps the fur round the silk, and it should be repeated with additional fur until a sufficient length of the silk has been covered. Press the finger and thumb together firmly during the rolling, *opening* them at the end of each individual roll. I stress this point so that you will not keep the finger and thumb together and just roll the fur backwards and forwards. It will be obvious that if rolling in one direction wraps the fur round the silk, rolling it back again will tend to unwrap it!

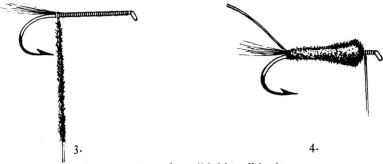

First stages in making "dubbing" bodies

The dubbing should now look like Fig. 3, and is then wound towards the eye of the hook, not forgetting to leave enough space at the eye end for any wings and hackles that have to be tied in.

The spacing of the winds will regulate the thickness of the body, and one usually overlaps them at the shoulder of the fly so that extra thickness is given at this point, Fig. 4. It is customary to give a tinsel rib of some sort to a dubbing body, and this is, of course, tied in at the tail before starting on the dubbing. This completes the durability of the body, and by the method I have shown it is possible to make bodies light and translucent, or thick and shaggy, that will put up with an almost unlimited amount of use. If the latter type of body is required, say, for a salmon fly, it is still far better to apply only a little dubbing to the silk at a time, adding more until a good thick "barrel" is achieved. After this is wound round the hook-shank, fibres can be pulled out from it with one's dubbing needle to give the hackle effect often needed.

If one is using a fur which has to be cut from the skin before use, it should be cut so that the staple is as long as possible. If the fibres are cut off so that they are only about ⅛ in. long, the difficulty of wrapping them around the silk is greatly increased.

It is also a fact that some furs are more easily applied than others. Seal's fur, for instance, being more difficult than rabbit or the synthetic Polymer dubbing. This is due to the fibres of the seal's fur being stiffer and more springy than the others. The procedure is exactly the same for all, however, and it just means that the points I have emphasised must be more strictly observed with the difficult furs.

Among the many very good suggestions given to me by Captain the Hon. R. Coke is his method of putting on dubbing bodies.

This method is particularly useful for those short-fibred dubbings which do not lend themselves easily to the "spinning" or rolling method I described. The procedure is as follows.

The fly is formed to the stage where the dubbing is required, which would bring the tying silk to the tail usually. At this point another piece of well-waxed tying silk is tied in. Place a portion of the dubbing between the two silks, and then twist them together embracing the dubbing. The silks and dubbing are then wound to form the body, care being taken to see that the silks remain twisted.

This brings me to a tip passed on to me by N. F. Bostock, an associate of the late G. E. M. Skues. Any material which has a twist imparted to it, as this method calls for, should be wound in the opposite direction to the twist imparted. In other words, if the two silks are twisted together anti-clockwise to embrace the dubbing, they will not untwist when wound clock-wise to form the body. This obviates the necessity of retwisting the silks during the process of forming the body. It will also be found useful when bodies are being formed of floss silks which have a twist in them when taken from the reel. Winding them on in one direction will continue to twist the silk into a tight cord, whereas winding them on in the opposite direction will untwist it so that a flat, well-shaped body is achieved. A small point, but a time saver.

CHAPTER TEN

MIXING DUBBINGS (FURS) FOR BODIES

IT IS OFTEN NECESSARY, to achieve some particular shade, that two or more furs have to be mixed together. This mostly happens when some particular shade of olive is required, and if one has two or three packets of dyed olive, ranging from light to dark, many variations can be produced.

These can also be tinted further with browns, reds, orange, etc., if warmer shades are required, and a very good fiery brown can be produced by mixing chocolate, red and orange.

It will, of course, be apparent that there is no end to the colours one can achieve.

The secret of success is to do only a little at a time. It is also important that the correct ratio of ingredients should be adhered to. A small portion of the smallest ingredient, about the size of a pea, should be selected, and teased out to make as large a bulk as possible, so that it is more like a piece of fluff. The correct proportion of the next ingredient should be treated in the same manner. The two heaps of dubbing, when sufficiently opened out, should then be placed one on top of the other, and thoroughly mixed together by breaking and refolding until a more or less uniform colour is obtained.

When the pile is well mixed small sections should be broken off and treated as was the pea-sized portion at the beginning. These should be mixed individually until the whole pile has been treated, and then all the separate piles of "fluff" mixed together again.

By this means it is possible to obtain one uniform colour, provided that clashing colours are not used, of course. I doubt very much if a very good grey could be obtained by trying to mix a black and a white. It is, however, possible to blend suitable colours so that a uniform shade is obtained.

When it is necessary to blend fluorescent material into a dubbing, it is better to use the wool rather than a floss. The wool should be cut in strips of about $\frac{3}{4}$ in., and then teased out into a very fine fluff. In this form it is very easy to mix into the main dubbing.

It often happens that when one comes to the actual mixing it is found that the staple of one ingredient is longer than the other. While it will not altogether prevent the mixing of the two ingredients, it is much easier to mix them if the fibres of each are more or less the same length. Therefore, the dubbing with the longer fibres should be cut across several times with a pair of sharp scissors until it is reduced to about the same consistency of the other fur to be mixed.

CHAPTER ELEVEN

MAKING HAIR BODIES AND HEAD OF "MUDDLER MINNOW"

THIS TYPE OF BODY is not in regular use in the United Kingdom, but in North America it is a favourite medium for the large lures used to attract large- and small-mouthed bass.

The reason for this is its floating qualities and the fact that it can be trimmed into shape after application. By this means, lures representing frogs, mice, shrews, etc., can be realistically reproduced, which can be worked across the surface of the water in a most lifelike manner.

The material used is the *body* hair of the common red deer, and as this varies from deep red brown through grey to a pale buff, several colour variations are possible. For instance, buff, brown, buff and so on will give a barred effect if required.

The reason I stress that it is the body hair which must be used is because it is the texture of these hairs which give the material its floating ability. The individual fibres are very stiff and quite thick. It is these qualities which enable the lure to float, and make possible the particular method of application. The finer hairs, say from the tail, will not spin round the hook-shank as will the stiffer and thicker body hairs.

The actual method of application is very simple and requires very little practice. It is as follows:

Place the hook in the vice (usually a stout long-shanked one), and fix the tying silk at the *bend* of the hook. No silk is run down the shank (Fig. 1).

Cut a small bunch of body fibres from the skin and hold them over the hook immediately above where the silk is tied in, and in line with the shank (Fig. 2).

Now take *two* loose turns round the fur and the hook-shank, just firm enough to hold the fur on to the hook, so that the fingers holding the fur can be released. When the fingers are released pull the silk tight and the fur will flare round the hook-shank just like a hackle (Fig. 3).

The silk should now be behind this "hackle", so, still keeping it tight, pass it through the "hackle", make a half-hitch round the hook-shank and press this close up to the "hackle".

The procedure is now repeated with another bunch of hairs, and another half-hitch as before. Carry on until the necessary amount of hook-shank has been covered, and the result should be a "flue-brush" anything from 1 in. to $1\frac{1}{2}$ in. in diameter (4).

This "brush" can be trimmed to shape, using a sharp pair of pointed scissors, resulting in a bristle body of most lifelike appearance (Fig. 5).

It is, of course, possible to dye the lighter-coloured hairs, and if a really dark body is required, the darker hairs can be dyed various browns, greens, or black.

A stout tying silk should be used so that the turns of silk can be pulled really tight, and although I advocate that the hook-shank should be left bare before commencing, an open layer of silk can be put over it when one has become adept at flaring the hairs. It is much easier to do on the bare hook.

This is the method used for making the distinctive head of the "Muddler Minnow". In this instance, however, only the front of the fly is treated as described, and this is trimmed giving the effect shown in Fig. 6.

Dressing of "Muddler Minnow".

Tail.   Two strips of "Oak" brown turkey wing quill.
Body.   Flat Copper or gold tinsel.
Wing.   Firstly, some fibres from a barred grey squirrel tail or similar marked hair.
         Secondly, two strips of "oak" brown turkey tail.
Head.   Deer body fibres applied as described in this chapter.
Hackle. Some of the fine pointed ends of the deer hair left on to form a "collar"
         hackle as shown in the illustration.

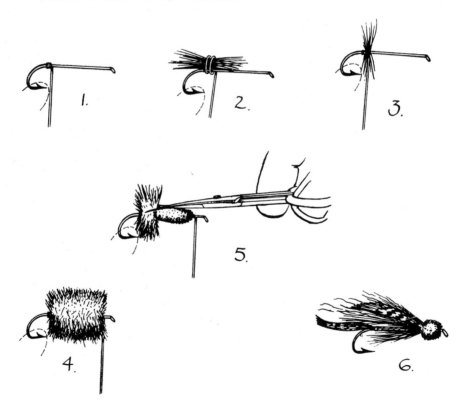

CHAPTER TWELVE
MAKING TINSEL BODIES

THE MOST PREVALENT CAUSE OF DISTORTION in tinsel bodies is the method by which the tinsel is first tied in. Unless it is so fixed that it can be wound evenly from the very start, an unsightly lump is formed at the tail end, and the spirals will not lie absolutely flat on the silk bed. The ribbing tinsel must also be tied in so that it starts neatly and has a good appearance at the tail end.

I have my own methods of achieving these objects, and although they may not be quite orthodox, if they are successful I am sure this will be overlooked. I feel rather strongly on this subject, as a clumsy tinsel body will ruin the appearance of any fly, no matter how well the rest of it may be made.

We have made the illustrations as large as we can for reasons of clarity, omitting items which do not concern the subject. We have included the tail so that the reader can know which aspect he is viewing.

Start the fly in the usual way, forming the tag (if it is a salmon fly), and tying in the tail. The latter should be so fixed that the turns of silk holding it are right up against the tag, with no gap. The ribbing is then tied in *underneath* the body, and pushed away to the left. The tinsel for the body is now cut off, and the usual diagonal cut is made across it as shown in Figs. 1 and 2.

This is now placed underneath the body as Fig. 1 (seen from above), and one turn of silk taken round it and the hook shank to hold it in position. Fig. 2. The cut edge of the tinsel should be at right-angles to the hook shank, *and this is most important*, so that the remaining length of tinsel will be angled to the right of the tyer. The importance of this will be seen as soon as one starts to wind the tinsel.

The cut end is then curled up and over the body, and two very tight turns made with the tying silk to hold it in position. Fig. 3. A piece of floss silk is now tied in at the shoulder of the fly, wound down to the tinsel and back again so that a smooth body of the desired thickness is achieved. Also as Fig. 3.

One complete turn of the tinsel is now taken round the body, covering the point of the cut end of tinsel. Looking down, the tinsel should now be as Fig. 4. It will be observed that the diagonal is still apparent, and this is very important as the next turn of the tinsel must be taken to follow this line, and it will also give the angle at which the tinsel must be held for the subsequent turns. Therefore, turn number two will be as Fig. 5. Each turn of tinsel must lie *edge to edge* with the preceding one. Any overlapping will distort the tinsel, and any gap will be unsightly. The tinsel must be pulled very tightly during the winding, and that is why it is so very important that the pointed end be tied in very securely at the start.

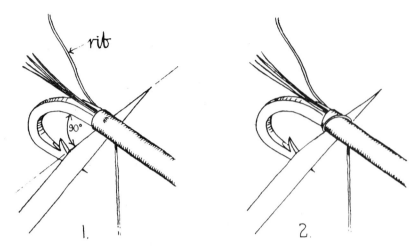

When the shoulder is reached, two turns of silk are put round the tinsel, and the surplus *broken* off. Breaking it off forms a ragged edge which will not slip out easily. If you prefer to cut it off, do not do so close up to the tying silk. The small surplus then remaining can be doubled back and fixed with a turn of silk.

Now back to the rib. This, you will remember, was tied in underneath the body. It is now wound one complete turn round the extreme edge of the tinsel body, and this should cover any gap between the tag and body. Bring it right round to the front, and then start the spiral as shown in Fig. 6. It is essential that the turns of this spiral shall all slope evenly and at the same angle. If they do not, this means that the tension of the rib is not equal along its entire length, and eventually the rib will slacken and lose its uniformity. When the end of the body is reached, the rib should be tied in underneath, and the surplus cut off.

It will be observed that in neither the script nor the illustrations has any butt been introduced. This is to point out that it is possible to form these tinsel bodies without the necessity of any butt being put in to conceal any untidiness at this point. This is an important factor when tying low-water patterns, for instance, although if a butt is used the procedure is not altered in any way.

If one uses wool for a tag, or ties a salmon fly with one or more items in the tail, an unsightly bump can form at the tail end of the tinsel body.

This bump cannot be avoided unless the tag and body are one smooth unit, so on small flies it is best to run the tag material the entire length of the body. It must be bound tightly and smoothly on top of the hook-shank with close turns of silk so that the tinsel will lie evenly. When the tag material will not reach the entire length of the body, and on larger flies, a short length of thin floss should be tied in at the shoulder and wound over the hook-shank and surplus tag material so that a smooth, even shape is formed, on which the tinsel can be wound easily and without distortion.

The following method of making tinsel bodies may appeal to some readers. It was among the many sent to me by Capt. the Hon. R. Coke.

The idea here is to use narrow or fairly narrow tinsel on all but very large salmon flies. This is tied in at the shoulder instead of the tail, and then wound to the tail and back again, winding very tightly and evenly with no overlap. It is essential that the jaws of one's vice grip the hook tightly, as there can be considerable leverage during this winding. It may be desirable to pad the hook-shank very lightly, and this should be done with split floss silk of white or grey, also wound very tightly and evenly.

I have found this to be a most excellent method for making tinsel bodies on small flies, as it produces a perfectly smooth body, completely devoid of bumps or distortions of any kind.

After winding the ribbing tinsel, if any, Capt. Coke advocates the use of a transparent cellulose paint to prevent tarnish.

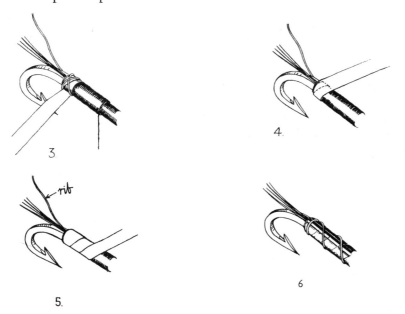

Tinsel can be polished before winding by pulling it through a folded rag on which some wetted plate powder has been smeared. It is then finished off by drawing it through a piece of folded chamois-leather, without powder, of course. A final polish with the chamois can be given after the body is wound.

The above method produces a bright, smooth tinsel body, with no gaps or lumps, and should be no thicker in appearance than those made in the orthodox manner. I would like to add that a very neat appearance at the tail end is assured.

CHAPTER THIRTEEN
MAKING TANDEM HOOK MOUNTS FOR LURES, ETC.

MANY FLY TYERS EXPERIENCE DIFFICULTY in making a multi-hook lure which can be relied upon.

These multi-hook lures are mostly used for sea-trout fishing, but smaller types can be used in lakes and reservoirs, while larger editions are often used for salmon fishing. They consist of two or three hooks in tandem, whipped to gut or nylon, with a long over-wing, Fig. 1. They are sometimes called "Demons" or "Terrors", and have their counterpart in the American streamer type of fly. They differ in the respect that the latter are usually tied on a single long-shanked hook.

Orthodox dressings are mostly used, two of the most popular being the "Peter Ross" and "Alexandra", although there is no limit to the variations which may be applied. An "Alexandra" would have its two or three hooks dressed with the usual flat silver body, and the long fibres of green peacock herl dressed over an under-wing of red goose or swan. Jungle cock eyes and a crest over the top are optional.

So much for the type of fly. The difficulty which arises is how to whip the hooks on to the gut so that they will stay put. The rear hooks are usually of the eyeless variety, but this is not essential as the gut can be threaded through the loop of an eyed hook, so that it lies flat on the shank. It is best to start with the rear hook first.

If the hooks are whipped on tightly and evenly there should be no trouble, but any slackness or uneven whipping can result in a lost fish.

Place the rear hook in the vice and wind the tying silk evenly from the bend to the end of the shank. The length of gut is then placed on top of the hook, and the tying silk wound in very tight, close turns back to the bend of the hook, and then back to the front end of the hook-shank again. Each turn must be very tight and close up against its neighbour. Uneven turns can result in the silk going slack. It is this tightness and uniformity which ensure that the hook will not slip. A couple of half-hitches are now made round the hook and the gut and the silk cut off.

If it is a three-hook lure being made, the middle hook is placed in the vice and a silk bed wound on as before. The gut is then placed on top with the rear hook to the top, and this will result in the centre hook being on top when the lure is completed, Fig. 1. The gut is now whipped to the centre hook as before. Now make the two half-hitches and cut off the tying silk. These half-hitches are necessary, as it is very difficult to make a whip finish with the end of the gut sticking out.

The front (eyed) hook is now put in the vice, and the procedure carried out as

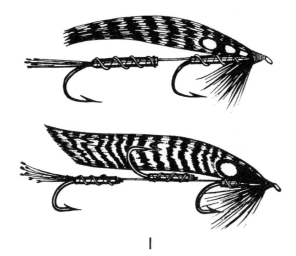

before. When all the hooks are tied on, their bindings must be well soaked in clear Cellire varnish, which must be allowed to dry hard before the bodies of the fly are put on.

If gut is used, this may be softened slightly in water before it is tied on, but if it is nylon, the portions which will be tied on to the hook-shank may be bitten lightly to form serrations on which the silk will grip. Twisted gut or nylon can be used to good effect, not only for extra strength, as the indentations formed by the twisting give the silk something to grip on.

Although this method may not seem to give a very robust anchorage for the hooks, it is surprising how tenacious close-whipped silk can be. Take half a dozen tight turns of silk round two closed fingers, and it will be found impossible to part them or break the silk.

Sometimes these lures are made with double hooks, particularly for salmon lures, only two doubles being used. With these it is possible to make an almost slip-proof lure. The method is as follows:

The rear double is placed in the vice and the tying silk wound up and down the hook-shank as before. One end of the length of nylon is then pushed through the bends of the hook until its end reaches the end of the hook-shank (Fig. 2). This is then fixed with a couple of turns of the tying silk. The long end is then doubled over and brought down on the hook-shank as Fig. 3, both sections of the nylon then being firmly tied in with the tying silk, which is wound down to the bend and back again. Take a half-hitch or two round nylon and hook at this point and cut off the tying silk.

The front hook is then placed in the vice and the free end of the nylon passed through its eye so that it protrudes sufficiently for a loop to be tied in it. It is then whipped to the hook as before. Incidentally, it is most important that these double hooks have the silk bed wound on first, so that the nylon is not whipped to the bare hook. The whippings are varnished as before, and a loop can be formed in the free end of the nylon. It will then be observed that even if the front hook should slip during use, it will be stopped by the rear hook, which is held firmly in the doubled end of the nylon. The completed mount is as Fig. 4. I think the illustration shows this quite clearly, and even if the front loop should be broken at any time, the cast can still be tied on to the eye of the front hook as normally.

The smaller lures can be tied by this method, using a small double at the rear and a single or singles in front of it.

Another most excellent method of making tandem hooks was given to me by Mr. A. K. Iles, of Fairford. The two hooks are whipped to fine trace wire, or stout nylon can be used, and the procedure is as follows:

Cut the wire (or nylon) so that it is a little more than double the length you require the tandem hooks to be. Divide the wire exactly in half by folding, and whip one half on top of the rear hook, as shown (Fig. 5), the half being tied down, being pushed through the eye of the hook first. The wire is then bound tightly to the hook, as I have described earlier in this chapter and then varnished.

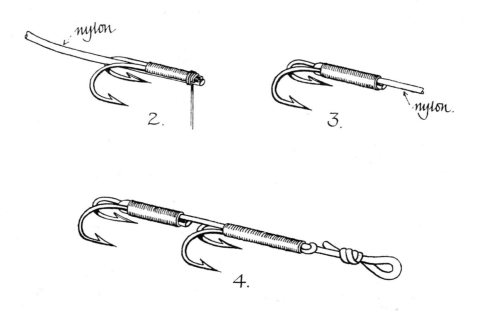

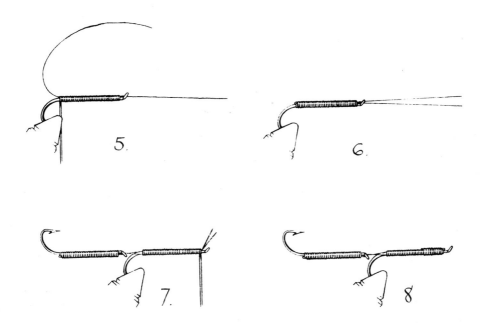

Now push the rear end of the wire through the eye of hook and bind this down and varnish it. We now have one hook with the two ends of wire protruding from the eye, both firmly bound down on to it. It is the binding down separately that gives the two ends of wire their immovable fixture, as stage two (Fig. 6).

The front hook is now put into the vice ready for the protruding ends of wire to be bound to it. Whether the rear hook points up or down is left to the preference of the tier, but for the purposes of this illustration the rear hook is shown in the "up" position.

The two ends of wire are now bound down on top of the front hook, but in this instance the ends are *not* pushed through the eye of the hook (Fig. 7).

Well varnish the silk bindings once again and then cut off the surplus wire so that the two ends project about $\frac{1}{4}$ in. beyond the eye. These two ends are then doubled back over the hook and firmly bound down as per Fig. 8.

To make the fixture even more breakproof, each arm of the wire can be tied down separately, including the bent back end.

All the silk bindings should be well varnished once again, building up several coats of the varnish, which should be allowed several days to harden. It is then ready for tails, bodies and hackles, and in use will be found practically indestructible.

The short lengths of wire between the two hooks can be twisted together before attaching the front hook, but this is not necessary with the nylon.

Badger Demon
BODIES. Flat silver tinsel.
TAIL. Rear hook only. Scarlet ibis or substitute.
HACKLE. Front hook only, dyed bright red.
WINGS. Two badger hackles back to back, their tips reaching to the end of the tail.
HEAD. Black varnish.

Black Leech—*see* "Black Lure"

Blue Terror
BODIES. Oval silver tinsel.
TAILS. (One at rear of each hook used.) Red wool or floss.
HACKLE. None.
WING. Two dyed bright blue cock hackles back to back, their tips reaching to end of rear tail.
SIDES. Strips of grey mallard flank feather —half length of hackle wing.
HEAD. Black varnish.

Crested Mallard
BODIES. Flat silver tinsel.
RIBS. Oval silver tinsel.
HACKLE. None.
TAILS. None.
WING. From brown mallard flank feather.
TOPPING. Golden pheasant crest over wing.
HEAD. Black varnish.

Dandy
BODIES. Oval silver tinsel.
HACKLE. Dyed red. (Blue as an alternative.)
WING. Strips from grey mallard flank feather.
HEAD. Black varnish.

Peacock Demon
BODIES. Embossed silver tinsel.
TAIL. Rear hook only—red wool or floss.

WING. A bunch of "herls" taken from the peacock "eye" tail. (Use the herls from the actual "eye", as they are usually of good shape, tapering nicely to the tips.)
HACKLE. Front hook only—dyed bright blue.
HEAD. Black varnish.

Junglecock and Silver
BODIES. Flat silver tinsel.
RIBS. Oval silver tinsel.
HACKLE. Usually none, but red, blue, black, etc., can be put in if required.
WINGS. Two large junglecock feathers back to back, their tips reaching to bend of rear hook.
HEAD. Black varnish.

Mary Ann
BODIES. Flat gold tinsel.
RIBS. Oval gold tinsel.
WING. Peacock "sword" herls.
SIDES. Scarlet goose.
TOPPING. Golden pheasant crest over wing.
HACKLE. None.
HEAD. Black varnish.

Black Lure (two-hook lure) (or "Black Leech")
BODIES. Black floss.
RIBS. Oval silver tinsel.
WINGS. Two black cock hackles, back to back, or splayed out in a "V".
HEAD. Black varnish.

Dunkeld
TAIL. Golden pheasant crest.
BODIES. Flat gold tinsel.
RIBS. Fine oval gold tinsel.
HACKLE. Orange.
WINGS. Long brown mallard.
CHEEKS. Small jungle cock feathers tied close to head.

CHAPTER FOURTEEN

TYING SILKS—COLOURS TO USE

MANY DRESSINGS GIVEN IN BOOKS do not state which tying silk should be used.

Tinsel-bodied flies, of course, do not present much difficulty, as the only place where the silk might show is at the head or through the hackle. Therefore, the colour to choose would be the colour of the hackle. Black for "Butcher", for instance, and red for "Bloody Butcher", "Red Spinner" or "Wickham's Fancy", and so on.

With dubbing bodies, I always use a colour approaching that of the dubbing fur used, claret for "Mallard and Claret", yellow for "Invicta", and olive for "Rough Olive", etc.

If a body is formed which will become semi-transparent when wet, a colour should be used which will have a neutral effect, such as white or grey.

CHAPTER FIFTEEN

MAKING DETACHED BODIES

IN SPITE OF THE FACT that the making of detached body flies creates a certain amount of difficulty, they are still popular, and I get many requests for the best ways of making them up. The advent of the long-shanked light wire hook has done much to oust this type of fly, but there is no doubt that the detached body looks very realistic.

Cork is a very popular material for making these bodies, especially for mayflies, and there are two methods of applying it. One is to use a fairly thin sheet of cork folded in half, or two pieces of greater thickness placed side by side. The method of fixing them to the hook is the same for both, and is as follows.

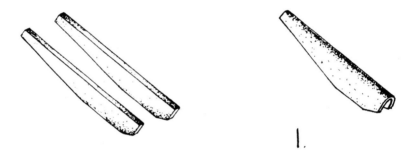

I.

If the two separate pieces are used, they are first cut to the approximate shape of the fly body as shown in Fig. 1. The shape of cork required to be folded is also shown. They are then trimmed to the exact shape. The tying silk is then tied in near the bend of the hook and wound to a point near the eye of the hook, or to a point where it is desired to tie in the body (Fig. 2). The colour of this tying silk should be neutral, and as near to the colour of the cork as possible. The two pieces of cork are now smeared on their inside surfaces with Cellire cement, and two or three turns of silk taken round their front end, placing them on the hook-shank so that they overlap it slightly, as shown in Fig. 2. Continue winding the silk at fairly wide intervals so that a criss-cross effect may be achieved instead of a close one, until point "A" is reached. Now separate the two sections with a dubbing needle and insert the tail fibres (Fig. 3). Position these and then squeeze the two sides together.

Now continue to wind the tying silk to the tail end of the body, and then back again to the front, keeping the same interval of width (Fig. 4). Allow the cement to set, and then finish the fly by adding wings and hackles.

To make detached bodies for small flies, the best material to use is nylon mono-filament of a thickness or slightly thicker than the hook-shank. This is tied tightly to the top of the hook-shank, and any excess of length clipped off. Apply a drop of cement to the tip of the nylon and fasten on the tail fibres, after which a piece of floss silk is tied in at the same point. Hold the nylon in the left hand and then wind the body material to the shoulder of the fly, incorporating the hook-shank in the windings at the appropriate place. Ribbing of silk or tinsel can also be added to these bodies if required. The finger and thumb holding the nylon can be brought into play to assist the winding of the body silks or ribbing.

I have also received several suggestions as to materials which can be used for

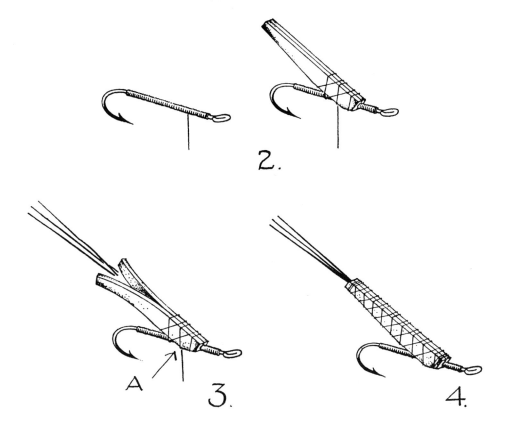

detached bodies, one being surgical oiled silk which is obtainable from chemists' suppliers. This material is cut into strips as wide as the body required, and then rolled round a needle to give it the required shape. The tail fibres are placed in the narrow end of the cylinder, and fixed with knotted tying silk, one end of which is continued round and down the body to form the rib. The thicker end is then tied tightly to the hook-shank. This material makes a very light, airtight body which is not only most translucent, but very natural looking.

Another ingenious suggestion was the use of feather quills. I have found that the best ones come from the quill tips of such flank feathers as brown mallard or teal, as these are both well shaped and translucent. Fig. 5 shows the portion to be used, and this is tied in with its closed end forming the tail end of the body. Tails and ribbings can be added as for the other detached bodies described in the foregoing.

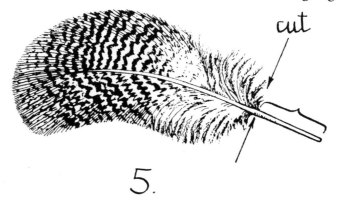

5.

Another most original method of making a detached-bodied fly was sent to me by W. R. Coffey, of Montreal. The originator of the method was Harry Darbee, a very well-known American fisherman and fly tyer.

Darbee's unique method requires only a single feather for body, wings and tail, and the feather is prepared as follows, and as shown in the first two illustrations.

All surplus fluff and fibres are removed, and the remaining fibres stroked outwards and then downwards, the feather ending up as Fig. 6B. The section of quill between the "wings" is then tied on to the hook as per Fig. 7A, and when the surplus quill is cut off a side view of our fly should be as Fig. 7B.

We now have a fly with cocked wings, but there is no reason why they may not be set in the open or "spent" positions.

Fibres can be cut from the tail section if it is too bushy.

A hackle is added in the usual way (Fig. 8A), two turns at the rear of the wings and two in front, and a finished fly should look like Fig. 8B.

The beauty of this fly is its extreme lightness, not only because only one feather is used for wings, body and tail, but because it can be tied on to the smallest dry-fly hooks.

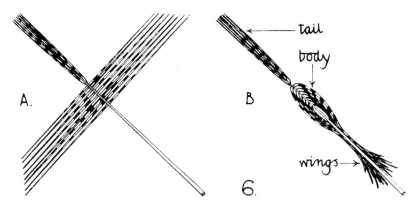

Darbee designed this fly for fish rising on a polished surface, and although it is elongated like a natural, because it weighs only about one quarter as much as a traditional fly, it floats down on to the water like gossamer.

I find that this method will produce a fine extra-light mayfly.

I use a No. 13 up-eyed hook, and feathers from the breast of teal, wood-duck, and mallard are ideal, both dyed and undyed. For hackles I use badger, grizzle, and various dyed shades in the olive group, and these can be of a size normally used for small dry-flies.

It is the use of these small hackles which gives the fly its very natural appearance, and their extreme lightness makes them ideal for those streams which have long slow glides where a minimum of disturbance is essential.

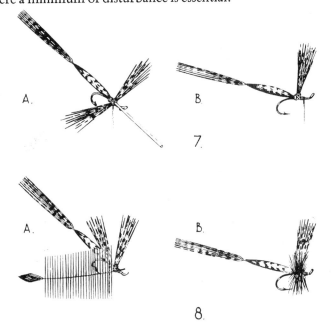

Since *Fly Tying Problems* was first published, science has come to the aid of the fly tyer once again, in the shape (literally) of moulded plastic bodies that are both realistic, light and translucent. They are also hollow, and providing the tyer ensures that they are airtight when tied on, they will float indefinitely.

Their size makes them ideal for use as detached bodies for mayflies and sedges, and they are particularly effective for "spent" patterns.

The usual long-shank mayfly hook may, of course, be dispensed with, Nos. 12 or 13 Redditch size being quite large enough.

Tails, if required, are added by cutting a very small hole at the extreme tip of the body, and then threading the tails point first through the main opening (Fig. 10). The hole in the tip must then be sealed with cement or clear varnish, otherwise the body will not be airtight.

The body, including the butts of the tail fibres, is then bound down on top of the hook in the middle of the shank. As fairly long fibres are used for tails on mayflies, there is always plenty of surplus at the butt end to be tied in.

Tying the body in the middle of the hook-shank leaves plenty of room for wings (if any are required), and hackle, and the turns of the latter can be kept to a minimum. This is because the hackle is not required to keep the fly afloat, so therefore its fibres can fulfil the true function—representation of the legs.

Lifelike segments are moulded into the bodies during manufacture, so no ribbing is required. The meticulous tyer can, if he wishes, accentuate the rib markings with varnish, and the result is really most lifelike.

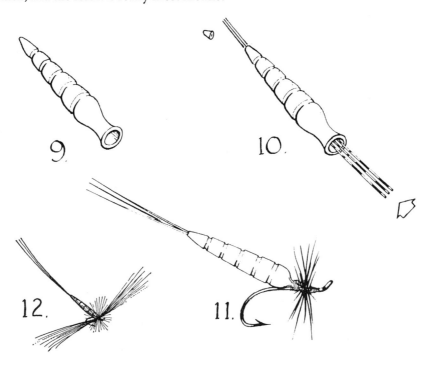

CHAPTER SIXTEEN

RARE HACKLES FOR DRY-FLIES—SUPPLY, DEMAND AND SUBSTITUTES

THE SUBJECT OF HACKLES, particularly those for dry-flies, is continually crop-ping up in my correspondence, not so much regarding the tying of them, but how to obtain certain types which are very scarce. To understand the problem fully, it is necessary to know the circumstances affecting supply, and the reasons for the shortage of some kinds.

In the first place, some of the more popular types are freaks, which means that birds cannot be bred to guarantee a certain type of hackle. Within this range of types we have the furnace hackles required for the popular "Greenwell's Glory", red/black for "Coch-y-Bondhu", and badger for "Grey Duster" and other flies. All these have one common feature, a black centre, and sometimes the tips of the hackles are also black. They are the outcome of crossing various strains of birds, usually by the introduction of game breeds into the flocks.

The main strains concentrated on by breeders for best egg- and flesh-producing results, are Red and Light Sussex, the Blacks and any other strains being introduced to improve the breed. The resulting birds, therefore, are nearly all Reds or Light Sussex, with now and again the improving breed cropping up in the plumage. A good furnace or a good badger may crop up only once in several thousand birds, which is the reason for the small number of required types, compared with the many hundreds of plain colours.

While breeders concentrate on these, to them, more profitable types, the number of freaks must continue to grow less. Added to this is the fact that many of the old breeds are no longer encouraged, which is the reason that Plymouth Rock (grizzle) hackles are now as scarce as were the coveted Andalusian types from which we obtained our Blue Duns, Iron Blues, Honey Duns, etc. This breed is now practically extinct.

Although there must be many birds killed every year, which would supply us with the hackles we require, modern methods of storing (cold store) and machinery plucking, render the hackles useless to the fly tyer. Many of them would be useless anyway, as few birds are allowed to reach the maturity that produces the hard hackles so necessary for the dry-fly.

With the greatly increased production of table birds, it might be thought that there were plenty of hackles made available to the fly tyer, but unfortunately this is not the case at all. The modern system of producing "broilers" results in birds covered by nothing but a stubbly down, absolutely useless for our purposes.

Before the war the British market supplied practically all the hackles we used, but the above-mentioned conditions have reduced this source of supply to a mere trickle. We also obtained many from what are now known as Iron Curtain countries, and even if these became available once again, no doubt we would find that they also have adopted the new methods of plucking and storing.

Consequently, new sources of supply had to be found, and the majority of our hackles now come from the East. Although quite a large number of the capes of hackles received from this source are excellent for dry-flies, the range of types is very limited for the same reasons as I have expounded at the beginning of this chapter. We must count our blessings, however, because if it were not for this source of supply there would not be enough good hackles of any kind to go round, and those available would be almost priceless. We can but hope that the aforementioned modern methods will not reach that part of the world for some time. Even now, it is becoming more noticeable that the strains are getting more concentrated, and the number of freaks growing smaller.

In an effort to overcome some of these shortages, dyed substitutes are taking the place of the Andalusian types, but it is, of course, impossible to dye a badger, and there are not enough badgers to spare for dyeing furnace.

The only ways to overcome the shortage of the freak hackles are: (1) use larger hackles; (2) cut hackles; or (3) resort to a substitute which I described in the *Fishing Gazette* several years ago. It is almost impossible to tell that the resulting fly has not been tied with a black-centred hackle, and although I know that the idea does not meet with the approval of purists, I can but say, "What else are we to do?"

My idea sprang from the method I had seen used by several fly tyers, amateur and professional, which incorporated a small, short-fibred black hackle with a red, white or ginger hackle, the black hackle being used, of course, to simulate the black centre. I replaced the black hackle with a strand of ostrich herl, and found it most effective. If one wishes to tie a "Greenwell" the method is as follows:

Form body with rib—with a tail if required, leaving plenty of room at the eye end of the hook. Tie in the strand of ostrich herl close up to the body and continue winding the silk until the eye is nearly reached. Tie in the ginger hackle and wind the silk back to the ostrich herl. Wind the hackle up to the ostrich herl, tie in its tip and cut off the surplus. Wind the tying silk back through the hackle to the eye. Now wind the herl through the hackle to the eye, holding it as taut as possible, so that the hackle fibres are not disturbed too much. When the eye is reached tie in the herl and cut off the surplus. Finish off fly with the usual whip finish.

The amount of black centre is, of course, governed by the number of turns given to the herl, and we found that for a lightly dressed fly, one turn at the back of the hackle, one or two through the hackle, and one in the front were all that was necessary.

Flies requiring a badger or a furnace hackle are tied in the same manner, using a white or a red hackle.

Winged dry-flies can also be tied, the wings being put on before the hackle and herl.

Wet-flies are treated in the same manner, by using hen hackles, or soft cock hackles.

CHAPTER SEVENTEEN
HOOKS—TERMINOLOGY

I HAVE MANY REQUESTS for information on hooks—the best to use for different types of fishing. Salmon flies do not present much difficulty as far as hooks are concerned, as the range is very limited these days, but trout flies can be tied on a wide variety of irons.

The kind of fish to be caught, where it lives, and the type of fly to be used, must, of course, determine the type of hook to use. A heavy hook in clear, placid water is as much out of place as a fine wire hook would be in heavy water where large fish can be expected. Furthermore, different kinds of hooks must be used for different flies, streamer patterns, nymphs, etc., as no hook is appropriate for all fly-fishing conditions.

The range of all types of hooks is much smaller than before the war, when it was possible to get a greater variety. If anyone worked out a new design which the manufacturers thought practical, they were often prepared to manufacture and market it. Such is not the case these days, as present-day costs of retooling, etc., make the introduction of a new pattern a costly business, and not a practical proposition unless a very big quantity is made. However, the range of types available for fly tying is still quite extensive, and one soon decides on preferred patterns for one's types of fishing. Fig. 1 illustrates the descriptive points of modern usage, and in this case it is a forged upturned-eye pattern.

Salmon flies can be divided up into four main groups: those using standard hooks which have a Dublin or Limerick Bend; summer or low-water hooks which are of lighter wire and longer in the shank for the same gape; dry-fly hooks which are of very light wire and which can also be used for low-water flies, and trebles for use with the now very popular tube flies. The standard and low-water hooks are also used as doubles.

The "shape" is the index to the hook pattern and I have illustrated one or two of the most popular of these. Incidentally, the "shape" is quite often referred to as the "bend". "Bend" really refers to any lateral offset to the point and barb, i.e. when the point is offset to the right it is called a "reverse bend" and when it is offset to the left it is called a "kirbed bend". Another misnomer is that of "snecked bend" instead of "kirbed", although it has been used so much now that it is an accepted description. The purpose of these bends is to direct the penetration of the point at an angle to the shank, which helps to prevent the release of the hook as the point and the shank are not parallel.

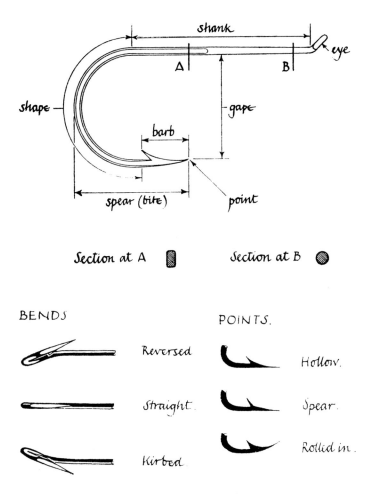

Section at A ▮   Section at B ◉

BENDS   POINTS.

Reversed   Hollow.

Straight.   Spear.

                         Rolled in.

Kirbed.

For dry-fly fishing, one of the best patterns to use is one with a sproat shape and turned-up eye, a slight reverse bend, and, of course, made of light wire. An alternative, and second in popularity, is the same type of hook with a turned-down eye, although I think that much of its popularity is due to the fact that it is considered easier by some tyers to dress a fly on a downturned eye hook. Hooks with the round shape are also popular for dry-flies in its smaller sizes, but as the wire increases in weight in the larger sizes they are also admirable for wet-flies.

A good hook for all-round types of wet-flies is the Limerick pattern, which is usually of quite stout wire. Another type of hook, which is self-descriptive, is the long-shanked. They are obtainable with either up- or down-eyes.

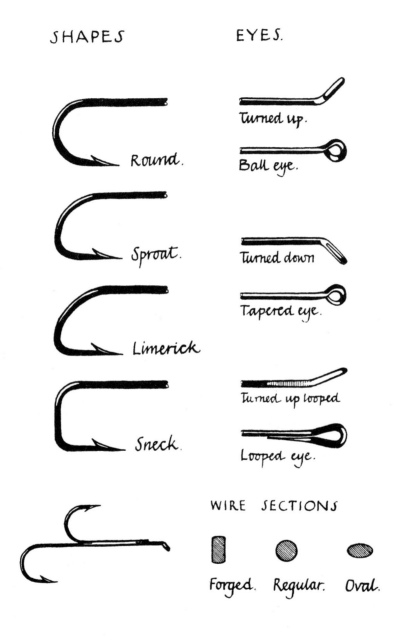

SHAPES

Round.

Sproat.

Limerick

Sneck.

EYES.

Turned up.

Ball eye.

Turned down

Tapered eye.

Turned up looped

Looped eye.

WIRE SECTIONS

Forged.   Regular.   Oval.

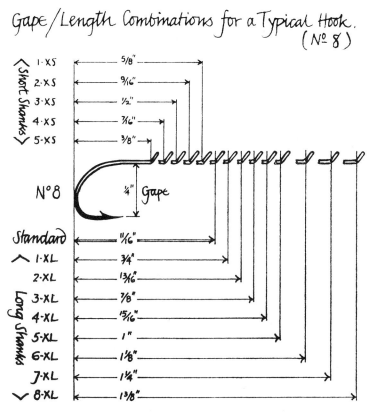

Gape/Length Combinations for a Typical Hook.
(Nº 8)

Short Shanks
1·XS — 5/8"
2·XS — 9/16"
3·XS — 1/2"
4·XS — 7/16"
5·XS — 3/8"

Nº 8   1/4" Gape

Standard — 11/16"
Long Shanks
1·XL — 3/4"
2·XL — 13/16"
3·XL — 7/8"
4·XL — 15/16"
5·XL — 1"
6·XL — 1⅛"
7·XL — 1¼"
8·XL — 1⅜"

NOTE. Measurements do not include the hook eye.

Further variations (not shown) include differences
in the gauge of wire, to suit hook purposes,
ie., for dry, wet & salmon flies.

I am grateful to Mr. S. A. Shrimpton, managing director of Messrs. Allcock & Co. Ltd., for the following notes on hook nomenclature.

"BEND". This is definitely a trade term for the shape of the hook, such as kirby bend, Limerick-bend, round bend, sneck bend, etc. To shape the hook, barbed and pointed wires were pulled round on a hand "peg-bend"; later the bend was fixed in a hand-operated machine, and the wire pulled round to shape.

As regards the different parts of a hook, we usually describe as the "depth" that part which you call "spear". The machine-point (as distinct from the old hand-filed point) is generally termed "spear point" so that there could be no confusion.

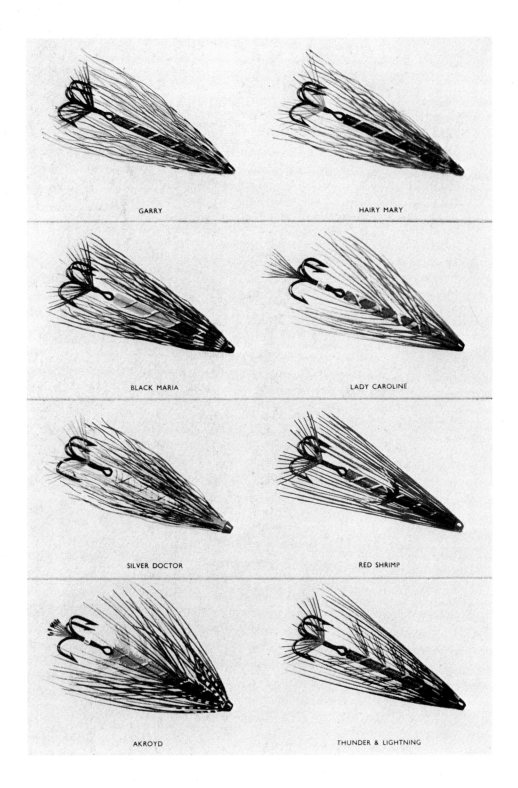

GARRY   HAIRY MARY

BLACK MARIA   LADY CAROLINE

SILVER DOCTOR   RED SHRIMP

AKROYD   THUNDER & LIGHTNING

TUBE FLIES

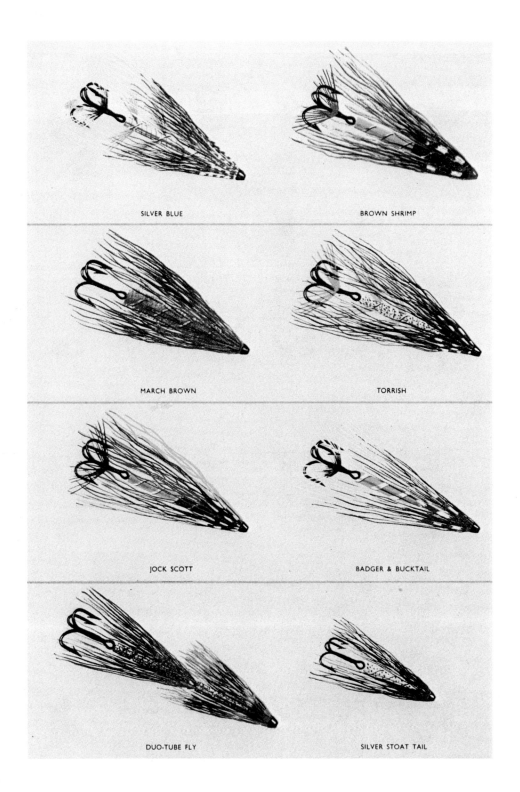

SILVER BLUE   BROWN SHRIMP

MARCH BROWN   TORRISH

JOCK SCOTT   BADGER & BUCKTAIL

DUO-TUBE FLY   SILVER STOAT TAIL

TUBE FLIES

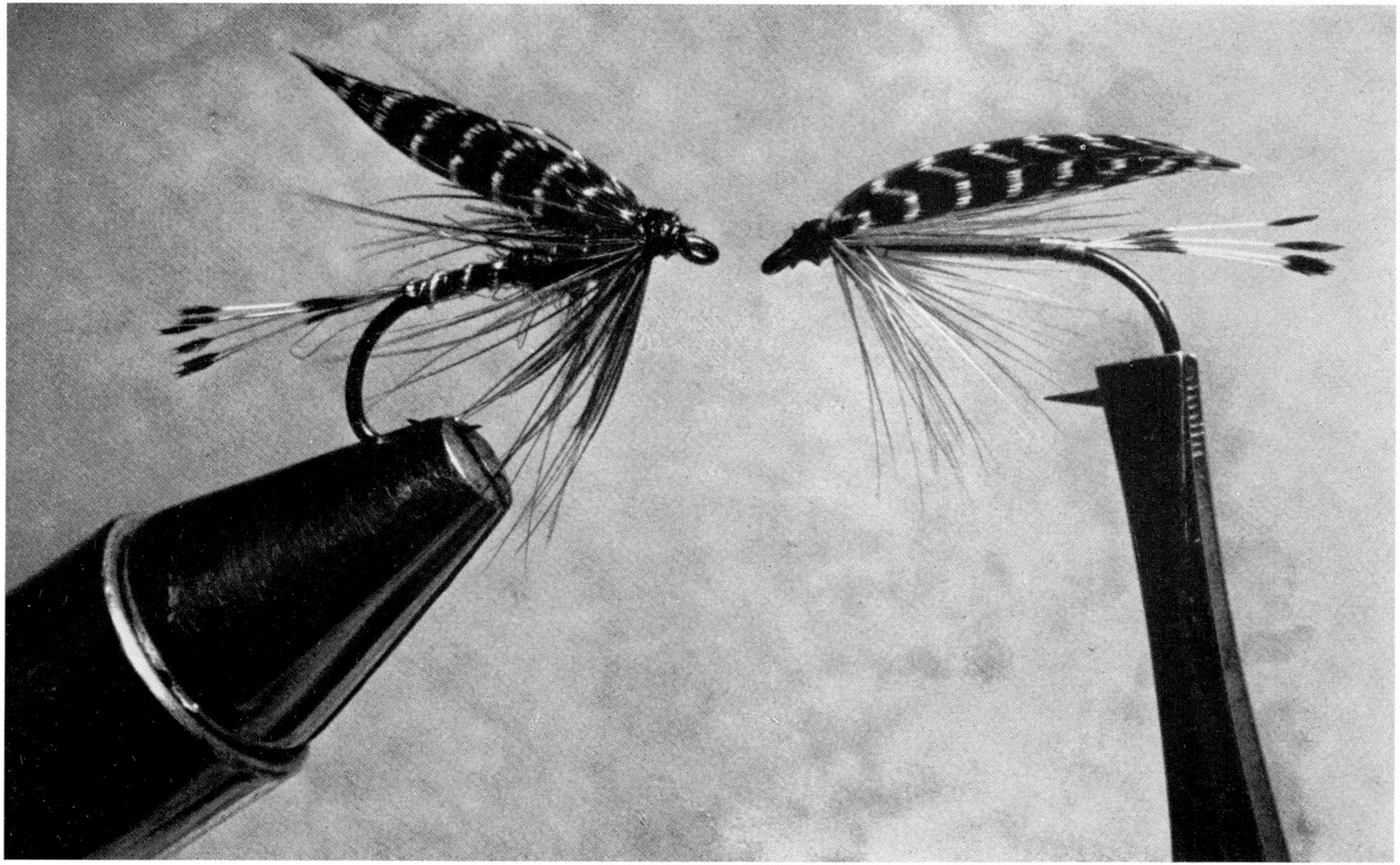

STYLES OF WINGING

TANDEM HOOK LURE

"FRENCH PARTRIDGE" MAYFLY

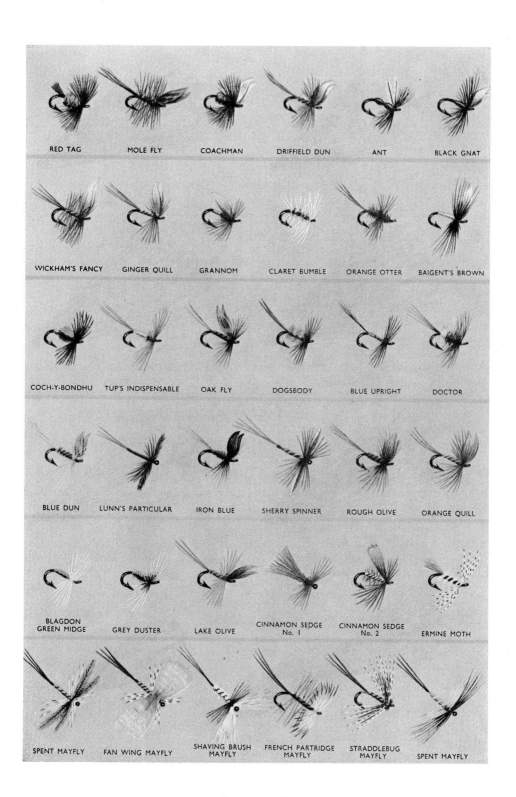

RED TAG   MOLE FLY   COACHMAN   DRIFFIELD DUN   ANT   BLACK GNAT

WICKHAM'S FANCY   GINGER QUILL   GRANNOM   CLARET BUMBLE   ORANGE OTTER   BAIGENT'S BROWN

COCH-Y-BONDHU   TUP'S INDISPENSABLE   OAK FLY   DOGSBODY   BLUE UPRIGHT   DOCTOR

BLUE DUN   LUNN'S PARTICULAR   IRON BLUE   SHERRY SPINNER   ROUGH OLIVE   ORANGE QUILL

BLAGDON GREEN MIDGE   GREY DUSTER   LAKE OLIVE   CINNAMON SEDGE No. 1   CINNAMON SEDGE No. 2   ERMINE MOTH

SPENT MAYFLY   FAN WING MAYFLY   SHAVING BRUSH MAYFLY   FRENCH PARTRIDGE MAYFLY   STRADDLEBUG MAYFLY   SPENT MAYFLY

DRY FLIES

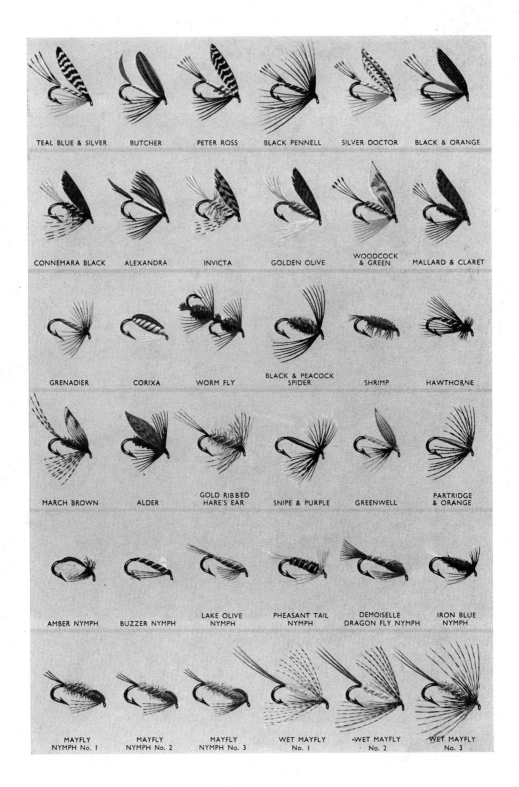

TEAL BLUE & SILVER	BUTCHER	PETER ROSS	BLACK PENNELL	SILVER DOCTOR	BLACK & ORANGE
CONNEMARA BLACK	ALEXANDRA	INVICTA	GOLDEN OLIVE	WOODCOCK & GREEN	MALLARD & CLARET
GRENADIER	CORIXA	WORM FLY	BLACK & PEACOCK SPIDER	SHRIMP	HAWTHORNE
MARCH BROWN	ALDER	GOLD RIBBED HARE'S EAR	SNIPE & PURPLE	GREENWELL	PARTRIDGE & ORANGE
AMBER NYMPH	BUZZER NYMPH	LAKE OLIVE NYMPH	PHEASANT TAIL NYMPH	DEMOISELLE DRAGON FLY NYMPH	IRON BLUE NYMPH
MAYFLY NYMPH No. 1	MAYFLY NYMPH No. 2	MAYFLY NYMPH No. 3	WET MAYFLY No. 1	WET MAYFLY No. 2	WET MAYFLY No. 3

WET FLIES

SECTION 2

THE USE AND APPLICATION OF FLUORESCENT MATERIALS IN FLY TYING

FLUORESCENT MATERIALS IN FLY TYING

THERE MUST BE FEW ANGLERS TODAY who have not been made aware of a new medium of attraction, not only in their sport, but also in everyday life. Examples may be seen on hoardings, buses, commercial vehicles, and in shops. It takes the form, usually, of printed matter that stands out clearly in any surroundings, and the gloom of "smog" seems to enhance its brilliance.

In our own sphere, attention has been drawn by articles in the angling press to the possibilities of this new material being advantageous to the fisherman.

The use of daylight fluorescent material for fly tying was first thought of by Eugene Burns, of America, during the Second World War, and now both the U.S. and Great Britain are producing these materials for use by the fly tyer.

Daylight fluorescent material, which we will call D.F.M. to save space and time, consists of specially treated fibres, and usually takes the three following forms: A thin floss, a wool yarn, and a chenille which is best described to the fly tyer as a "herl" of silk.

It is also possible to obtain hackles and furs dyed with this new medium, or dyes to carry out one's own ideas.

First, a little simple theory. It has been suspected, and there is much to indicate it, that fish have sight which is sensitive to the light rays at the "blue" end of the spectrum. In fact, that they may be able to record with their eyes ultra-violet rays, or at any rate a different range of colours activated by ultra-violet rays. In order that we humans may see the appearance of objects when exposed to these rays, special scientific instruments are needed, but the fish may see these effects in their normal sight. It is an interesting theory and a likely one. With D.F.M. we have a material which relies upon ultra-violet and blue and green light for its brilliance, and if it can be blended into the body of an imitation fly it may well be that the exact imitation, from a fishy point of view, might be possible. This would benefit the trout fisherman.

In deep or coloured water, particularly moving water, no matter what degree of sight be possessed by fish, they must obviously be very limited in their seeing distance. All food they capture must therefore be such as they happen to see passing close to them, and such as they detect by other senses. As we are dealing with non-tasting or smelling foods, then we anglers must give the fish the best possible chance of seeing our offer. Fluorescent objects, capturing the very weakest of light rays, no matter what their wave length, will automatically give the best chance.

D.F.M. therefore is ideal for any lure to be used "wet" and thus holds potentialities for the sea-trout, salmon and wet-fly trout angler.

Although much information has been gathered as to the efficacy of D.F.M., the materials are still so much in the experimental stage for fly tying that one or two misconceptions have arisen. If I can dispel those with these notes it may save many from using flies which are supposed to be fluorescent, but which are not. For instance, I have read that on certain days fish would only take flies incorporating D.F.M. in the body or wings, and colours such as "dark olive" and "claret" were mentioned. I have even heard "black" quoted in connection with fluorescent material. From experiments carried out during the production of the British materials, I know that it is only pastel shades of the primary colours that can be imparted to the materials. The colours found to react the best were: white, blue, yellow, lime green, orange, scarlet, pink and grey. Darker colours went black under the fluoroscope. The imparting of a dark colour to a fluorescent material is the equivalent of giving a coat of paint to a piece of strip lighting, and very opaque paint at that. The darker the shade, the more it masks the fluorescence.

This does not mean that flies with dark-coloured bodies (even black) cannot incorporate D.F.M., as I hope the rest of this chapter will show. It has been the proving of the adaptability of D.F.M. which has made experimental progress so slow. We have to thank M. A. Wardle, the well-known fly tyer, of Broxbourne, in Hertfordshire, and the late John E. Hamp, of Farnham, Surrey, for most of the information recorded here. Combinations of D.F.M. were worked out and natural insects were copied, but what is more important, the flies were tried out!

Firstly we must know what is meant by fluorescence. It is the property of a material to glow when exposed to light rays of a certain type, and to have something more than just plain "colour". The effect to the human eye when viewing a fluorescent object is that of a headlamp picking out a reflector at night. The reflector does not just appear red or white as a piece of painted wood or paper might, but literally glows with colour. Full advantage was taken of this property during the war years, when identification armbands of specially treated material were worn by troops engaged in the misty regions of the Aleutians; and shirts and signalling devices on aircraft carriers were also of this new material.

To sum up then, the new material at our disposal is a reflector, and when it is exposed to the ultra-violet and other light rays which are always present in daylight (hence D.F.M.), it reflects back its own colour. Under a fluoroscope, or ultra-violet ray lamp, a reel of this material looks as though it is illuminated from inside the reel itself.

When it was first introduced in the U.S. glowing reports were made of its success, and it appeared that many were under the impression that a new wonder material had arrived which would solve all our problems, and provide every novice with the means of gathering huge baskets of fish. Although the material is here to stay, fortunately for the fish, our fishing, and ourselves, baskets still cannot be filled merely by casting in a fly. What we have got, however, is a new material which we believe will give the angler a much better advantage in the unequal battle.

The development of D.F.M. must take its evolutionary course in the scheme of things, and it is up to the anglers who are fly tyers, or those who can collaborate with fly tyers, to develop this newly found asset.

Before going on to the uses of D.F.M., one point must be made clear. The material is not active when no light is present. This is usually from one hour after sunset until one hour before sunrise, the ultra-violet light being the last to leave the atmosphere owing to its greater refraction. D.F.M. cannot therefore be expected to attract any better than any other material of similar colouring when night fishing.

HOW D.F.M. MAY BE USED WITH SUCCESS

In the earliest experiments D.F.M. was used as a substitute for body materials in general use. If the body of a fly was normally tied green or red, for example, then green or red D.F.M. was used instead of the fur, silk or chenille normally used. As was bound to happen, some fish were caught on the flies, including some that would refuse all other offers at the time. This, of course, aroused enthusiasm at once, but when the same patterns proved utterly worthless at another time it became obvious that all was not well. All idea of a "wonder" material, irresistible and unfailing, vanished at once. Yet, the spasmodic success indicated that there was something attractive to fish which could be harnessed perhaps in some other way. It is these "other ways" which fly tyers, waiting to use this substance, want to know about, if only to give them a lead as to which direction in which to experiment.

USE IN PRACTICE

1. **Mixing with silks, wools, herls, or chenilles.**—This is the simplest way of incorporating D.F.M. in wet- or dry-flies, where brilliance is normally part of the pattern.

The normal body material is simply twisted with a piece of D.F.M. of like texture, into a rope and tied in and wound as a body. The amount of brightness is of course governed by the ratio of the mixture, at least two strands of ordinary material being used with one of D.F.M. to keep the brightness reasonable. The effect with this method is that of a brightly ribbed fly.

A more even mixture may be obtained by unlaying either the wool or silk and really mixing it with fibres of D.F.M., and then twisting together. This is very suitable for many flies, particularly salmon and sea-trout patterns. For example: a "Jock Scott" salmon fly can be made very much more attractive with a little D.F.M. added: (1) at the tail, a small wisp of fluorescent floss interspersing the Indian crow and golden pheasant crest; (2) in the yellow half of the body, the silk may be wound until the thickness is all but right, and then one layer of D.F.M. over to make the finishing touch; (3) at the centre, orange, or orange and yellow mixed D.F.M. fibres to replace the toucan veiling. The yellow tag, so common in many salmon-fly patterns, may be usefully made of yellow D.F.M.

This mixing of a scant amount of fluorescent material can be used with advantage on many salmon and sea-trout flies without using too much of the material or making the fly too gaudy. Flies tied in this manner have proved successful, although insufficient evidence is yet available to prove great superiority over orthodox patterns. We have proved, however, that they give the angler a much better chance in cloudy and swift water. We also know that such flies retain their fresh-tied appearance and brightness even after considerable use, accidents and wear and tear being considered.

This straightforward method of combining D.F.M. with wool or silk to enliven its appearance can be applied in so many cases and patterns that it would be a formidable task to mention them all, and experiments have by no means been exhaustive. Apart from salmon and sea-trout flies, brown trout flies, both wet and dry, may be treated similarly. Any pattern having a wool or silk body: e.g. Palmer flies, "Little Marryat", etc., or any having a bright tag: e.g. "Red Tag", "Treacle Parkin", etc., may be improved, in some cases with killing effect, by the careful addition of D.F.M. blended into the tie. But please note: always the accent on "careful"! The secret is to use just enough of the fluorescent materials to tint the orthodox materials, as it were. To swamp the fly in radiant brilliance does not work consistently well.

2. **Mixing with fur, hair and fluff, and the iridescent effect.**—One of the easiest, and certainly one of the proved effective methods of using D.F.M.

Furry bodies have always been good ones for trout, sea-trout and salmon flies, because under water the fibres float out and give a translucent appearance. Above water, the light playing on the projecting fibres gives much the same effect. Now, add to these already excellent materials a little extra sparkle and glow, and there you have one of the deadliest materials for general use.

Again, the possible combinations are legion, but many have been tried with very satisfactory results when otherwise poor sport would have been had. The method here is to cut the D.F.M., silk or wool according to body texture being used, into short lengths comparable with those of the body material, and mix together to obtain a uniform result. Whatever D.F.M. is added, the result is little different from the original, but it glows with little points of light wherever the tips of fluorescent strands show themselves, especially if the D.F.M. is the same colour.

This method can be used either merely to enrich the colour of the body, or to obtain iridescent effects. For example, in sea-trout or any other flies having a seal's fur body, the mixing of a little D.F.M., ratio 1 to 4, with the fur improves the fly, and the results, considerably. With seal's fur the fluorescent wool is the best medium to use, of a similar colour where possible.

With other furs, such as hare's ear, D.F.M. can be added similarly, although not in the same colour. This is where tinted and iridescent mixtures come in. If one wishes to strike a particular tone of colour there is no better way than to choose a fur near to the required tone and add D.F.M. until the right tone is obtained. A practical example is this: a copy of the larva of the lady-bird was required, a beetle-like creature with a dark back and a green-white belly and orange tip. It sounds complex, but proved easy. The back, of dark green heron herl, was tied in at the tail ready to lay over beetlewise. The body was made of natural off-white seal's fur mixed with green to obtain the depth of colour, and then a sprinkling of white and green fluorescent wool was added. When it was all mixed, it was spread out like a small cigar and a little orange fluorescent wool was kneaded into one end. A pinch of the resulting fur, orange tip first, was spun on to the tying silk, and the body wound. The back was laid over and tied in, and a small Coch-y-bondhu hackle and black silk finished the head. This pattern took brace after brace of fish so long as the larvae fell from the trees on that river, the Coln, but similar flies with no D.F.M. gave mediocre results. The foregoing dressing explains the principle of tinting existing furs to give better results.

Besides enriching specific colours or using D.F.M. to obtain a particular degree of colour, iridescent effects may be obtained with any type of fur, and are simple to obtain. A little pinch of cut D.F.M., of as many colours as desired, is mixed together and then added to some natural fur. By adding or subtracting certain colours the resulting iridescence may be given a bias towards one end of the spectrum or the other. If the D.F.M. is mixed thus with natural seal's fur, a light grey iridescent fur results. If mixed with hare's ear, a drab brown, and so on with any fur. The result does not look in the least bright, but glows from every point with a fiery pin prick of colour. The idea of iridescence is not new, and trout have a fancy for iridescent flies under certain conditions, a fact which was much appreciated by that wonderful angler and tyer Leonard West, who often used iridescent wings. One has only to examine a few natural insects in a beam of sunlight to appreciate how many of them shine with the colours of the spectrum as the light is refracted in the membranes of their wings and the hairs on their bodies. For this reason iridescent flies, even with D.F.M., give their best results under sunny conditions, but D.F.M. gives the best iridescence of any material.

Now that the fluorescent dyes are obtainable, the logical conclusion to draw is

"Why not dye the furs instead of mixing them with other fluorescent materials?' Unfortunately, natural furs do not react so well as artificial materials such as Nylon, Mohair being the only exception. To obtain the best results therefore, it is better to mix the natural furs with the established fluorescent materials.

It must be stressed that there can be no guarantee that this new material will solve all our problems and turn every fly into a killer, but it is worth while adding some iridescent mixture to the body of any fly to see if it improves the efficacy of the pattern, particularly in sunshine. It has done so in some cases which have been test-proved and may do so in many more.

3. **Mixing with hackle fibres for wings.**—Another method of using D.F.M., with once again unknown limits, is that of creating iridescent wings with its aid. Flies tied with these wings have rewarded time and time again under otherwise poor conditions. After considerable trial and error the best system is this: Select some first-quality cock hackles with long shiny fibres in white, grey, light and dark blue dun and light and dark claret. Lay these out on a flat surface. Take from each one in turn a few fibres, about six to ten, less of the claret than the others, and gather together in a bunch. Mix the fibres up carefully and add short lengths of white, grey, blue and a very little pink D.F.M. floss. This floss is better unlaid so that the fibres will separate and mix with the hackle fibres. When all are mixed well, dip the root end of the bunch in varnish and leave to dry. In this way a few dozen wing sets may be made at a time, and when the varnish is dry they may be stored in a box, and will keep thus for years.

This method, unlike the one utilising furs, is simplified by the advent of the new fluorescent dyes. Hackles dye up very well and fluoresce excellently, a large range of delicate olives and duns being available by mixing the dyes accordingly. They can also be dyed in all the eight pastel shades previously mentioned, and blended with the other hackle fibres as laid down in this section of the booklet. I would not suggest that the floss/hackle fibre method be dispensed with entirely, as this has proved to be successful.

When tied into a fly, they are treated in the same way as a hackle point or hair wing. Care should be taken to see that if the wing is split to form a double wing, an even distribution of the colours is maintained, particularly of the reds. The tyer may well consider fitting these wings to almost any dry-fly. In general they have proved remarkably successful on imitations of natural insects normally showing iridescence in sunlight and in particular on the Black Gnat, which thus dressed has proved the undoing of many brace of "smutting" fish.

4. **Use with horsehair for translucency.**—This is one of the most fascinating and not the least successful of the uses of this remarkable substance. Again it must be pointed out that the field in this direction has not been fully probed, but it has been sufficiently tried to show great possibilities.

The aim of many tyers of trout flies has been to obtain natural translucency, and horsehair has been one of the mediums used to produce it. Not only will D.F.M. with horsehair produce translucency, but such a good degree of it as to equal that of the natural insect in many cases, despite the ever-present hook-shank. The method is simply to use D.F.M. floss wound along the hook-shank as a base over which horsehair is then wound, either a single or double layer. The whole is then lightly varnished with very thin clear varnish. The colour of the body is graded and controlled either by clear hair over coloured D.F.M., or coloured hair over white D.F.M., or a combination of colours in both. The reason for the translucency is that the light passing through the hair instead of striking the opaque hook-shank is reflected back by the fluorescent core, thus giving the illusion that the whole is a semi-clear homogeneous substance. These flies when finished are amazingly faithful copies of the natural, and are deadly when fished during a rise. Experiments have shown that imitations tied with horsehair and D.F.M. which look good copies of the natural insect to the tyer will almost certainly look so to the fish. One tip to remember with this method is to use horsehair that is quite clear before dyeing, and not to dye it too deeply. *N.B.*—The horsehair/floss combination may be varied to obtain a variety of shades of olive, such as clear hair over yellow floss, or olive hair over white floss, and so on.

As has been stressed, we anglers are only on the threshold of a new discovery in the science of fly dressing. Up till now, only a handful of tyers have experimented seriously with this new substance, and still fewer have made their findings public. Consequently it is too early to be dogmatic about good and bad "fluorescent" patterns; all we can do is to say such patterns have been very successful with some anglers on some rivers, then to give the patterns to the angling world and let it get on with them for a bit until improvements and modifications are forthcoming and standard recipes are then laid down.

The dressings which follow are all ones which have been actually tried out under as many different conditions as possible, and have proved superior to any other flies of like pattern. There is no reason why the required hues and colours may not be obtained by other combinations of materials than those given, or that the wings and hackles should be strictly as described. The reason why most of the patterns are "naturals" is purely because Mr. Wardle prefers to stalk and hunt for trout rather than to hunt for a "master" fly.

It is of course unnecessary to use D.F.M. for many imitations such as the Willow Fly, Hawthorn Fly, etc., which are quite opaque and taken so greedily by the fish when they are present that no great research is called for.

Just one last word of advice: do not hesitate to use even the most fantastic combinations of D.F.M., do not expect great results, but do not be surprised if you get them.

PROVED PATTERNS OF "FLUORESCENT" FLIES

(Devised and proved by Michael A. Wardle)

KEY: W—Wing (Hackle point in every case where used); B—Body; H—Hackle; T—Tails or Whisks; S—Silk.

Dark Olive Dun

W—Dark grey; B—Grey-green horse-hair over white or grey D.F.M. floss, varnished; T—Dark grey; H—Dark olive "cree" cock's; S—Dark olive.

Spinner Male

W—Rusty dun; B—Orange tip of silk; then pale blue horsehair over orange D.F.M. floss, varnished; T—Pale grey or dun; H—Claret-brown; S—Dark claret.

Spinner Female

W—Dark grey; B—Claret and clear horsehair wound side by side over white D.F.M. floss and varnished; T—Cream; H—Natural brown; S—Dark claret.

Medium Olive Dun

W—Medium grey; B—Medium olive horsehair over yellow D.F.M. floss, varnished; T—G.P. yellow breast; H—Cream or pale honey; S—M.O.

Spinner Male (Brown and Yellow)

W—Medium grey; B—Cinnamon horsehair over yellow D.F.M., with last third brown silk and varnished; T—Olive badger or cree; H—Olive cree; S—Brown.

Spinner Female

W—Paler grey; B—As for male, but no brown tip (may be yellow tip); T—Olive badger; H—Badger; S—Brown or M.O.

Spinner Male

W—Pale blue dun; B—Primrose tip of silk; then clear horsehair over white D.F.M. floss, varnished; T—White; H—Pale blue dun; S—Primrose.

Spinner Female (Little Amber)

W—Pale blue dun; B—Pale cinnamon horsehair over white or yellow D.F.M. floss and varnished; T—Cream; H—Cream; S—Yellow.

Pale Watery Nymph

B—Clear horsehair over white D.F.M. or white D.F.M. mixed with white "cellu-lite" floss; T—Cream; Thorax—Cream herl or white silk; Legs—Cream.

Iron Blue Spinner Male (Jenny)

W—Pale blue dun; B—Light claret tip of silk; then clear horsehair over white D.F.M. floss, varnished; T—White; H—Pale blue dun; S—Light claret.

Iron Blue Spinner Female (Claret)

W—Dark blue dun; B—Claret horse-hair over white D.F.M. floss and varnished; T—Dark claret; H—Dark claret-brown; S—Brown.

Sherry Spinner Male

W—Medium grey; B—Reddish claret horsehair over white or grey D.F.M. floss, varnished; T—G.P. yellow/orange breast feather; H—Grey badger; S—Dark claret.

Pale Watery Dun

W—Pale blue dun; B—Clear horsehair over white or grey D.F.M. floss and varnished; T—White; H—Badger; S—Dark green.

Black Gnat

W—Iridescent; B—Crow's herl; H—Black natural; S—Black natural.

Red Ant

W—Iridescent; B—Cinnamon horsehair over red or orange D.F.M. floss and varnished (should be ant-shaped); H—Gamecock; S—Red or orange.

Cow Dung

W—Blue dun set sloping back; B—Dirty orange herl mixed with fibres orange D.F.M. wool; H—Gamecock; S—Orange.

Green Insect

B—Green heron herl twisted with green D.F.M. floss or wool and fine gold wire rib; H—Greenwell; S—M.O.

Green Caterpillar

B—Two strands of heavy green floss silk twisted green D.F.M. floss laid top and bottom of shank with yellow or green D.F.M. floss strand along each side. All tied on with green silk; H—Blue dun tied palmer.

Sherry Spinner Female

W—Pale grey or ginger; B—M.O. horsehair over orange D.F.M. floss and varnished; T—G.P. yellow breast; H—Ginger; S—Orange.

Greenwell's Glory

Tied as orthodox but with waxed and dirtied green or yellow D.F.M. floss for body. It may be varnished.

Houghton Ruby

W—Medium grey (spent); B—Cinnamon horsehair over pink D.F.M. floss and varnished; T—Red cock's; H—Red cock's; S—Red.

Brown Bug

This is tied as a beetle. B—Iridescent hare's ear; Back—Dark brown strands of a wing feather; H—Coch-y-bondhu; S—Black.

Wardle's B.W.O.

W—Iron Blue hackle points; B—Yellow-olive horsehair over orange D.F.M. floss and varnished; T—G.P. yellow/orange breast; H—Dark blue dun or iron; S—Red.

Alternatives to B.W.O.

W—Iron Blue; B—Orange hair over white or yellow D.F.M.; T—G.P. yellow/orange breast; H—Ginger, dark blue dun or iron, or may be entirely hackled in iron, no wings (this has been tried for Kennet and Test to float in fast turbulent water, by Mr. Hamp); S—Red.

Further successful experiments based on the foregoing, were carried out by that well-known angler Gordon Hay, and the results published in his article in the *Fishing Gazette* of 16 April 1955. He incorporated D.F.M. to give more lifelike brilliance to the bodies of his flies, and to help to produce a greater amount of translucent light effect. He also confirmed the theory that flies tied with a proportion of D.F.M. were most effective on dull days, or at dawn or dusk.

Most of Wardle's experiments were carried out on southern dry-fly waters, whereas Gordon Hay did his on our northern swift rivers where dry-fly is seldom possible. The valuable work they have done, therefore, has considerably reduced the probability of our using useless methods of incorporating D.F.M., no matter what our type of fishing.

The methods used by Hay, and the five patterns he described in his article, are well worth studying, and I only hope I can do them justice.

One of his most successful patterns (over four seasons) was a "Partridge and Red". This was tied on a long-shanked up-eyed hook size 14–11, with a wool-mix body, three turns of orange D.F.M. as a tag, and a brown partridge hackle. Red tying silk was used throughout. The wool-mix for the body was made up of equal lengths of nigger brown and fawn ordinary skein wool, mixed with similar lengths of orange and pink D.F.M. wool. All the lengths must be thoroughly teased out before mixing, and one of the best ways to do this is to hold the wool firmly in one hand, take a pair of tweezers in the other hand, grip the wool firmly about $\frac{1}{2}$ in. from its loose end and draw the tweezers along the wool. This will produce a fluffy end to the wool which can be cut off, and the process repeated until the whole length of the wool has been so treated. To mix the four shades of wool thoroughly, hold them all in the left hand and tear out a pinch at a time, pulling all four colours with each pinch. Let all the pinches form a little pile on the table until all the wool has been teased out, and repeat the process until an even mix has been obtained.

The orange D.F.M. floss for the tag is tied in just above the point of the long-shanked hook, three turns to the rear, and then back over itself. Hold the floss taut when tying it off, as it has a tendency to slip. The wool-mix is now spun very lightly on to the tying silk, tapering it off so that there is practically nothing where the silk meets the hook. Wind along the shank of the hook to form a tapering body, slim throughout, but with a thickening at the thorax. Now tie in the partridge hackle, and secure. Next, take the hackle between the finger and thumb of the left hand, and draw all the fibres upwards and backwards towards the bend of the hook. Hold in this position and secure with a few turns of the tying silk, so that all the fibres are set above the hook. Black cellulose varnish finishes the head.

The hackle fibres for these flies should be short and need not be longer than will reach from the head of the fly to the point of the hook. Rib with fine gold wire for lake use.

Another successful pattern, originally tied for evening use, is the "Twilight Grey". Captain J. Hughes Parry, in August 1951, took eight fish out of a total catch of ten, on this fly, and dressed on a No. 5 long-shank hook; he also took a

$2\frac{1}{2}$ lb. sea trout, and a $1\frac{1}{4}$ lb. brown, when no other flies would move a fish. Dressed on sizes 00 to 1 and 2, it has taken many trout, lake and river, throughout the season. The dressing is:

Hackle: Grizzle (Plymouth Rock) cock.
Body: Grey wool-mix.
Tying Silk: Grey or olive.

The wool-mix is made up of a length of medium grey tapestry wool, and a length of white fluorescent wool only one-third as long as the grey wool. The two should now be thoroughly mixed as for the "Partridge and Red". Grey fluorescent wool can also be used to vary the shade of the body. The wool-mix should be very thin and tapering when spun on to the tying silk, and a tapering body formed—slightly thicker at the thorax.

Two or three turns of hackle are sufficient for wet-flies, but more may be added if they are to be used dry. For sea trout, No. 5 long-shank hooks are recommended, with a slightly longer hackle for the extra length of hook.

The third dressing given by Mr. Hay is the ever-popular "Black Gnat", tied both wet and dry. A stiff black cock hackle is used for the dry pattern, and a starling hackle for the wet, and they are tied on sizes from 00 to 1.

The tying silk is black, of course, and this is whipped from the eye towards the bend of the hook. The stem of the hackle is then placed on these turns, and the silk whipped back the eye, leaving enough space in front for the hackle to be wound. The silk is then wound back towards the bend, finishing opposite the point. At this stage a piece of white D.F.M. floss is tied in. Secure it firmly and then take two turns towards the bend, and then two or three back to cover the first two, so as to form a small pea about the size of a pin head. Keep the floss as tight as possible. Tie in the waste end of the floss with the tying silk and cut off. Now take two turns of the tying silk over the floss, each turn lying next to its neighbour, so as to form a slight bulge towards the tail. Now whip back over all the tying silk up to the point required for winding the hackle. Wind the hackle and tie in its tip, cut off surplus and seal off the head with black cellulose varnish.

The last dressing is a variation of the "Coch-y-bondhu". When the tying silk is wound down to the bend for tying in the peacock herl body, a small loop of white D.F.M. floss is first tied in. The loop is then cut and then teased out with the tying silk to form a small fluffy tassel, and trimmed with the scissors so that only about one-sixteenth of an inch projects from the herl body. Mr. Hay's preference is for a dark red game cock's hackle in place of the more usual Red/Black, but only because he found it more successful on the particular waters he fished. A fine gold tinsel rib was found to be an asset on cold dull days.

During the past few years I have had a great deal of correspondence with the late William Bannerman, an expert fisherman and fly tyer, of Buckie, Banffshire. He was always a valuable source of information when one was looking for lesser-known trout and salmon patterns, and some of his suggestions and patterns are given in Section 6, page 183.

He devoted a great deal of time to experiments with fluorescent material, and I could not do better than quote his conclusions verbatim.

"I have done quite a bit of experimenting with D.F.M. this season, and although disappointed with the length of time taken to try out the ideas, I am quite pleased with some of the results. Some of the experiments proved most successful, but there still remains the doubt that the originals may have done quite as well under the same circumstances. Following are some of the new ideas, at least original in my case, which were tried out and in my opinion were an improvement on the standard pattern.

"Floss silks rolled in chopped D.F.M. of various colours, and then wound on the hook-shank before building the bodies called for in the pattern. This was very good on such patterns as Coch-y-bondhu and Rough Olive, and patterns calling for seal's fur and other dubbings.

"Single strands of D.F.M. floss dividing and shading quill bodies.

"Single strands ribbed the same as tinsel.

"Hair and spade hackle wings with a minute quantity of D.F.M. floss strands to give flash.

"A single strand of blue floss twisted round the ribbing tinsel on such flies as the 'Teal Blue and Silver'. This method can be applied to any fly with a silver body.

"The only conclusions I would stick my neck out for are:

"That combined with horsehair translucency can be obtained to a satisfactory degree.

"That floss silks rolled in chopped D.F.M. can obtain many combinations which seem attractive to fish.

"That tails of yellow D.F.M. shading short tails of orange D.F.M. are at least as successful if not more so than standard tails.

"That D. F. M. should be used more sparingly in low clear water than in deep coloured water.

"In case you are interested in sea and bait fishing, I must tell you about the uses of D.F.M. with these.

"Sea flies. Use as with ordinary flies.

"Minnows, especially wooden devons in the spring, lend themselves to use with D.F.M., the most successful being single strands of D.F.M. laid parallel along the belly on wet varnish, and then thoroughly re-varnished with clear Cellire. In some cases the strands were stiffened with varnish and fixed to extend beyond the minnow body and almost covering the treble hook.

"Metal sea baits. The most easily worked, of course, are the lead type. Holes are bored through the flat sides of the bait, and D.F.M. floss threaded in and out. Or the holes can be filled with short lengths of the floss and wool, which are then cut quite close to the body. In both systems the bodies are varnished after the D.F.M. has been added. Many variations can be made, the best I found being one with spots of red or blue.

"Sea fishing may well provide a useful field for this type of experiment. My only regret is that I have neither the time or health to experiment with this type of material as much as it deserves."

A FLUORESCENCE DETECTOR

ALTHOUGH THE BEST TEST for fluorescent fly-tying materials is to use them when fishing, it is, of course, desirable to know the amount of fluorescence present in the fly to be used, or the amount of fluorescence being given off by the material which is to go into the fly.

The normal method adopted is to use a quartz mercury vapour lamp, with the visible light screened by means of a special nickel glass filter, but this is an expense to which few fly tyers can be prepared to go. It is, however, possible to use the ultra-violet light present in sunlight to operate a simple detector, one of which is illustrated (p. 98). It is a small wooden box with a sliding lid, the inside of which is blackened with indian ink. A hole is cut into the lid, which takes a piece of special nickel glass to form a screen 2 in. × 2 in.

The material or flies to be tested are put into the box, and with the eye close to the hole in the front of the box to exclude all light, allow sunlight to fall on the screen. Artificial light does not produce much fluorescence, but there will be sufficient for demonstration purposes. Incandescent electric light is the best source, should there be no sunlight.

A few remarks as to the lasting powers of fluorescent materials will no doubt be helpful. Tests were carried out over nine weeks June/July 1954, which, incidentally, was the wettest summer for half a century.

D.F.M. exposed to daylight only was still as good as ever after twelve months, and flies used throughout the season still reacted as well as when they were first tied.

The continuous exposure test began on 1 June, and a complete range of D.F.M. was exposed to the elements (sun, wind, rain) with the object of seeing just how much they would stand.

During the month of June there was 3 in. of rain and an average $5\frac{1}{2}$ hours sunshine per day. Coupled with the high winds, these conditions were very severe, but they made little impression on the D.F.M. There was very little fading either in the actual colours of the materials or in the fluorescence, which was very encouraging, as these conditions must have been as severe, if not more so, than any fly would have to contend with.

The tests were carried on into July with the same materials, and during that month we had a further $2\frac{1}{2}$ in. of rain and an average of $4\frac{1}{2}$ hours of sunshine. By the end of the month most of the materials had begun to wilt, and the accompany-

96

ing chart shows to what degree. It should be borne in mind that any dyed material would have faded after two months' exposure to such conditions, and also that for maximum fluorescence D.F.M. is only dyed in light pastel shades.

Results at the end of Continuous Exposure Test on D.F.M. Materials
(9 weeks—June/July 1954)
Conditions: Heavy Rain (5.44 inches), Wind and Bright Sunshine
(297.4 hours)

	HACKLES	WOOL	CHENILLE	FLOSS
WHITE	Complete loss of fluorescence	Complete loss of fluorescence	Complete loss of fluorescence	Complete loss of fluorescence
BLUE	Complete fading and loss of fluorescence	Some fading and complete loss of fluorescence	Some fading and complete loss of fluorescence	Complete fading and loss of fluorescence
GREY	Complete fading and loss of fluorescence	Some fading and complete loss of fluorescence	Some fading and complete loss of fluorescence	Complete fading and loss of fluorescence
LIME	Severe fading, but fairly good fluorescence	Some fading and slight loss of fluorescence	Some fading and slight loss of fluorescence	Severe fading (see note regarding fluorescence)
YELLOW	Severe fading, but fairly good fluorescence	Slight fading, but fairly good fluorescence	Slight fading, but fairly good fluorescence	Severe fading (see note regarding fluorescence)
ORANGE	Slight fading, but fair fluorescence	Slight fading, but fair fluorescence	Slight fading, but fair fluorescence	Severe fading (see note regarding fluorescence)
SCARLET	Very little fading and very good fluorescence	Slight fading, but good fluorescence	Slight fading, but very good fluorescence	Severe fading (see note regarding fluorescence)
PINK	Severe fading, but quite fair fluorescence	Slight fading, but fair fluorescence	Slight fading and slight loss of fluorescence	Severe fading (see note regarding fluorescence)

Note: Severest loss of colour was found in the floss, and colours which retained fluorescence in this material were dominated by Yellow.

A fluorescence detector

This detector enables any material or fly to be tested for the presence of daylight fluorescence.

The material or fly is placed in the box and the screen on top exposed to sunlight when the ultra-violet rays falling on it will expose any fluorescence that is present.

MAKING TUBE FLIES

WITH A SUGGESTED LIST
OF DRESSINGS

*Sixteen illustrated in colour
between pages 80 and 81*

*Patterns for the colour plate
supplied by John B. Price,
Weymouth*

HOW TO MAKE TUBE FLIES

ALTHOUGH I ADDED A CHAPTER on the making of tube flies to the 1960 impression of *Fly Dressers' Guide*, space did not allow me to give it the coverage I would have liked. I have therefore enlarged on this subject here, plus two coloured plates, which I trust will enable the reader to have a much clearer idea of the "know-how" of making these flies. (See illustrations between pages 80 and 81.)

The coloured illustrations are shown in enlarged form for clarity, and although flies of this size are used quite regularly in conditions that call for large sizes, the tube fly can also be utilised for low-water conditions, for sea-trout fishing, and for lake flies.

I would suggest that the very fine tubes or tubing be used for the smaller patterns, and I hope the instructions and suggestions will enable the individual fly tyer to achieve patterns of his own particular style and "fancy" as well as the more orthodox ones.

The dressings given were produced by myself in conjunction with my friend John Price, of Weymouth, who also tied the patterns used by the artist to produce the coloured plates. He has also fished this type of fly regularly, and has done much to popularise it on rivers in the southern counties and in his native Wales. I add this note so that the reader will know that the flies have a practical background and are not just blind reproductions in tube form of well-known patterns.

Because the fly's rise to popularity is so recent, available literature on its use, how to make it, and dressings, is very scarce. This chapter covers one method of making them, and I hope the short list of dressings will be a basic guide as to what one can produce. The standard names I have used ("Jock Scott", "Blue Charm", etc.) are merely given to illustrate the effect I have tried to achieve. The "Blue Charm", for instance, has the normal black floss body and silver rib, while the effect of the barred teal feather of the original wing is obtained by using a grey squirrel tail. The blue hackle in front can be added in "collar" fashion as described later or omitted altogether.

One of the first patterns of tube fly to become very well known was the "Stoat Tail", which in its original form consisted merely of fibres from the tail of a stoat, whipped round one end of a tube. As with all patterns which achieve popularity, variations very soon began to appear. These usually took the form of additions to the tube body itself (silk and tinsel coverings), or by additions of different-coloured hair fibres to those of the stoat tail. The "Hairy Mary" is

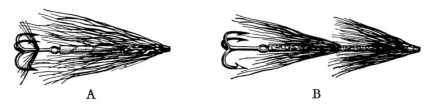

Fig. 1. Single and double tubes

another popular tube-fly adaptation, being a standard hair-winged salmon fly in its original form. The tube version is given in the list of dressings.

For the uninitiated, the tube fly, as its name denotes, consists of a length of polythene or metal tubing, round which are whipped hair fibres from the tails of different animals. Orthodox salmon-fly bodies are sometimes added to the tubes, and long-fibred hackles may be used in conjunction with the hair fibres, or even in place of them. Heron and guinea-fowl hackles are good examples of feathers which may be used for this purpose.

The tube flies are fished in conjunction with a treble hook which is attached to the end of the cast. The tube is slid down the cast tail first until it is stopped by the eye of the hook. For colour variations or increase in size, two tubes can be used instead of one, and Fig. 1 illustrates the two methods.

Ordinary fly-tying implements are all that are required to make tube flies, plus two or three sizes of tapered (no eye) salmon hooks on which the tubes can be slid to facilitate the tying. I would suggest sizes 4, 2, 1, 1/0 and 3/0, as these should cope with most of the sizes of tubes one is likely to come up against. If a tube with a very large interior diameter is used, I suppose a special mount would have to be made for it if the flies are to be tied in a vice.

To tie a "Hairy Mary" the first step is to press the tube on to the tapered hook-shank, firmly enough to hold it well, but not so hard as to split or damage the end of it. The bend of the hook is then placed in the vice as per Fig. 2. Tying silk is then run down the tube in the usual manner, and the body silk and tinsel rib tied in at what would be the tail end of a normal fly. Wind the tying silk back to the front, and then follow with the body silk and tinsel rib in that order. We should now be as Fig. 3. Now put a layer of the tying silk on the remaining portion of the tube, to form a bed for the ends of the hair fibres which are to be tied in.

The "wing" of the "Hairy Mary" is made from the brown fibres taken from a deer's tail (bucktail), or in the smaller patterns, fibres from a barred brown squirrel tail can be used. No matter what kind of tail is used for making tube flies, it will be found that the best fibres for small flies will be found at its base. For larger flies the fibres should then be taken from that part of the tail which suits them best,

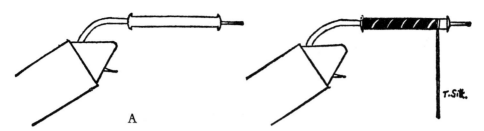

Fig. 2. First stages in tying a "Hairy Mary"

so that for very large flies the fibres would be taken from the tip. In this manner best use is made of any variegated colourings the tail may possess.

The hairs are cut off by twisting a small bunch of them together, and then cutting off as near to the root as possible. Any fluffy fur, which is found at the base of most hair fibres, should be combed out with the point of a dubbing needle. This fur has no use in the wing, and only causes the head of the fly to finish thicker than need be. Every effort should be made to keep down the size of the head to prevent a bow-wave, and to facilitate rapid entry into the water.

Do not try to put on too many hairs at a time, and a good measure of quantity is their thickness when they are twisted together. A thickness of about $\frac{1}{16}$ in. is maximum, even for large flies.

Fig. 3. A further stage in tying a "Hairy Mary"

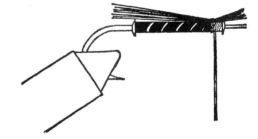

The bunch of fibres is now tied in on top of the tube as per Fig. 3, and the old and faithful method of making the loop of tying silk over the fingers as used for tying-in normal wings can be very helpful here.

The waste ends should now be cut off, and this should be done after each bunch of fibres is tied in. This enables one to follow each stage of the tying-in more closely, as a large bunch of splayed-out waste fibres will obscure the head of the tube.

The tube is now rolled round the hook-shank, bringing to the top the next portion which is to be covered by the hairs. Another bunch of fibres is now tied in, the turns of silk being immediately to the right of those which tied in the first bunch. Carry on in this manner until the complete circumference of the tube has been covered.

The reason for placing the silk turns to the right as each bunch is tied in is to keep down the size of the head. If all the turns were in one place it would be quite bulky. One should endeavour to fix the "steps" of tying silk so that when the last bunch of fibres is tied in, the end of the tube is reached. A single layer of silk is then taken round all the fibres where they are tied in. This forms a neat head and gives a uniform slope to the fibres. As all the waste ends of the fibres were cut off as we went along, all that is now necessary is a whip finish and the addition of varnish to the head. I would suggest one or two coats of thin clear Cellire soaked well into the silk whippings, for strength. When these are dry, a final coat of black or red as desired.

If the tube fly requires a hackle in front, this is wound in front of the fibres at the same point as where the first bunch of fibres was tied in. All the hackle fibres are then drawn to the rear by the fingers of the left hand, and a few turns of silk wound over their base so that they envelop the hair as closely as possible.

If heron hackles are used in the place of hair, one hackle is wound at the front and all its fibres pulled to the rear, or on a larger pattern it can be wound "Palmer" fashion.

In some cases, the appearance of a fly, as well as its "taking" qualities, can be improved by dressing the treble hook. This usually takes the form of a few turns of tinsel or floss (or both), which on an orthodox fly would be the "tag" wound underneath the tail. Two or three golden pheasant crests can be added to form a tail, or the treble can be masked with a hackle as shown in the coloured illustrations.

One fault with the tube fly is the tendency for the treble to hang at an angle to the tube, or even catch on to the cast during the actual casting of the fly. This can be overcome by fixing a small piece of bicycle valve rubber over the end of each tube when it is completed. The "eye" of the treble can then be drawn into the valve rubber before one starts casting. This is illustrated below. (Fig. 4.)

Fig. 4. Preventing snags when casting

SUGGESTED DRESSINGS FOR TUBE FLIES

Illustrated in colour between pages 80 and 81

Silver Blue
TREBLE HOOK. Hackle. Badger cock.
BODY. Flat silver tinsel.
RIB. Oval silver tinsel.
WING. Grey squirrel tail.
HEAD HACKLE. Teal flank or breast, according to size of fly.
HEAD. Black varnish.

Brown Shrimp
TREBLE HOOK. Hackle. Orange cock.
BODY. First half yellow floss, remainder black floss.
RIB. Oval silver tinsel.
WING. Hot orange bucktail, well mixed with brown bucktail. (The brown fibres can be taken from the dark part of the dyed orange bucktail, as the dyeing gives them a good rich colour.)
HEAD HACKLE. Natural guinea fowl.
HEAD. Red varnish.

Garry
TREBLE HOOK. Hackle. Black cock.
BODY. Black floss.
RIB. Oval silver tinsel.
WING. Yellow bucktail, with a few red fibres underneath.
HEAD HACKLE. Dyed blue guinea fowl.
HEAD. Black varnish.

March Brown
BODY. Hare's fur.
RIB. Oval silver or gold tinsel.
WING. Barred brown squirrel tail.
HEAD. Black varnish.

Torrish
TREBLE HOOK. Hackle. Yellow cock.
BODY. Embossed silver tinsel.
RIB. Oval silver tinsel.
BODY HACKLE. Yellow cock.
WING. Dyed black bucktail.
HEAD HACKLE. Natural guinea fowl.
HEAD. Black varnish.

Black Maria
TREBLE HOOK. Hackle. Black cock.
BODY. Tail half yellow floss, remainder black floss.
RIB. Oval silver tinsel.
BODY HACKLE. Black cock, over black floss only.
WING. Black bucktail.
HEAD HACKLE. Natural guinea fowl.
HEAD. Black varnish.

Lady Caroline
TREBLE HOOK. Embossed silver tinsel, and a golden pheasant breast feather wound as a hackle.
BODY. Olive green (1 strand) and light brown (2 strands) wool, wound together.
RIB. Flat gold tinsel, and oval silver holding down the turns of hackle.
HACKLE. Grey heron's hackle, wound the length of the body.
FRONT HACKLE. Golden pheasant breast feather.
HEAD. Black varnish.

Hairy Mary

TREBLE HOOK. Hackle. Dyed blue cock.
BODY. Black floss.
RIB. Oval gold or silver tinsel.
WING. Brown bucktail hair.
HEAD HACKLE. Dyed blue guinea fowl.
HEAD. Black varnish.

This fly now has many variations, the original version being an orthodox "Blue Charm" salmon fly, the wing of which was replaced with brown bucktail fibres. Any colour of hair can be used, to suit local conditions, and the body silk can be varied. Coloured tinsel (Lurex) bodies are very popular for Scots rivers, particularly blue and red.

Badger Bucktail

TREBLE HOOK. Hackle. Badger cock.
BODY. Golden yellow floss.
RIB. Flat silver tinsel.
WING. Badger hair, mixed with white bucktail, plus a few fibres of natural brown bucktail.
HEAD HACKLE. Natural guinea fowl.
HEAD. Black varnish.

Silver Doctor

TREBLE HOOK. Hackle. Dyed blue cock.
BODY. Flat silver tinsel.
RIB. Oval silver tinsel.
WING. Alternating stripes of natural grey squirrel tail, and grey squirrel tail dyed red, blue and yellow.
HEAD. Red varnish.

A head hackle of natural guinea fowl is sometimes added.

Jock Scott

TREBLE HOOK. Hackle. Black cock.
BODY. Tail half yellow floss, remainder black floss.
RIB. Oval silver tinsel.
BODY HACKLE. Black cock over black floss only.
WING. Black squirrel or bucktail, alternating with strips of red, yellow and blue bucktail.
FRONT HACKLE. Natural guinea fowl.
HEAD. Black varnish.

Duo-Tube Fly

This is only one example of this type of fly, as the combinations are practically limitless. No treble-hook hackle is shown, but this could vary with type of combination used. i.e. Yellow, orange or red on a light-coloured fly, black or dyed blue on a dark one.

First Tube

BODY. Embossed silver tinsel.
WING. Black squirrel tail

Second Tube

BODY. Embossed silver tinsel.
WING. Alternating stripes of natural grey squirrel tail, and grey squirrel tail dyed orange and blue.
HEADS. Black varnish.

Red Shrimp

TREBLE HOOK. Hackle. Scarlet cock.
BODY. Tail half red floss, remainder black floss.
RIB. Oval silver tinsel.
MIDDLE HACKLE. Badger or hot orange.
WING. Dyed red bucktail (natural red golden pheasant breast feather could be used on small flies).
HEAD. Red varnish.

Silver Stoat Tail
TREBLE HOOK. Hackle. None.
BODY. Embossed silver tinsel.
RIB. Oval silver tinsel.
WING. Stoat tail fibres, or natural black squirrel tail fibres on large flies.
HEAD. Black varnish.

Thunder and Lightning
TREBLE HOOK. Hackle. Orange cock.
BODY. Black floss.
RIB. Oval gold tinsel.
BODY HACKLE. Hot orange.
WING. Black heron hackle.
FRONT HACKLE. Dyed blue guinea fowl.
HEAD. Black varnish.

Akroyd
TREBLE HOOK. Flat silver tinsel, and golden pheasant tippet fibres projecting just beyond bends of hooks.
BODY. First half orange seal's fur, remainder black floss.
RIB. Oval silver tinsel over seal's fur, flat silver over floss.
HACKLE. Yellow cock over seal's fur, black heron over floss.
THROAT HACKLE. Teal duck flank.
HEAD. Black varnish.
(As this fly is popular for heavy conditions, the tube could be wrapped in lead wire, or a heavy brass tube used.)

NOT ILLUSTRATED

Blue Charm
BODY. Black floss.
RIB. Oval silver tinsel.
WING. Grey squirrel tail fibres.
HACKLE. (Optional) blue cock.

Blue Doctor
As Silver Doctor, but with a blue floss body, ribbed with oval silver tinsel, and the guinea fowl hackle dyed blue.

Black Doctor
As Silver Doctor, but with a black floss silk body, ribbed oval silver tinsel.

Stoat Tail
BODY AND RIB. As desired, or just the bare tube.
WING. Fibres from a stoat's tail.

Teal Blue and Silver
BODY. Flat or embossed silver tinsel.
RIB. Oval silver tinsel.
WING. Grey squirrel tail fibres.
HACKLE. Blue cock or hen.

Grey Eagle
The details for the "Akroyd" also apply to this fly.
TREBLE HOOK. Silver tinsel, and a golden pheasant breast feather wound as a hackle.
BODY. Light orange, deep orange, scarlet and light blue seal's fur in equal sections. Well picked out.
RIB. Flat silver tinsel and twist.
HACKLE. An eagle hackle (or substitute) from third turn of tinsel.
FRONT HACKLE. Light teal flank.

In addition to the patterns given here, most of which are designed for salmon fishing, I would like to give some of the dressings evolved by Mr. K. Stewart of Stevenston, Ayrshire, for trout and sea trout.

They were originally worked out for his ARCAS "Slim Jim" flies, which were tied on a mount similar to those used for the Waddington "Elverine" lures. This is a metal shank attached to a treble hook, but I see no reason why they could not be adapted to tube flies.

They differ from tube flies as we have so far discussed them in that the wings are put on as for orthodox trout flies, one wing up and one down, so that the fly with a line drawn through its centre becomes a mirror of itself. I think the illustrations given here best describe this aspect. Once the tyer has the general idea, any pattern can be adapted to this type of fly, and to facilitate this I am giving the dressings of one or two very well-known patterns as applied to the "Slim Jim".

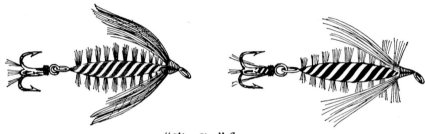

"Slim Jim" fly

DRESSINGS

Alexandra

BODY. Flat silver tinsel as a ribbing over black floss or dubbing.

BODY HACKLE. Black soft fibred cock.

WINGS. Peacock sword herl with insets of ibis, and golden pheasant crests over.

TREBLE HOOK. Flat silver tinsel, with two or three turns of black ostrich herl at front.

TAILS. A few fibres of ibis.

Blae and Black

BODY. Black floss.

RIB. Flat or oval silver tinsel.

BODY HACKLE. Soft black cock.

WINGS. From grey mallard wing quill.

TREBLE HOOK. Black floss ribbed with oval silver tinsel, with black ostrich herl at front.

TAILS. Tippet fibres.

Bloody Butcher

BODY. Blood-red floss or dubbing.

RIB. Flat silver tinsel.

WINGS. From white-tipped blue mallard quill.

BODY HACKLE. Blood-red cock.

TREBLE HOOK. Flat silver tinsel, with black ostrich herl at front.

TAILS. Ibis or substitute.

Black Spider

BODY. Dark purple floss or seal's fur.

RIB. Flat silver tinsel.

BODY HACKLE. Soft black cock.

WINGS. Blue dun hackle.

TREBLE HOOK. Flat silver tinsel, with ostrich herl at front. Either black or same colour as body.

Blue Zulu
BODY. Black floss or seal's fur.
RIB. Flat silver tinsel.
BODY HACKLE. Black cock.
WINGS (OR FRONT HACKLE). Blue cock.
TREBLE HOOK. Black floss ribbed with fine oval silver tinsel and black ostrich herl at front.
TAIL. A tuft of red floss silk.

Coachman
BODY. Bronze peacock herl.
BODY HACKLE. Natural red cock.
WINGS. White duck wing quill.
TREBLE HOOK. Bronze peacock herl.
TAILS. Few fibres of natural red cock hackle.

Coch-y-bondhu
BODY. Bronze peacock herl.
BODY HACKLE. Furnace cock.
WINGS (OR FRONT HACKLE). Furnace cock.
TREBLE HOOK. Oval gold tinsel, with bronze peacock herl at front.
TAILS. A few fibres of furnace cock hackle.

Partridge and Orange
BODY. Orange floss or seal's fur.
BODY HACKLE. Orange cock.
THROAT HACKLE. Orange hen or soft cock.
WINGS. A dark partridge back feather wound in front of the orange throat hackle.
TREBLE HOOK. Orange floss.
TAILS. A few fibres of dark partridge back feather.

Partridge and Yellow
As "Partridge and Orange", but with light partridge breast feathers, and yellow hackles instead of orange.

Peter Ross
BODY. Half silver tinsel, remainder red seal's fur.
RIB. Oval silver tinsel.
BODY HACKLE. Black cock.
THROAT HACKLE. Black hen.
WINGS. Teal flank feather.
TREBLE HOOK. Flat silver tinsel with red ostrich herl at front.
TAILS. Golden pheasant tippet fibres.

March Brown
BODY. Hare's fur.
RIB. Flat gold tinsel.
BODY HACKLE. Brown partridge back.
THROAT HACKLE. Brown partridge back.
WINGS. From partridge, hen pheasant, or grouse wing quill. (The wing is optional on this pattern.)
TREBLE HOOK. Oval gold tinsel with brown ostrich herl at front.
TAILS. Fibres of brown partridge back feather.

TYPES OF SLIPSTREAM TUBES

1¼ in.

Type "A"
Plastic tube with moulded ends which prevent the dressing from slipping off.

¾ in.

Type "B"
A stouter plastic tube with cavity in tail to take eye of treble hook so that it is always in perfect alignment.

1¼ in.

Type "C"
Plastic-lined aluminium tube which cannot chafe cast or "skid" on surface of water.

Type "D"
As type "C", but plastic-lined brass instead of aluminium, to ensure rapid sinking.

Sizes: ½ in., ¾ in., 1 in., 1¼ in., 1½ in., 2 in.

(Suggested Eyed Treble Hook Sizes: Nos. 16, 15, 14, 13, 12 and 10.)

SECTION 4

———

A LIST OF
BRITISH TROUT-FLY PATTERNS
TRIED FAVOURITES
AND SUCCESSFUL MODERN ADDITIONS

INTRODUCTION

BECAUSE OF THE PRESENT-DAY INCREASE in trout-fly fishing (and fly tying) in this country, it has become very evident that an illustrated list of dressings covering flies for all types of water is an absolute necessity. Particularly to those who may be new to the art of fly tying, and who may wish to make themselves patterns they have heard of but have never seen.

To produce an illustrated book of dressings in colour to satisfy the needs of all fly fishermen would be a prodigious task, particularly financially. As a book of that nature would price itself out of the reach of most of them, I had to come to some compromise.

What I have endeavoured to do is to give an illustration of the most popular or well-known example of a particular group of flies, and then the dressings of the rest of the group. By this means, a quite comprehensive collection of dressings can be compiled, and the tyer also has a coloured illustration to act as a guide to any particular pattern he may wish to make. (See illustrations between pages 80 and 81.)

This is particularly true of such groups as the sedges, duns, spinners, nymphs, mayflies etc. in the dry-fly section, and the "teal", "mallard", "woodcock", and "grouse" series in the wet-fly.

Some individual flies, of course, have no counterparts, but had to be included because of their popularity and success. I am referring to flies such as the "Grey Duster", "Dogsbody", "Coch-y-bondhu", "Orange Otter", "Worm Fly", "Alder", and others which are all familiar names to the fly fisherman.

The collection was built up by knowledge of demand for materials, and I feel sure that there can be few fly-tying anglers who will not be able to select patterns from it, suitable for all the waters they fish.

Although the collection is divided roughly into two equal sections—dry-flies and wet-flies—in some instances I have given the wet version of a dry-fly and vice versa, i.e. the "March Brown" is included in the wet-fly section, but dry patterns are also included. This is another means by which I have managed to increase the range of the collection.

In addition to this general list are many patterns of recent development, evolved or sponsored by the band of enthusiastic fly fishermen and fly tyers that is ever present in this country. Fortunately for the art, their ranks never seem to dwindle, and I am very pleased to say that the modern members of the band are making contributions of as lasting importance as those of their predecessors over the centuries.

I have devoted a special chapter to their work, starting on page 161. Mostly in abbreviated form, of course, as some of them have produced, or will be producing, books of their own.

A LIST OF BRITISH TROUT FLIES

for which patterns are given on pages 116–148

(Those in bold type are illustrated between pages 80 and 81)

THE DRESSINGS ARE GIVEN in the same sequence as they appear on the coloured plates. An alphabetical list is given on pages 114–115.

Red Tag

Although more famous as a grayling fly, this is also very useful for trout. It can be fished both dry and wet.

HOOK. 12–14.
TAG. Bright red wool, red ibis feather, or red floss.
BODY. Bright bronze green peacock's herl from the moon feather.
HACKLE. Bright red game cock's.

A turn or two of silver or gold flat tinsel under the tail is sometimes added, and with an alternative tag of orange wool, floss or fibres of an orange feather, it becomes the "Orange Tag". Another common name for this fly is the "Treacle Parkin".

Mole Fly

Although predominantly popular in Europe, particularly in France, this fly is of English origin, taking its name from the River Mole in Surrey. Very effective on slow-flowing rivers, where its forward style of winging enables it to cock up very nicely. It will take fish during a hatch of olives, mayflies or sedges.

HOOK. 14–16.
BODY. Dark olive tying silk.
RIB. Gold wire.
WINGS. Mottled hen pheasant tied forward.
HACKLE. Red/black (Furnace) wound from shoulder to tail.

Another pattern, and the one most popular in France, is as follows:

HOOK. 14.
TAIL WHISKS. Coch-y-bondhu.
BODY. Mustard—yellow floss.
RIB. Gold wire.
WINGS. Speckled hen wing quill (as light as possible).
HACKLE. Coch-y-bondhu, ribbed down body.

This dressing makes it a very good imitation of the Oak Fly.

Coachman

This very well-known fly is thought to be the invention of a coachman to the British Royal family many years ago, although there are other versions of its origin. It can be used dry or wet, but has been found to be most successful as a dry-fly for lake fishing, particularly in the smaller sizes.

HOOK. 16–10.

BODY. Bronze peacock herl.

WINGS. White duck wing quill.

HACKLE. Natural red cock's hackle.

When tied with wings of starling wing or grey duck wing quill, it becomes the "Lead-winged Coachman".

This fly is as popular, if not more so, in North America as it is in Great Britain, and has several variations in those parts. One of these variations is the "Royal Coachman", which differs from the original in that it has a centre section of the body composed of red floss silk, the peacock herl forming a "butt" and a "thorax".

The Americans are particularly fond of fan-winged examples of this fly, and any variations can be thus formed by using the round breast feathers of the Mandarin Duck as wings. An illustration of a fan-winged fly is shown between pages 80 and 81.

Driffield Dun

A very popular north-country fly, named after the famous Driffield Beck.

HOOK. 14–16.

WHISKS. From a ginger cock's hackle.

BODY. Lead-coloured or very pale blue seal's fur.

RIB. Yellow tying silk.

WINGS. Pale starling.

HACKLE. Ginger cock's hackle.

Ants

Flying ants do not appear very often, but when they do fish rise to them very freely. Not only trout, but practically every species. It is always very wise, therefore, to have one or two examples in one's box.

Black Ant

HOOK. 15–16.

BODY. Black tying silk, well waxed, and tied to the shape of an ant's body. Varnishing with Cellire varnish can be an improvement.

HACKLE. Black cock.

WINGS. Two pale blue dun cock hackle tips tied to slope backwards.

Red Ant

Tied as for the Black Ant, but with a dark orange tying silk body, and a natural red cock's hackle.

Black Gnat

To call this fly a gnat is a misnomer as it is a member of the Diptera family. The male is darker and slimmer than the female, and it is as well to have patterns of each as trout will often feed on one in preference to the other.

Male Black Gnat

HOOK. 15–17.
BODY. Black quill, horsehair or tying silk.
HACKLE. Black cock or starling's neck feather.
WINGS. Pale starling or two small pale blue dun hackle tips tied flat on the back.

Female Black Gnat

BODY. A strand of brown turkey tail feather, or brown quill.
HACKLE. Black cock's hackle or a starling's neck feather.
WINGS. Pale starling or two small pale blue dun cock hackle tips, tied flat on the back.

Another pattern which is a good imitation of the Black Gnat is the "Baby Sun Fly", the dressing of which is as follows.

HOOK. 14–16.
TAIL WHISKS. Three strands from a Coch-y-bondhu cock hackle.
BODY. Hair from a rabbit's poll, using only the black and brown fibres from between the eyes and nose.
HACKLE. Short fibred Coch-y-bondhu cock hackle.

Wickham's Fancy

A first class "fancy" fly which is not designed to imitate any particular species, but will be found most useful under practically any circumstances. It can be used wet or dry, but is better as a floating fly, for trout, grayling, dace and chub flies. It can even be used as a sea-trout fly, and I personally have found a fairly large specimen most useful when the sedge flies are "on".

HOOK. 14–16. Larger for sea trout and during the sedge rise.
TAIL WHISKS. Red-game cock's hackle fibres, or guinea fowl dyed red-brown.
BODY. Flat gold, ribbed with fine gold wire.
HACKLE. Red-game cock's hackle.
THROAT HACKLE. One, or two, red-game cock's hackles.
WINGS. Starling wing quill—grey duck wing quill in the larger sizes.

Some anglers prefer this fly without the wings, and it becomes a hackled pattern merely by the omission of the wings.

Ginger Quill

I have included this one as a good example of the quill-bodied type of fly so popular on most dry-fly streams. Hackled patterns are also much used.

HOOK. 15–16.

TAIL WHISKS. From a ginger cock's hackle.

BODY. Undyed quill from the "eye" part of a peacock's tail, with the flue stripped off. This reveals a dual marking which simulates the segmented body of many natural flies.

HACKLE. Ginger cock's hackle.

WINGS. Starling wing quill.

It is turned into a hackled pattern by omitting the wings and winding a light blue dun hackle in front of the ginger one.

Red Quill

Exactly the same as for the "Ginger Quill", but using a bright red-game cock's hackle, and tail whisks of the same colour.

Blue Quill

As for the first two, but using medium to dark blue dun cock's hackles for hackle and tail whisks.

Another very well-known version of quill-bodied fly is the "Blue Upright" dealt with on page 122.

Grannom

This is one of the smaller sedge flies, appearing early in the season on most of the rivers in the U.K. but seldom on lakes, although I have seen it hatching in large numbers on a reservoir in Sussex.

HOOK. 13–14.

TYING SILK. Bright green.

BODY. Fur from the base of a hare's ear spun on brown silk.

EGG SAC. This is a very distinctive feature of the female fly, and should be shown by winding a short length of either green wool or floss at the tail end.

WINGS. From a hen pheasant or partridge's wing feather, tied full.

HACKLE. Greyish-brown—rusty dun if available, or dark Cree.

It is sometimes profitable to have one or two nymph patterns handy, and these can be tied in the nymph style, using the same materials, i.e. the wing material would form the wing cases in this instance.

Claret Bumble

Bumbles are very well-known Derbyshire patterns, and I have also included them because they are an illustration of flies tied in the "Palmer" style, i.e. with the hackle ribbed down the body. Other bumble dressings are also included.

HOOK. 12–14.

BODY. Claret floss ribbed with a strand of peacock herl, green or bronze.

HACKLE. Medium blue dun cock's hackle wound from tail to shoulder.

Orange Bumble

BODY. Orange floss ribbed with a strand of peacock herl and flat gold tinsel.

HACKLE. Honey dun cock's hackle from tail to shoulder.

Yellow Bumble

BODY. Yellow floss ribbed with bronze peacock herl.

HACKLE. Blue dun cock's hackle wound from tail to shoulder.

All the bumbles are excellent grayling flies anywhere.

Orange Otter

I have included this little-known pattern, as it is one of the best grayling flies I have ever used.

HOOK. 16.

TAIL WHISKS. Fibres of bright red-game cock's hackle.

HACKLE. A small bright red-game cock's hackle tied in the centre of the body.

BODY. In two parts divided by the hackle, of seal's fur dyed a very deep orange, almost scarlet. The original dressing stipulated fur from an otter's throat, but this is difficult to get. The seal's fur should therefore be as soft as possible, or very short fibred.

Baigent's Patterns

Designed by the late Dr. Baigent, of Northallerton, to represent a series of dry-flies instead of any particular pattern. Their special feature is the large natural old game cock hackles which are used. This method of dressing, particularly with the type of hackles used, enables the flies to stand well on the water and give them a most natural appearance.

Dr. Baigent went even further with his theory, and produced what became known as the "Refracta" dry-flies. These used the original long-fibred game hackle of a neutral shade for the floating hackle, but also had the short-fibred hackle which represents the legs of the fly. The advantages of this fly is the light manner in which they fall on the water, their good floating capabilities, and the long-fibred hackles disturb the surface of the water, giving an altered refraction which makes the fly more lifelike. For the large hackles of the "Refracta" patterns, natural light blue dun or Badger hackles should be used, and the dressings for the "Quill" patterns can be used with success merely by adding one of these hackles to the original dressing.

Baigent's Brown

HOOK. 15–12.

BODY. Yellow floss silk.

WINGS. Hen pheasant wing quill.

HACKLE. Light furnace cock's hackle, long in fibre and very stiff.

Baigent's Dark Olive

TAIL WHISKS. Fibres from a stiff dark olive cock's hackle.

BODY. Stripped peacock quill from "eye" part of tail, dyed olive.

WINGS. Starling wing quill.

HACKLE. Large stiff dark olive cock's hackle.

Baigent's Black

BODY. Orange floss ribbed with peacock herl.

HACKLE. Black cock's, very stiff and long in fibre.

Baigent's Red Variant. (So called because it is merely a variation of an established dressing.)

BODY. Stripped peacock quill.

WINGS. Starling wing quill feather.

HACKLE. Stiff light furnace cock's hackle, long in fibre.

Dark Variant

Same as above, but with a dark dun hackle.

Rusty Variant

Same as above, but with a rusty dun hackle.

Light Variant

BODY. Stripped peacock quill.

HACKLE. Light blue dun, very stiff and long in fibre.

Baigent's March Brown Spinner

BODY. Stripped peacock quill.

HACKLE. Brown partridge back feather, with a long-fibred natural brown hackle behind it.

Baigent's Red Spinner

BODY. Stripped peacock quill.

HACKLE. Large ginger cock's hackle.

Baigent's Dark Olive Dun Spinner

BODY. Dark olive stripped peacock quill.

HACKLE. Large dark olive dun.

Baigent's Light Olive Dun Spinner

BODY. Undyed stripped peacock quill.

HACKLE. Pale ginger, very stiff and long in fibre.

Coch-y-bondhu

This fly, a beetle representation, is so well known and popular, particularly in the west and north, that all I intend to do is give the standard dressing.

HOOK. 12–14.

BODY. Two or three strands of bronze peacock herl, with one or two turns of fine flat gold tinsel forming a tip.

HACKLE. Coch-y-bondhu cock. Deep red with black centre and tips.

When the gold tip is carried on down the body to form a rib it is called the "Marlow Buzz", and with a feather from the neck of a cock pheasant instead of the usual hackle, it becomes the "Bracken Clock".

Tup's Indispensable

This very popular fly can be fished either dry or wet, as an imitation of pale wateries, duns, spinners and nymphs, throughout the season.

HOOK. 15–16.

TAIL. Fibres from a stiff bright honey dun cock's hackle.

BODY. Tail end—about one-quarter of the length—yellow floss or tying silk. The remainder is a mixture of dyed pinkish lamb's wool and cream-coloured seal's fur.

HACKLE. Honey or honey dun.

For a nymph pattern, the dubbing should be taken right down to the tail, and a short fibred blue dun hen's hackle substituted for the honey cock hackle.

Oak Fly (downlooker)

A largish land-bred fly, very good on brooks, particularly from April to June.

TAIL. Two strands from a natural red hackle.

BODY. Orange floss silk or dyed orange raffia, ribbed with a stripped quill from the stem of a peacock tail, not from the "eye".

WINGS. From a woodcock wing feather, tied low over back, or two dark grizzled cock hackles.

HACKLE. Coch-y-bondhu cock's hackle.

Dogsbody

A very useful general-purpose fly invented by the late Mr. Harry Powell, the famous Usk angler and fly tyer. The original body material was taken from a local dog (hence the name, obviously) and the nearest substitute for this material is seal's fur dyed camel colour. A very good fly when fish are feeding on natural flies, but will not take a close imitation. Good for both trout and grayling.

HOOK. 14–16.

BODY. Brown tying silk dubbed with camel-coloured seal's fur.

RIB. Oval gold tinsel.

HACKLE. Barred Plymouth Rock (Grizzle) with a stiff red cock's hackle in the front.

TAIL WHISKS. Three strands from a cock pheasant's tail.

Blue Upright

A very famous west country pattern that will take fish anywhere in the United Kingdom—fished wet or dry. It is one of the well-known "Quill" type of flies, and although most modern reproductions use the stripped quill from the "eye" of the peacock's tail, the following is the correct dressing.

HOOK. 10–14.

TYING SILK. Purple.

BODY. Undyed peacock quill, stripped, taken from well down the tail feather, using a quill that is lighter coloured at the root. This lighter part will represent an egg sac if tied and wound in the right proportion.

HACKLE. Steely blue cock's hackle, nearly black, but with a definite blue centre. It can be wound at the head only or from shoulder to tail.

TAIL WHISKS. Fibres from the same coloured hackle.

Doctor

A fly designed to imitate beetles, which can be used throughout the season on rivers or lakes.

HOOK. 12–14.

BODY. Rear quarter, white rabbit fur dyed yellow, remainder black rabbit fur. It should be dressed full to represent a beetle-like body.

TAIL WHISKS. Fibres from a large stiff Coch-y-bondhu cock's hackle.

HACKLE. One large Coch-y-bondhu cock's hackle wound full—ten or eleven turns.

The "Devonshire Doctor" from which the above pattern was derived, is usually ribbed with flat gold tinsel and does not have the yellow rear quarter. This is also a very good wet fly.

Blue Dun

This is a very famous pattern, used to imitate the dark olive dun and iron blue dun. With variations in colour and size it can be used to imitate almost the whole range of duns used in various parts of the United Kingdom. There are many variations, but I trust the list I give will be found comprehensive enough for most British tyers, for both wet- and dry-fly fishing, and the first one is about the most popular dry-fly pattern.

HOOK. 14.

TAIL WHISKS. Fibres from a medium blue dun cock's hackle.

BODY. Mole or water rat fur spun on yellow tying silk.

HACKLE. Medium blue dun cock's.

WINGS. Dark starling or snipe wing quill.

Alternative body materials for use with above hackles: Dark peacock quill, olive tying silk with a gold rib, natural peacock quill from "eye" of tail, or herl from a heron wing quill.

Hackled Pattern

BODIES. As for winged flies.

WHISKS. From a dark olive cock hackle.

HACKLES. (2) Medium blue dun cock's, with a small dark olive cock hackle behind it to represent the legs.

Heron Blue (dry)

BODY. Natural heron herl.

HACKLE AND TAIL WHISKS. Hackles dyed to same colour of body.

Rough Olive (dry)

BODY. Heron herl dyed olive.

RIB. Gold wire.

HACKLE AND TAIL WHISKS. Dark blue dun cock's hackle.

WINGS. Optional—Dark starling wing quill.

Rough Olive (wet)

BODY. Heron herl dyed dark green olive.

RIB. Gold wire.

HACKLE. Small feather from outside a coot's wing.

Half Stone (dry)

BODY. Tail half yellow tying silk, remainder blue rabbit or mole fur.

HACKLE AND TAIL WHISKS. Medium to dark blue dun cock's hackle.

Waterhen Bloa (wet)

BODY. Mole or water rat fur spun on yellow silk.

HACKLE. Shiny feather from underneath a waterhen's wing.

Blue Dun Spider

BODY. Two or three turns of yellow tying silk at tail end, remainder blue rabbit's fur spun on yellow silk.

HACKLE. Small shiny feather from underneath a waterhen's wing.

Lunn's Particular

One of the finest flies for general use on chalk streams. It is invented by Mr. W. J. Lunn, the famous river keeper on the Test during the end of the nineteenth and the beginning of the twentieth century. It is a good fly to use if the fish are "shy" or taking spinners.

HOOK. 14.

TAIL WHISKS. Four fibres from a stiff natural red cock's hackle.

BODY. The undyed hackle stalk of a natural red cock hackle.

WINGS. Two medium blue dun cock hackle tips tied "spent".

HACKLE. Natural medium red cock hackle.

Iron Blue

This is a small fly which appears in the early part of the season, particularly on cold days, and it is always taken well by the fish.

HOOK. 16.

BODY. Stripped peacock quill dyed purple or claret.

WINGS. Cock blackbird, or starling dyed inky blue.

HACKLE. Dark blue dun cock's hackle.

TAIL WHISKS. Fibres from a pale blue dun cock's hackle.

Or:

BODY. Dark peacock quill dyed olive.

WINGS. As above.

HACKLE. Dark brown olive cock's hackle.

WHISKS. Fibres from a rusty dun cock's hackle.

Hackled Pattern

BODY. Purple or claret quill.

HACKLE. Dark blue dun cock's hackle.

TAIL WHISKS. Fibres of pale blue dun cock's hackle.

Dark Watchet (north-country west pattern)

BODY. Mole fur dubbed on orange and purple tying silk, which should be twisted together to make alternate ribbings.

HACKLE. Small feather from a jackdaw's throat.

Infallible (west country wet-fly pattern)

BODY. Mole fur spun on claret or crimson silk.

HACKLE AND TAIL WHISKS. Dark blue dun cock or hen.

Sherry Spinner

The spinner of the blue-winged olive, deriving its name from the colour of the body.

HOOK. 15.

TYING SILK. Hot orange.

BODY. Amber-coloured seal's fur with a gold rib, or amber tying silk with clear horsehair wound over.

WINGS. Two pale blue dun cock hackle tips tied "spent".

HACKLE. Palest ginger, or (if available) natural honey dun cock's.

TAIL WHISKS. Three strands from a honey cock's hackle.

Other useful spinners are as follows:

Blue Dun (Early Olive) Spinner

HOOK. 14.

TAIL. Fibres of natural red cock's hackle.

BODY. Dark reddish brown quill, or reddish brown seal's fur.

RIB. Gold wire (over the seal fur only).
HACKLE. Natural red cock's hackle.
WINGS. Tied spent, of fibres of medium blue dun cock's hackle, or the tips of two hackles of the same colour.

March Brown Spinner

Sometimes called the Great Red Spinner.

HOOK. 12–13.
TAIL. Fibres of natural red cock's hackle.
BODY. Red seal's fur.
RIB. Gold wire.
HACKLE. Natural red cock's hackle.
WINGS. Tied spent, of fibres of medium blue cock's hackle, or the tips of two hackles of the same colour.

Iron Blue Spinner (female)

HOOK. 16–17.
TAIL. Fibres of medium blue dun cock's hackle.
BODY. Claret quill, or claret seal's fur.
HACKLE. Medium blue dun cock's hackle.
WINGS. Tied spent, of fibres of medium blue dun cock's hackle, or the tips of two hackles of the same colour.
RIB. Gold wire (over seal fur only).

Iron Blue Spinner (male)

HOOK. 16–17.
TAIL. Fibres of white cock's hackle.
BODY. White horsehair or quill, showing a tip of bright red silk at tail and shoulder.
WINGS. Tied spent, of glassy white cock hackle fibres.
No hackle.

Olive Spinner (female)

HOOK. 15.
TAIL. Fibres of medium olive cock's hackle.
BODY. Horsehair dyed yellow, or yellow olive seal's fur ribbed with gold wire.
HACKLE. Medium olive cock's hackle.
WINGS. Tied spent, of pale blue dun cock's hackle fibres, or two small pale blue cock hackle tips.

Olive Spinner (male)

HOOK. 15.

TAIL. Fibres of brownish olive cock's hackle.

BODY. Yellow horsehair, showing a tip of brown at tail and shoulder.

HACKLE. Brownish olive.

WINGS. Tied spent, of medium blue dun cock hackle fibres, or two small medium blue cock hackle tips.

Orange Quill

A good representation of the "Blue Winged Olive" and a great favourite of the late G. E. M. Skues. Freely taken during a "B.W.O." rise by both trout and grayling.

HOOK. 13–14.

TAIL WHISKS. Fibres from a natural bright red or medium ginger cock's hackle.

BODY. Pale ginger quill, with no dark edge showing.

WINGS. Light starling tied "full".

HACKLE. Natural bright red or medium ginger cock's hackle.

Blagdon Green Midge

A still-water fly, hatching in June and lasting throughout the rest of the season. A good dry-fly for all pools, lakes and reservoirs.

HOOK. 14–16.

BODY. Emerald green wool.

HACKLE. Stiff white cock hackle wound at shoulder only.

Or:

BODY. A strand from a swan's feather dyed emerald green.

HACKLE. A Plymouth Rock (Grizzle) cock's hackle wound from tail to shoulder, cut to shorten the fibres.

WINGS. Two light grey cock hackle points.

Blagdon Olive Midge

Another fine dry-fly for lake fishing.

HOOK. 14–16.

BODY. Natural heron's herl.

HACKLE. Stiff olive cock's hackle at shoulder only.

WINGS. Two blue dun cock hackle points.

Grey Duster

One of the best all-round dry-flies, which will take fish throughout the season, being particularly good during the mayfly hatch.

HOOK. 12–14, larger for mayflies and lake fishing.

TYING SILK. Brown.

BODY. Dubbing of light rabbit's fur mixed with a small amount of the blue under-fur.

HACKLE. Stiff badger cock's hackle with a good dark centre.

Tail whisks can be added on smaller patterns if the "Duster" is used during a hatch of olives.

Lake Olive

This is the dressing of this fly invented by Mr. J. R. Harris the well-known Irish entomologist, and recommended by Col. Joscelyn Lane in *Lake and Loch Fishing.*★

HOOK. 12–13.

WINGS. Dark starling tied forward.

BODY. Pale blue heron herl dyed brown olive.

RIB. Gold wire.

HACKLE. Green olive cock's hackle.

TAIL. Fibres from a brown olive cock's hackle.

During the autumn the hackle should be brown olive, and the body swan herl dyed brown olive.

The nymph dressing of this fly is given on page 144.

Cinnamon Sedge (1)

I have chosen this pattern as it illustrates the rather unique method of dressing recommended by Col. Joscelyn Lane, and I can vouch for its floating capabilities from experience.

HOOK. 5.

TYING SILK. Golden olive.

TAIL. Pale ginger cock hackle fibres.

BODY. Ginger cock's hackle.

WINGS. Pale ginger cock hackle fibres.

THORAX. Ginger cock's hackle.

LEG HACKLE. Ginger cock.

The full tying method is graphically described in *Lake and Loch Fishing* by Col. Lane, but I trust the brief description given here will suffice.

TAIL. A thick bunch of cock hackle fibres.

BODY. A long hackle wound close and then clipped close on top, and trimmed underneath and each side to a length equivalent to the gape of the hook. Taking up the tail half of the body.

WINGS. A bunch of fibres tied in as was the tail, the broader the better. There should be no daylight between wing, body and tail.

THORAX. Tied in and treated as was the body, the whole fly now trimmed to a conical shape. Room should be left for the front hackle.

LEG HACKLE. Four or five turns of a short-fibred hackle.

★ Seeley Service

I trust this description together with the illustration will show how this fly should look. (See colour plates between pages 80 and 81.)

Cinnamon Sedge (2)

BODY. Light olive quill.
BODY HACKLE. Light olive.
WINGS. Light brown hen wing quill. Lightly speckled if available.
FRONT HACKLE. Natural light red cock's hackle.

Cinnamon Sedge (3)

BODY. Fibre from a cinnamon turkey tail.
RIB. Gold wire.
BODY HACKLE. Dark ginger.
WINGS. Brown henwing quill.
FRONT HACKLE. Dark ginger.

See also the "Grannom" on page 119, which is a good imitation of a smaller sedge fly.

Ermine Moth

A good imitation of the light-coloured moth, as are the "Grey Duster" given on page 127, and "Feather Duster" given here also.

HOOK. 14–12.
TAG. A loop of orange wool tied in flat and then cut to form a fork about $\frac{1}{4}$ in. long.
BODY. White rabbit fur.
RIB. Coarse black thread.
HACKLE. Two large grey speckled partridge feathers.

Feather Duster

BODY. Light grey seal's fur mixed with blue rabbit fur.
HACKLE. Blue dun.
Both body and hackle should be dressed full.

White Moth

HOOK. 10–14.
BODY. White wool rather thick.
RIB. Silver wire.
HACKLE. White cock from shoulder to tail.
WINGS. From a light-coloured owl's wing.

Spent Mayfly

TAIL. Three cock pheasant tail fibres.
BODY. White floss silk or natural raffia.
WINGS. Dark blue dun hackle points tied "spent".
HACKLE. Badger cock hackle.

Fan Wing Mayfly

The illustration on the colour plate between pages 80 and 81 is the "Yellow Drake" fan wing, but other colours of wing and hackle can be used for this type of fly.

HOOK. 10–11, long shank.
TAIL. Three fibres from a cock pheasant tail.
BODY. Yellow raffia.
RIB. Oval gold tinsel.
WINGS. Duck breast feathers back to back, dyed yellow.
HACKLES. 1ST. Yellow cock hackle. 2ND. Grey partridge back feather, or a grizzle cock hackle.

Shaving Brush Mayfly

This fly derives its name from the peculiar wing formation, and is a good imitation of the hatching fly. The "Barret's Brown" is also of the same type, and the "Grey Wulff", both dressings being given here.

HOOK. 10–11, long shank.
TAIL. Three long black cock hackle fibres.
BODY. Kapok.
RIB. Black tying silk.
WINGS. A large grizzle hackle wound and divided to slope forward.
HACKLE. Black cock's hackle.

Barret's Brown Mayfly

HOOK. 10–11, long shank.
TAIL. Three long black cock hackle fibres.
BODY. Brown raffia.
RIB. Oval gold tinsel.
WINGS. Fibres from a brown bucktail, divided and sloping forward.
HACKLE. NO. 1. Medium olive cock's hackle. NO. 2. (Nearest to eye) hen pheasant neck feather.

Grey Wulff Mayfly (hair winged)

HOOK. 10–11, long shanked.
TAIL. Fibres from a brown bucktail.
BODY. Blue-grey seal's fur.
WINGS. Brown fibres from a bucktail, divided and sloping forward.
HACKLE. Blue dun cock's hackle.

Tied on a size 15 hook, and using fibres from a brown barred squirrel tail for the wings, this makes an excellent representation of smaller hatching nymphs.

French Partridge Mayfly

This is a mayfly of the "Straddle Bug" type, as also is the pattern immediately following. (See illustrations between pages 80 and 81.)

HOOK. 10–12, long shanked.

TAIL. Three fibres from a cock pheasant tail.
BODY. Natural raffia ribbed with oval gold tinsel.
BODY HACKLE. Olive cock's hackle.
FRONT HACKLE. French partridge breast feather.

Straddle-Bug Mayfly (Summer Duck)
HOOK. 10–12, long shank.
TIP. Very fine gold oval or twist tinsel.
TAIL. Two or three fibres from a black cock's hackle.
BODY. Natural raffia.
RIB. Brown tying silk.
HACKLES. NO. 1. Orange cock's hackle. NO. 2. Brown speckled summer duck
feather.
HEAD. Bronze peacock herl.

Spent Mayfly
This is a personal favourite which I have used with much success during the
height of the hatch.
HOOK. 10–11, long shanked and of fine wire.
TAIL. Three fibres from a cock pheasant tail.
BODY. Natural raffia.
RIB. Oval silver tinsel.
WINGS. A very stiff black or dark blue dun cock's hackle wound in the normal
way, the fibres then being split into two equal halves and tied "spent".
HACKLE. None. I rely on the stiffness of the wings to float the fly, but if a hackle is
preferred I would recommend a short-fibred stiff badger hackle. (As shown.)

Teal Blue and Silver
The Teal series are standard wet-fly patterns for both sea-trout and lake-trout
flies. This fly and the "Peter Ross" (described on pages 132-133), are the two best-
known of the series.
HOOK. 8–14.
TAIL. Two or three golden pheasant tippet fibres.
BODY. Flat silver tinsel.
RIB. Oval silver.
HACKLE. Bright blue.
WINGS. From teal breast or flank feathers, according to size of fly. The flank
feathers producing longer fibres than the breast.
There are many colour combinations for this series of flies and the following
two will give some idea what may be achieved.

Teal and Black
HOOK. 8–14.
TAIL. Fibres of golden pheasant tippet, or from a black cock's hackle.

BODY. Black wool, silk or seal's fur.
RIB. Oval silver, or fine flat in the smaller patterns.
WINGS. Teal breast or flank feathers.
HACKLE. Black.

Teal and Mixed

HOOK. 8–14.
TAIL. Fibres of golden pheasant tippet.
BODY. One third each of yellow, red and blue seal's fur.
RIB. This is optional, but can be of either silver or gold tinsel.
HACKLE. Black cock or hen.
WINGS. Teal breast or flank.

The colour combinations for the "mixed" flies can, of course, be varied, the rule being to have the darkest one at the front and the lighest at the tail end.

Butcher

With the "Peter Ross" and "Alexandra", this is undoubtedly one of the most well-known flies in the world. It is deadly, particularly early in the season, for lake, river and sea trout.

HOOK. 10–14.
TAIL. Red ibis or substitute.
BODY. Flat silver.
HACKLE. Black cock or hen's hackle.
WINGS. From the blue-black section of a feather from a mallard drake's wing.

This fly is sometimes referred to as the "Silver Butcher" to distinguish it from the "Gold Butcher", which obviously has a gold tinsel body and rib, and the "Bloody Butcher", which differs only in the fact that it has a dyed red hackle instead of a black.

Another lesser-known variation, very popular in Scotland for loch fishing, is the "Kingfisher Butcher".

WINGS. Slate coloured, from the primary wing feathers of the mallard or coot.
HACKLE. Orange cock or hen's.
TAIL. Two or three fibres from the wing of the kingfisher.
BODY. Flat gold tinsel.
RIB. Oval gold.

Peter Ross

Undoubtedly the most popular pattern for wet-fly fishing ever invented. Its originator was Peter Ross of Killin, Perthshire, and although he only produced it as a variation of the "Teal and Red", the slight variation turned a good fly into one of the most killing patterns known to anglers. Its main reputation is as a lake fly, but is reckoned by many to be equally good for sea trout.

HOOK. 8–14.
TAIL. Fibres from a golden pheasant tippet feather.
BODY. In two halves, the tail half of flat silver tinsel, and the front half of dyed red seal's fur.
RIB. Oval silver over both halves.
HACKLE. Black cock or hen's.
WINGS. From the breast or flank feather of a teal.

Black Pennell

The "Pennell" series were the invention of H. Cholmondeley Pennell, English poet, sportsman and author, who also had much to do with the evolution of our present-day hook styles.

These flies should be dressed with the hackle rather longer than is usual, and the number of turns kept to a minimum. Pennell himself recommended three patterns besides the Black, Brown, Yellow and Green.

HOOK. 10–13.
TAG. Fine silver tinsel.
TAIL. Tippet fibres, to which are sometimes added a small golden pheasant crest feather.
BODY. Very thin, of black floss silk.
RIB. Oval silver—fine.
HACKLE. Black cock, long in fibre and dressed sparsely.

For the other patterns it is merely necessary to alter the colour of the body silk and hackle, natural light red game hackles sometimes being preferred for the yellow and green patterns.

The "Pennell's" are primarily lake- and sea-trout flies, and dressed much heavier in the hackle are very much in demand for "dapping".

Silver Doctor

This is the trout version of the popular salmon fly of the same name, dressed much simpler, of course. Ideal for lake and sea trout when big fish are expected, and for this reason it is particularly popular in North America.

HOOK. 10–6.
TAIL. Fibres of golden pheasant tippet.
BODY. Flat silver tinsel.
RIB. Oval silver.
HACKLE. Bright blue.
WINGS. Strips of goose or white duck wing feathers, dyed green, yellow and red, with a strip of mallard's grey breast or flank feather each side.

A small golden pheasant crest feather is sometimes added to the tippet fibres of the tail, and in larger patterns a few fibres of speckled guinea fowl neck feathers are added in front of the blue hackle.

Black and Orange

A very effective fly for sea trout, particularly during low-water conditions. It is very well thought of in Ireland for summer conditions.

HOOK. 10–6.
TAIL. Fibres of golden pheasant tippet.
BODY. Orange floss silk.
HACKLE. Black hen's.
WINGS. Originally from the tail feather of a black cock, but any black shiny feather will do.

Variations of the pattern are the "Black and Silver", which has a flat silver body and oval silver rib, and the "Black and Claret", which has a claret floss silk body. They are all worth a try for sea trout.

Connemara Black

Although, as its name denotes, originally an Irish lake- and sea-trout pattern, it has proved a successful fly in every part of the British Isles.

HOOK. 12–8.
TAIL. Small golden pheasant crest feather.
BODY. Black seal's fur.
RIB. Fine oval silver tinsel.
HACKLE. Black cock's hackle, with the blue feather from a jay's wing in the front.
WING. Brown (bronze) mallard shoulder.

On larger patterns, the black hackle is wound from tail to shoulder.

Alexandra

A fly that needs little or no introduction, being one of the most well-known lake- and sea-trout patterns. Lauded by some and condemned by others, I personally have found it a real "killer" in lakes stocked with Rainbow trout, particularly the "Jungle" version.

HOOK. 10–12.
TAIL. Red ibis, to which is sometimes added a strand or two of green peacock herl.
BODY. Flat silver tinsel.
RIB. Fine oval silver (optional).
HACKLE. Black hen's.
WINGS. Strands of green herl from the "sword" tail of the peacock, usually with a thin strip of ibis each side.

The "Jungle Alexandra" is exactly the same, but instead of sides of ibis these are replaced with small jungle cock feathers. Tied in "short".

Invicta

Always a very popular fly for lakes, this famous pattern is now having a run of success on the large reservoirs that have come into being since the Second World War. This, I think, is mainly due to the large hatches of sedge to be found on them, of which the Invicta is a fine imitator for wet-fly fishing. When used for this purpose, good results can be expected right through the season.

HOOK. 10–14.

TAIL. Golden pheasant crest feather.

BODY. Seal's fur dyed yellow.

RIB. Oval or round gold tinsel.

BODY HACKLE. Red game from shoulder to tail.

FRONT HACKLE. Blue jay, from the wing.

WINGS. From a hen pheasant's centre tail.

A variation designed by the late Mr. John Eastwood for sea trout, is tied as follows:

HOOK. 7–10.

TAIL. Golden pheasant crest feather.

BODY. Flat silver tinsel.

HACKLE. Blue jay wing feather, rather long in fibre.

WINGS. From a hen pheasant's centre tail.

Golden Olive

A very old and famous sea-trout fly, and also regarded very highly as a good imitation of the lake olive when tied on the smaller sizes of hook.

HOOK. 10–12.

TAG. Orange floss.

TAIL. A golden pheasant crest feather.

BODY. Rich golden olive seal's fur.

RIB. Oval gold tinsel.

HACKLE. Golden olive cock or hen's.

WINGS. Golden pheasant tippet fibres with strips of brown mallard over.

Woodcock and Green

The "Woodcock" series resemble the "Teal", "Mallard", and "Grouse" series in that they are standard patterns for lake- and sea-trout fishing. The "Woodcock and Yellow" is particularly successful as a lake or reservoir fly, as a sedge imitation.

HOOK. 8–14.

TAIL. A few fibres of golden pheasant tippet.

BODY. Green seal's fur.

RIB. Oval silver.

HACKLE. Natural medium red, or a green one the same colour as the body.

WINGS. From the wing feather of a woodcock.

Woodcock and Yellow

BODY. Seal's fur dyed yellow.
HACKLE. Natural ginger, or one dyed the same colour as the body.
WINGS AND TAIL. As for "Woodcock and Green".

Woodcock and Red

BODY. Dyed red seal's fur.
HACKLE. Natural dark red, or one dyed the same colour as the body.
WINGS AND TAIL. As for "Woodcock and Green".

Woodcock and Hare's Ear

TAG. Flat gold tinsel.
TAIL. Two fibres of brown mallard.
BODY. Dark fur from the hare's ear.
HACKLE. Longer fibres of hare's flax picked out to form hackle.
WINGS. Woodcock wing feather.

Ribbing is optional for this fly, but fine flat gold tinsel is recommended for keeping the body in place.

Grouse Series

By substituting grouse tail feathers for woodcock wing quills, this entire series may be converted to the "Grouse" series, i.e. "Grouse and Green", "Grouse and Yellow", etc. The "Grouse and Purple" has been particularly successful in Scotland, both for loch and river trouting.

Mallard and Claret

The best known of the "Mallard" series of lake- and sea-trout flies, and probably the most successful pattern ever invented for wet-fly fishing. Its reputation is high in every part of the British Isles, both for lake- and sea-trout fishing. Tied in the smallest sizes it can be also used for nymph fishing for brown trout. In fact, the best all-rounder one is likely to find.

There are several patterns in the "Mallard" series, but it is the "Claret" which reigns supreme.

HOOK. 10–14. (Up to size 8 for sea trout.)
TAIL. Golden pheasant tippet fibres.
BODY. Claret seal's fur.
RIB. Oval gold tinsel. (Fine gold wire in very small sizes.)
HACKLE. Natural red cock's, or one dyed the same colour as the body.
WINGS. Bronze speckled feathers from the mallard flank, usually referred to as "Bronze Mallard".

"Mallard and Mixed" is another good lake pattern, and is tied as follows:
TAIL. Tippet fibres.

BODY. In three equal sections of orange, red and fiery brown seal's fur, tied in from the tail in that order.

RIB. Oval gold tinsel.

HACKLE. Natural dark red cock or hen's.

WINGS. Bronze mallard.

Mallard and Green

Tied as for the "Mallard and Claret", but with a body of green seal's fur, a silver rib, and a natural light red or dyed green hackle.

Mallard and Silver

Tied as for "Mallard and Claret", but with a silver tinsel body.

Dunkeld

This trout-fly version of the famous salmon fly of the same name has had a very large measure of success during the last few years, particularly in the reservoir type of lake such as Chew, Blagdon and Weir Wood. It is now an established member of the "Mallard" series, and I consider it a "must" for the boxes of all lake- and sea-trout fishermen.

TAIL. Golden pheasant crest.

BODY. Flat gold tinsel.

RIB. Gold wire or gold oval tinsel.

HACKLE. Dyed orange, from shoulder to tail.

WINGS. Brown mallard.

"EYES." Two small jungle cock feathers tied close to head.

Freeman's Fancy

A lesser known but none the less very effective fly for lake fishing, which also uses the bronze mallard feather for its wings.

HOOK. 12–10, and up to size 8 if used for sea-trout fishing.

TAIL. A bunch of orange toucan breast feathers, or substitute. (A small golden pheasant crest is good.)

BODY. Flat gold tinsel.

WINGS. Bronze mallard, with a very small jungle cock feather each side.

HACKLE. Dyed bright magenta.

Grenadier

This pattern is one of several described by Col. Esmond Drury in an article in the *Fishing Gazette* of April 1958. They were designed by Dr. Bell, of Wrington, particularly for the lakes and reservoirs of Chew Valley and Blagdon. The other patterns are the "Large Amber Nymph", "Small Amber Nymph", "Buzzer Nymph" and "Corixa", and the dressings of all these are included in this book. (See Index)

HOOK. 13.
BODY. Hot orange floss or seal's fur.
RIB. Oval gold tinsel.
HACKLE. Two turns of ginger or light furnace cock.

Corixa

One of the patterns mentioned above, the dressing being as follows:
HOOK. 12 or 13.
BODY. White or cream floss silk dressed very fat.
RIB. Beige or brown silk.
WING CASE. A strip of woodcock wing fibres tied in at the tail, brought over to lay on top of the body and tied in at the head.
LEGS. A few fibres of white or cream hen's hackle tied in under the head.
Note: If the hook-shank is first painted white, it will prevent the white floss body becoming dull when wet.

Worm Fly

This is another pattern which has come very much to the fore with the advent of reservoir fishing, and is another of the flies mentioned in Col. Esmond Drury's list of patterns. It is best described as two "Red Tag" flies in tandem.
HOOKS. Two tied in tandem—No. 12 or 13.
(TAIL FLY)
TAG. Red floss silk.
BODY. Bronze peacock herl, with a small tip of flat gold tinsel wound under the tail (optional).
HACKLE. Dark red cock or hen.
(FRONT FLY)
Same as for tail fly, but without the red tag.

Black and Peacock Spider

Also one of the patterns recommended for reservoirs by Col. Drury.
HOOK. 7–11.
BODY. Bronze peacock herl.
HACKLE. A relatively large and soft black hen's hackle.

Shrimp

One of the most difficult creatures to imitate, and the following dressing is by Col. Joscelyn Lane, given in his book *Lake and Loch Fishing for Trout*.
HOOK. 12 or 13.
TYING SILK. Medium olive.
TAIL. A bunch of speckled brown partridge hackle fibres $\frac{3}{16}$ in. long, tied on the bend of the hook with fibres pointing downwards.
BODY. Of hare's ear dubbing tied well round bend of hook, padded to suggest the

humped back, and as fat as possible without obstructing the gape of the hook.
HACKLE. One or more brown partridge hackles wound over the body, spaced as
for ribbing, with fibres upright. Trim off closely all fibres at the sides and top, and
then trim the ends of the fibres below the body level with the point of the hook.
Touch the coils of quill on top of the body with varnish.
Note: For deep fishing, coils of fine wire can be wound over the hook-shank before
the fly is dressed.

Hawthorn (sometimes spelt Hawthorne)
Another of the patterns given by Col. Joscelyn Lane, although there are several
others to choose from. His dressing is as follows:
HOOK. No. 10.
TYING SILK. Black.
BODY. Black floss tapering finely towards the tail. This can be varnished.
RIB. Fine silver wire widely spaced.
HACKLE. Three or four turns of glossy black cock's hackle, tied in behind the
thorax and sloping backwards. Fibres to be as long as the hook.
THORAX. Conspicuous. Tied in last of all, using two strands of black ostrich herl.
A dry pattern of this fly is the one designed by Roger Woolley; the dressing as
follows:
HOOK. No. 13.
BODY. Two black strands from a turkey tail feather tied in so that the bright black
quill of them shows up most. The ends of the two strands are tied back after form-
ing the body, to represent the two long trailing legs of the fly.
HACKLE. Black cock.
WINGS. Palest part of a jay's wing feather.
A wet-fly pattern popular in Ireland has the following dressing:
HOOK. No. 12, larger for sea trout.
TAG. Flat gold tinsel.
BODY. Rear two-thirds black horsehair, remainder black ostrich herl.
HACKLE. Black cock's—two or three turns.
WINGS. Starling.

March Brown
One of the most universally used flies, some dressings of which date back to the
seventeenth century. More popular on the rocky streams of northern England and
of Wales, it is sometimes called the "Cob Fly", "Brown Drake", or "Dun Drake".
Dressings are numerous, and variations are many, but I think the following range
will cover most anglers' needs.
Winged Wet-Fly (northern dressing)
HOOK. 13–11.

TAIL. Fibres from a brown speckled partridge hackle or tail feather.
BODY. Sandy fur from a hare's neck, or brown seal's fur.
RIB. Yellow silk or gold wire.
HACKLE. Brown partridge.
WINGS. Fibres from a speckled partridge tail feather.

Winged Wet-Fly (male)
TAIL. Two strands of brown speckled partridge feather.
BODY. Dark hare's fur from ear.
RIB. Yellow tying silk or gold wire.
HACKLE. Brown speckled partridge, or brown grizzled (Cree) hen's hackle.
WINGS. Mottled secondary feather from hen pheasant's wing.

Winged Wet-Fly (female)
TAIL and HACKLE. As male.
BODY. Ginger hare's fur from neck.
RIB. Gold wire.
WINGS. Same as for male, but lighter in colour.

Hackled Wet-Fly
TYING SILK. Hot orange.
BODY. From a hare's poll, dyed hot orange
HACKLE. A snipe's rump feather.

March Brown Spider
TAIL. Two strands from a speckled partridge tail.
BODY. Dark hare's ear, mixed with a little claret wool or seal's fur.
RIB. Yellow or primrose tying silk.
HACKLE. Brown speckled partridge, fairly long in fibre.

March Brown Spider (Welsh pattern)
BODY. As above.
RIB. Silver.
HACKLE. As above.
I understand the name of this pattern to be Petrisen Corff Blewyn Ysgyfarnog.

March Brown Nymph
TAIL. Two short strands of a cock pheasant's tail, or fibres of brown mallard shoulder feather.
BODY. Herls from a cock pheasant's tail.
RIB. Gold wire.
THORAX. Hare's ear fur at shoulder.
WING CASES. From a woodcock wing feather. (Sometimes omitted.)
LEGS. One turn of a small brown speckled partridge hackle.

Winged Dry-Fly (male)

TAIL. Fibres from a brown grizzled (Cree) cock's hackle.

BODY. Hare's ear fur, mixed with a very small amount of yellow seal's fur.

RIB. Yellow tying silk.

WINGS. Darkish mottled hen pheasant or cock pheasant wing quill, tied upright.

HACKLE. Brown grizzled (Cree) cock's hackle—stiff and bright.

Winged Dry-Fly (female)

Tied as for the male, but with wings of a lighter shade.

Hackled Dry-Fly

TAIL. Stiff fibres from a brown grizzled (Cree) cock's hackle.

BODY. As for winged dry-flies.

HACKLES. Same as for winged dry-flies, but with the addition of a bright red-game cock hackle (short in fibre) tied behind the cree hackle. Alternatively—a brown speckled partridge hackle wound mixed with a darkish bright blue dun cock's hackle.

March Brown Variations

Silver March Brown

TAIL. Two fibres from a brown speckled partridge hackle or speckled partridge tail feather.

BODY. Flat silver tinsel.

RIB. Oval silver.

HACKLE. Brown speckled partridge feather.

WINGS. From the hen pheasant's mottled secondary wing feather.

Gold March Brown

Same as above, but with gold body and rib.

Both these patterns are excellent for lake- and sea-trout fishing.

Claret March Brown

A good lake fly only differing from standard dressings in that it has a claret hackle.

Purple March Brown

A pattern of recent innovation, very popular in Scotland and practically always fished wet. The only deviation from the standard pattern is its purple wool or seal's fur body, ribbed with yellow silk or gold wire.

Alder

As this is the only representative of its class, there can be no derivatives. Although a waterside insect, it is not bred in the water, but on rocks and rushes nearby. It is also one of the fisherman's most popular patterns, particularly as it appears in May and June, when one can reasonably expect the best fishing to start. It is sometimes fished dry, but takes most of its fish as a wet-fly.

HOOK. 13–11.

BODY. Thin peacock herl dyed magenta, or claret wool or silk ribbed with undyed bronze peacock herl.

HACKLE. Black hen wound in front of wings. Cock hackle for a dry-fly.

WINGS. Speckled brown hen wing quill, tied low over body to give the characteristic humped shape of the wings.

TYING SILK. Crimson.

Gold Ribbed Hare's Ear

Another "champion" fly with a fine reputation all over the U.K., fished wet or dry. It is thought to represent the nymph in the process of shedding its shuck, and should therefore be fished only slightly submerged for the best results.

HOOK. 14–16.

BODY. Dark fur from the root of the hare's ear spun on yellow silk.

RIB. Fine flat gold tinsel.

HACKLE. Long strands of the body material picked out with the dubbing needle.

WHISKS. Three strands as hackle.

If a winged pattern is preferred, these should be formed of fibres from a starling's primary wing feather, low over the body for the wet-fly, upright and double for the dry-fly.

Snipe and Purple

A standard pattern for Yorkshire and the north generally, and a particularly good lake pattern elsewhere.

HOOK. 14–15.

BODY. Purple floss.

HACKLE. Small feather from the outside of a snipe's wing, taken from as near the joint as possible.

Another version is the "Snipe and Yellow", not quite as popular, but often more effective on very cold days. The hackle is a dun feather from the back of the wing, and the body is formed of either yellow or straw-coloured silk.

Greenwell (Greenwell's Glory)

Invented by Canon William Greenwell of Durham, this is probably the best known of this whole list. In fact it is more likely the most well-known fly of all! It is effective no matter which of the duns the fish may be taking, and is a pattern which can be fished with confidence during the entire season. The dressing can be varied to suit particular conditions, but the original was as follows:

HOOK. 14.

BODY. Yellow silk (sometimes ribbed with fine gold wire).

HACKLE. Light Coch-y-bondhu, cock or hen.

WINGS. Hen blackbird wing feather.

The yellow silk of the body is more often than not waxed with cobbler's wax to impart an olive hue, and what is called a "Furnace" hackle is usually used in place of the Coch-y-bondhu. The furnace hackle does not have the black tips of the Coch-y-bondhu.

For a dry hackled pattern, a blue dun cock's hackle should be wound with a furnace cock, and tail consisting of a few fibres of furnace cock hackle also added.

This fly is also a successful lake pattern, and larger versions (up to size 8 old scale) are very popular in New Zealand. The New Zealand anglers add either a bright red tag or a tail of golden pheasant tippet fibres.

Partridge and Orange

Another standard north-country pattern for both trout and grayling, and also effective as a lake fly.

HOOK. 14.

BODY. Orange floss or tying silk.

HACKLE. Small feather from the back of a partridge, brown in colour and with dappled markings.

The "Partridge and Yellow" is another version, having a yellow silk body and a lighter hackle, usually from the breast of the partridge. It is also sometimes referred to as the "Partridge Spider".

Amber Nymph

Another of Dr. Bell's patterns for lake fishing, of which there are two versions. They have been very successful in both Blagdon and Chew Valley lakes.

Large "Amber Nymph" for use in May and June and usually the first dropper, and the "Small Amber Nymph" for use in July.

HOOK. 11–10. For the large pattern No. 12 for the small.

BODY. Amber yellow floss silk or seal's fur tied rather thick.

THORAX. Brown floss silk or seal's fur, approximately one third the length of the body.

WING CASE. A strip of any grey-brown feather, tied in at the tail and finished behind the thorax.

LEGS. A few fibres of pale honey hen's hackle, tied in under the head and extending backwards.

The only difference in the smaller pattern is that the thorax should be of hot orange floss silk or seal's fur.

Buzzer Nymph

From the same stable as the Amber Nymph, this should be fished in June and from mid-August to the end of September.

HOOK. 12–10.

BODY. Black floss silk taken partly round the bend of the hook.

RIB. Flat gold tinsel.

WINGS. A short tuft of white floss silk tied in just behind the head, about ⅛ in. long.
LEGS. A few fibres of brown mallard shoulder feather tied in under the head and sloping backwards.

Lake Olive Nymph

This is another of Col. Joscelyn Lane's patterns, and a "must" for all lake fishermen.

HOOK. 12.
TYING SILK. Golden olive.
TAIL. A bunch of dyed olive cock hackle fibres, about ¼ in. long.
ABDOMEN. Olive silk or 3X nylon, very thin at tail end and thickening gradually up to thorax.
THORAX. Darker and thicker than the body, but not ball-shaped.
RIB. Fine gold wire.
HACKLE. A small bunch of dyed olive cock hackle fibres, tied in under the throat, and with most of the fibres lying back close along the body.

Col. Lane recommends a darker variation of the dressing for spring fishing, and for an imitation of the nymph on the point of hatching he plumps for our old friend the "Gold Ribbed Hare's Ear" discussed earlier.

Pheasant Tail Nymph

The "Pheasant Tail" is best known as a very fine all round wet- or dry-fly, being a very good representation of a number of flies, but the nymph pattern has also proved its effectiveness, its virtues being extolled by such well-known anglers as the late G. E. M. Skues and Frank Sawyer, the famous river-keeper of more modern times.

HOOK. 16–13.
BODY. Fibres from a cock pheasant's centre tail. Only the richly coloured reddish fibres should be used.
RIB. Gold wire.
HACKLE. Brassy or honey dun cock or hen very short in the fibre.
TAIL. Two or three strands as hackle.

The body should be wound more thickly at the shoulder to form the thorax.

Frank Sawyer dispensed with the hackle altogether in one of his patterns, the body being formed of the cock pheasant tail fibres twisted together with very fine copper wire. This combination was doubled back and then forward again at the shoulder to form the thorax.

Demoiselle Dragon-Fly Nymph

Regarded by Col. Lane as one of the most useful all-round patterns for lake fishing, together with the "Large Dragon-Fly Nymph", the dressing of which I also give here.

Demoiselle

HOOK. 10.

TYING SILK. Golden olive.

TAIL. A big bunch of dyed olive cock's hackle fibres, cut off square to a length of $\frac{1}{4}$ in.

BODY AND THORAX. Carrot shaped. Of olive floss silk or 3X nylon, tapering from tail up to a full $\frac{1}{8}$ in. at thorax.

RIB. Finest gold wire ending short of thorax.

LEG. A bunch of dyed olive cock hackle fibres, tied in under the throat to lie close beneath body.

Large Nymph

HOOK. 10–9.

TYING SILK. Green.

TAIL. Three lengths of thick knitting wool $\frac{1}{4}$ in. long. One medium green and two nigger brown.

BODY. Two pieces of the same wool, one medium green and the other nigger brown, twisted together and wound on tightly. The body should be $\frac{1}{4}$ in. thick in the middle and taper at both ends, and be tied down with open turns of the tying silk.

HACKLE. One turn of a brown partridge back feather dyed very dark green.

Iron Blue Nymph

There are far too many natural nymph imitations for me to show them all, but the method of tying this one is universal and can be applied to others, the dressings of one or two of which are also included here.

HOOK. 16.

WHISKS. Three short fibres from a white cock's hackle.

BODY. Mole fur spun on claret tying silk.

THORAX. Mole fur.

WING CASES. Waterhen's secondary wing feather.

LEGS. One turn of a short-fibred dark blue dun hen's hackle.

Early Olive (Blue Dun) Nymph

HOOK. 14–13.

TAIL WHISKS. Three short strands from a dark olive hen hackle.

BODY. Dark olive seal's fur, or dark olive quill.

RIB. Fine gold wire.

THORAX. Dark olive seal's fur.

WING CASES. Dark starling wing feathers.

LEGS. One turn of a short-fibred dark olive hen hackle.

F.G.F.D.–K

Olive Dun Nymph

HOOK. 15.
TAIL WHISKS. Three short fibres from a dyed medium olive hen hackle.
BODY. Olive seal's fur.
RIB. Fine gold wire.
THORAX. Olive seal's fur.
WING CASE. Starling wing feather undyed or dyed olive.
LEGS. Short-fibred medium olive hen hackle. One turn.

Blue-Winged Olive Nymph

HOOK. 15–14.
TAIL. Fibres from a grizzle hackle, dyed yellow.
BODY. Heron herl dyed greenish olive.
RIB. Fine gold wire.
THORAX. Darkish olive seal's fur.
WING CASES. Goose breast dyed pale olive.
LEGS. Grizzle hen hackle dyed yellow. Short fibred, and one turn only.

Pale Watery Dun Nymph

HOOK. 16–15.
TAIL WHISKS. Pale ginger or very pale olive hen hackle fibres.
BODY. Pale ginger seal's fur or undyed lamb's wool spun on pale yellow tying silk.
THORAX. As body.
WING CASE. Pale starling wing feather.
LEGS. Palest ginger or very pale olive hen hackle.

Mayfly Nymphs

These should be tied fairly heavily, as the mayfly nymph is a good-sized insect. There are many patterns, but the following three should meet most requirements.

NO. 1
HOOK. 11–9, long shanked.
TAIL. Three short strands from a cock pheasant's tail feather.
BODY AND THORAX. Brown olive seal's fur.
RIB. Oval gold tinsel.
WING CASE. From a hen pheasant's tail feather. Dark as possible.
LEGS. Brown partridge back feather.
NO. 2
TAIL. As for No. 1.
BODY. Three turns at tail end of dirty yellow seal's fur. The remainder and thorax of brown olive seal's fur.
RIB. Yellow silk, thicker than the normal tying silk.

WING CASE. As for No. 1.
LEGS. A mottled feather from a hen pheasant's neck.

NO. 3

TAIL. As for Nos. 1 and 2.
BODY AND THORAX. Pale buff seal's fur.
RIB. Oval gold tinsel.
WING CASE. As for Nos. 1 and 2.
LEGS. Dark brown grouse hackle.

Wet Mayflies

More often than not these are used at the commencement of the rise while the fly is hatching, and should therefore be fished semi-submerged.

NO. 1

HOOK. 11–9, long shanked.
TAILS. Three strands from a cock pheasant's tail.
BODY. Dyed yellow lamb's wool.
RIB. Oval gold tinsel.
LEGS. Hen pheasant neck feather dyed yellow, or undyed.
WINGS. Speckled grey mallard feather dyed yellow.

NO. 2

TAILS. As for No. 1.
BODY. As for No. 1.
RIB. As for No. 1.
LEGS. Ginger cock's hackle, dyed yellow.
WINGS. Speckled grey mallard feather dyed greenish-yellow.

NO. 3

TAILS. As for Nos. 1 and 2.
BODY. Buff yellow floss silk.
RIB. Oval gold tinsel.
LEGS. Brown grouse hackle.
WINGS. Grizzle cock hackle dyed greenish-yellow.

Dapping Flies

A form of "dapping" practised mainly on the wind-swept lakes of Scotland and Ireland is a most interesting and rewarding method of angling.

A long (14 ft.) rod is the customary weapon used, the reel loaded with plenty of backing, to which is attached a length of light but stout floss silk. The floss line should be quite long, so that the backing does not have to be let out during the actual "dapping".

The fly is attached to the "blow line", as the floss is called, by a short length of gut or nylon, fairly stout, as this method of fishing seems to bring the big ones to the surface.

The line is not laid on the water as in normal casting, but should belly out in the wind, allowing the fly "dap" on the surface like a natural insect.

Mayfly imitations can be used at the appropriate time when fishing the Irish lakes, but the usual patterns for this type of fishing are large heavily hackled ones.

Sometimes they are of the "palmer" type or hackled in the front only, but whichever type is used, several hackles must be wound together to ensure full and heavy hackling.

One or two patterns are given here for guidance, but a range of different-coloured types can be made merely by altering the hackle colour. Usual mayfly hackled patterns can be used, adapting them by increasing the amount of hackle used.

Scots Grey

TAIL. Fibres from a stiff grizzle hackle.
BODY. Blue dun seal's fur.
RIB. Fine flat silver tinsel (for lightness).
HACKLE. Three grizzle cock hackles, at front only.

Red Palmer

TAIL. None.
BODY. Dyed red seal's fur.
RIB. Fine gold wire.
HACKLE. Several natural red game hackles wound "palmer" from bend to eye of hook.

Black Pennell (other colours—brown, yellow, green)

TAG. Fine flat silver tinsel.
TAIL. Tippet fibres.
BODY. Black floss silk, very thin.
RIB. Fine flat silver tinsel.
HACKLE. Two or three black cock hackles at front only (natural red game or furnace as alternatives).
HOOK SIZES. 8-10.12.

AN ADDITIONAL LIST OF BRITISH PATTERNS

TROUT AND SALMON

SUPPLIED BY PRIVATE INDIVIDUALS

Not illustrated

CHAPTER ONE

ADDITIONAL BRITISH TROUT FLY PATTERNS

Black Duck Fly (dry)
(Alternate names: "Black Midge" or "Black Buzzer".)
HOOK. 13 or 14.
BODY. Black floss, thicker at shoulder.
WINGS. Two dun or cream cock hackle points tied sloping backwards.
HACKLE. Rusty black cock, short in fibre, tied in front of wings.

Black Duck Fly (wet)
(See also "Buzzer Nymph".)
HOOK. 12–14.
BODY. Black silk or wool, wound thicker at shoulder.
HACKLE. Black cock.
WING. Starling wing quill fibres, tied short, divided, and inclined towards tail.

Large Olive Midge ("Olive Buzzer") (dry)
HOOK. 12–14.
BODY. Hare's ear mixed with olive seal's fur.
BODY HACKLE. Cream cock, or cream badger cock (light centre).
SHOULDER HACKLE. Cream badger cock tied spent.

Olive Buzzer
(See "Large Olive Midge".)

Black Buzzer
(See "Black Duck Fly".)

Gold Zulu
TAIL. Red wool.

BODY. Bronze peacock herl.
RIB. Fine flat gold tinsel.
HACKLE. Coch-y-bondhu from shoulder to tail.

Black Midge
(See "Black Duck Fly".)

Olive Midge
(See "Olive Duck Fly".)

Black Lure (two-hook lure)
BODIES. Black floss.
RIBS. Oval silver tinsel.
WINGS. Two black cock hackles, back to back, or splayed out in a "V".
HEAD. Black varnish.

Olive Duck Fly (dry)
BODY. Olive floss silk or swan herl dyed pale green olive.
WINGS. Two blue dun or cream cock hackle points tied sloping backwards over hook.
RIB. Gold wire.
HACKLE. Pale grizzle or rusty dun cock, tied in front of wing.
HOOK. 12–13.

Bridgett's Black
(Wet lake fly—for chironomid representation.)
TAIL. Two fibres from a guinea-fowl hackle.
BODY. Black ostrich herl.
RIB. Fine silver wire.
HACKLE. Guinea fowl.

Burleigh (Loch Leven fly)
TAIL. Ginger hackle fibres (or Tippet).
BODY. Yellow tying silk well waxed to make it olive.
RIB. Silver wire.
HACKLE. Ginger.
WINGS. Starling wing feather, tied low over body in sedge style.

Dunkeld (trout version)
TAIL. Golden pheasant crest.
BODY. Flat gold tinsel.
RIB. Fine oval gold tinsel.
HACKLE. Dyed orange from shoulder to tail.
WINGS. Brown mallard flank.
CHEEKS. Small jungle-cock feather.

Cran Swallow (Clyde fly)
HOOK. No. 14.
TAIL. None.
BODY. Pale yellow tying silk waxed to darken it.
WING. Swift wing or substitute rolled with inside outside, and tied low over body.
HACKLE. Bronze-green feather from starling breast, one turn only.

A. C. Allen's Mayfly
TAIL. Three fibres from a cock pheasant tail.
BODY. Yellow floss.
RIB. Fine oval gold tinsel.
BODY HACKLE. Badger.
HEAD HACKLE. Guinea fowl dyed yellow.
A successful pattern for Hampshire rivers.

The "Marquis" Mayfly
TAIL. Three fibres of black bear hair, or dyed hog bristles as a substitute.
BODY. Brown floss silk.
RIB. Oval gold tinsel.
WINGS. Grey drake breast (fan wing).
HACKLE. Brown cock's hackle.

Ke-He (Orkney sea-trout fly)
TAIL. Bright red wool and about four tippet fibres.
BODY. Bronze peacock herl over floss silk to make it good and thick.
HACKLE. Rhode Island Red, with ginger as an alternative.

Blanchard's Abortion
TAIL. Fibres of natural red cock hackle.
BODY. Brown silk, or heron herl.
WINGS. Fibres of honey dun cock sloping forward.
HACKLE. Natural red.
HOOK. No. 12–14.

Lansdale (Mayfly)
TAIL. Three fibres from a cock pheasant tail.
BODY. Dark brown wool.
HACKLES. Ginger cock hackle, with French partridge in front.

Kite's Pale Watery
HOOK. No. 15.
TYING SILK. White.
TAIL. Fibres from a cream cock hackle.
BODY. Three herls from a grey goose wing primary feather.
HACKLE. Cream cock hackle.

"Footballer" Nymphs
HOOK. 12–16.
BODY. Alternate windings of black and white horsehair, wound well round bend of hook. A black and white barred effect is required.
THORAX. Mole fur.
HEAD. Two turns of bronze peacock herl.

Coloured Versions
Same as above, but with clear horsehair wound over various colours of tying silk. Red, Olive, Yellow, Orange, etc.

John Storey
TAIL. Fibres from a red cock's hackle.
BODY. Thin peacock herl.
RIB. Scarlet tying silk.
HACKLE. Red.
WING. Grey mallard flank.

Kite's Imperial
HOOK. 14–15.
TYING SILK. Purple.
TAIL WHISKS. Grey-brown or honey dun hackle fibres.

BODY. Herl from undyed heron primary feather.
RIB. Gold wire.
HACKLE. Honey dun.

Bates Badger
TAIL. Three fibres from lemon badger hackle.
BODY. Natural raffia.
RIB. Red tying silk.
HACKLE. Lemon badger cock hackle.

WELSH PATTERNS

A selection of Welsh patterns which he recommends, for the Llanberis lakes in particular, and for other lakes and streams of North Wales, by Mr. G. O. Jones, 1957 captain of the Welsh International Fly Fishing Team:

Ceiliog Hwyaden a Chorff Gwin
TAIL. Fibres from brown mallard flank.
BODY. Claret seal's fur.
RIB. Gold wire.
WINGS. Brown mallard.
HACKLE. Black or claret.

Brech yr Iar (Alder)
BODY. Peacock herl dyed magenta.
WINGS. Speckled hen wing quill.
HACKLE. Black.

Starling Corff Du
TAIL. Blue dun hackle fibres.
BODY. Black silk.
RIB. Flat silver.
HACKLE. Blue dun.
WING. Starling wing quill. ("Blae & Black"(?))

Petrisen Corff Paun
BODY. Bronze peacock herl.
HACKLE. Brown partridge back.

Petrissen Corff Twrch
TAIL. Brown partridge back fibres.

BODY. Mole fur.
RIB. Silver.
HACKLE. Brown partridge back.

Ceiliog Hwyaden Corff Piws
BODY. Purple seal's fur.
RIB. Gold.
WINGS. Bronze mallard.
HACKLE. Black or purple.

Petrisen Corff Blewyn Ysgyfarnog
BODY. From hare's ear.
RIB. Silver.
HACKLE. Brown partridge.

Ceiliog Hwyaden a Chorff Melyn Budr
BODY. Dirty Yellow seal fur, or medium olive.
RIB. Gold or silver.
WINGS. Bronze mallard.
HACKLE. Ginger or yellow.

Cyfflogyn Corff Gwyrdd
BODY. Green seal's fur.
RIB. Silver.
WINGS. Woodcock wing quill.
HACKLE. Ginger or green.

A selection of Welsh salmon and sea-trout flies was given to me by the well-known Llanwrst fly tyer, R. H. Hughes. They will be useful to any angler contemplating a trip to these waters.

SEA TROUT

Torby Coch

TAIL. Red ibis or substitute.
BODY. Hare fur.
RIB. Oval silver tinsel.
HACKLE. Brown hen.
WING. Plain brown hen wing quill.

Hugh Nain

TAIL. Golden pheasant tippet fibres.
BODY. Tail half golden olive seal's fur, remainder grey seal's fur.
RIB. Oval silver tinsel.
WING. From hen pheasant wing quill.
HACKLE. Brown partridge wound as a collar.

Teal and Blue (Welsh)

TAIL. Golden pheasant tippet fibres.
BODY. Embossed silver tinsel.
HACKLE. Dyed blue cock hackle.
WING. Tip of a teal breast or flank feather tied in to form a "roof" over the body.

Spider (Welsh)

TAIL. Red ibis or substitute.
BODY. Grey seal's fur.
RIB. Oval silver tinsel.
HACKLE. Badger cock, long in fibre.

SALMON

Conway Blue

TAG. Round silver tinsel and golden yellow floss.
TAIL. Golden pheasant crest.
BUTT. Black ostrich herl.
BODY. Royal blue seal's fur.
RIB. Oval silver tinsel.
HACKLES. Two—at throat only. Blue jay wing feather at front, with a dyed royal blue cock hackle behind it.
WING. Two golden pheasant tippet feathers back to back, with a "roof" of brown mallard flank feather over. A golden pheasant crest feather over the brown mallard.
HEAD. Black varnish.

Shrimp Fly (Welsh)

TAG. Yellow floss silk.

TAIL. Golden pheasant crest feather.

BUTT. Black ostrich herl.

BODY. Yellow floss.

RIB. Oval silver tinsel.

WING. Tip of a red golden pheasant body feather tied over body of fly, with jungle cock each side.

HACKLE. White cock, wound as a "collar".

HEAD. Black varnish.

Brown Turkey

TAG. Round silver tinsel and yellow floss.

TAIL. Golden pheasant crest and ibis or substitute.

BODY. Hare fur.

RIB. Oval gold tinsel.

HACKLES. Two—at throat only. Blue jay wing feather in front, with a dark furnace cock hackle behind it.

WING. From cinnamon turkey tails.

ADDITIONAL BRITISH SALMON FLY PATTERNS

Haslam (salmon fly)
TAG. Flat silver tinsel.
BUTT. White wool or floss silk.
TAIL. Small golden pheasant crest.
BODY. Flat silver tinsel.
RIB. Oval silver tinsel.
THROAT HACKLE. Blue jay, or guinea fowl dyed blue.
WING. From hen pheasant tail and tied slim.
HORNS. Blue/yellow macaw tied in so that they curve along the sides of the wings and so that the tips cross over each other above the tail.
HEAD. Black varnish.
This fly can be tied in all sizes, and the smaller ones are good for sea trout.

Skin the Goat (Irish salmon fly)
TAG. Fine round silver tinsel and yellow floss.
TAIL. Golden pheasant crest and Indian crow.
BUTT. Black ostrich herl.
BODY. Violet floss silk.
RIB. Oval silver tinsel.
BODY HACKLE. Golden olive.
THROAT HACKLE. Blue jay.
WING. Mixed fibres of golden pheasant tippet, golden pheasant tail, red, yellow, blue goose, grey mallard flank, with brown mallard flank over. A golden pheasant crest over all.
CHEEKS. Blue chatterer or kingfisher.
HEAD. Black varnish.

Hairy Mary (original)
TAG. Round silver tinsel.
TAIL. Golden pheasant crest.
BODY. Black floss silk.
RIB. Oval silver or gold tinsel.
HACKLE. Dyed blue.
WING. Fibres from brown part of bucktail.
HOOK. No. 6 standard salmon.
Modern variations add various dyed coloured fibres to the wings, and coloured tinsel bodies are popular in Scotland.

Sir William (salmon fly)
HOOK. No. 5 double long shank.
TAIL. None.
TAG. Round silver tinsel.
BODY. Flat silver tinsel.
RIB. Oval silver tinsel.
HACKLE. Blue.
WING. Grey squirrel tail dyed hot orange.

Lady Gwen (salmon fly)
HOOK. No. 5 double long shank.
TAG. Round silver tinsel.
TAIL. Golden pheasant crest.
BODY. Black floss silk.
RIB. Flat silver tinsel.
HACKLE. Black or bright blue.
WING. Grey squirrel tail dyed lemon yellow.
HEAD. Black varnish.

Thurso Copper King (low-water salmon fly)
TAG. Fine oval silver tinsel.
BODY. Flat gold tinsel.
RIB. Fine oval gold tinsel.
BODY HACKLE. Grizzle dyed yellow.
FRONT HACKLE. Golden pheasant red breast feather.
HEAD. Black varnish.

Beauty
TAIL. Fibres from a guinea-fowl hackle.
BODY. Grey wool.
RIB. Flat silver tinsel.
HACKLE. Guinea fowl.
WING. From guinea-fowl wing or tail quill.
HEAD. Black varnish.

Black Dragon
TAIL. Fibres of black squirrel tail.
BODY. Black chenille.
RIB. Embossed silver tinsel.
WING. Black squirrel tail fibres.
HACKLE. Black cock—wound as a collar.
HEAD. Black varnish.

Black Heron
TAIL. Red ibis.
BODY. Black floss silk.
RIBS. Oval silver tinsel.
HACKLE. Black heron.
WINGS. Teal flank.
To be tied as a low-water pattern on 6–9 hooks.

Sweep
TAIL. Golden pheasant crest.
BODY. Black floss.
RIB. Oval gold tinsel.
HACKLE. Black cock.
WING. Any black feather such as crow or dyed goose.

CHEEKS. Blue kingfisher.
HEAD. Black varnish.
HOOK. 6–8 standard.

Black Maria (standard salmon fly)
HOOKS. 4–8 single or double.
TAG. Fine oval silver tinsel.
TAIL. Small golden pheasant crest.
BODY. Tail half yellow floss, front half black floss.
RIB. Fine oval silver tinsel.
BODY HACKLE. Black—over black floss only.
WING. A slender bunch of any black hair—bucktail, bear hair, squirrel, etc.
HEAD. Black varnish.

Yellow Dog (Irish salmon fly)
TAG. Round silver tinsel.
TAIL. Golden pheasant crest.
BUTT. Black ostrich herl.
BODY. Yellow floss.
RIBS. Scarlet floss and fine oval silver tinsel.
BODY HACKLE. Yellow—over front third of body only.
THROAT HACKLE. Dyed red.
WING. Tippet in strands, red, yellow, blue goose, florican bustard, brown mallard over, crest over all.
CHEEKS. Teal flank.
HEAD. Black varnish.

Goat's Toe
TAIL. Scarlet wool.
BODY. Bronze peacock herl.
RIBS. Scarlet floss silk.
HACKLE. Green peacock breast feather with fairly long fibres.

Gold Sylph
TAIL. Fibres of red golden pheasant breast and ibis.
BODY. Flat gold tinsel.

RIBS. Oval gold tinsel.
1ST HACKLE. Yellow.
2ND HACKLE. Red golden pheasant breast feather—both at throat only.
WINGS. Brown mallard.

Poacher
TAG. Orange floss.
TAIL. Fibres from red golden pheasant breast feather.
BODY. Peacock herl. (Green).
RIB. Oval gold tinsel.
HACKLE. Dark furnace, long in fibre.
HEAD. Black varnish.

Dragon Lady
TAIL. Golden pheasant crest.
BODY. Black chenille.
RIB. Embossed silver tinsel.
WINGS. Grey squirrel tail fibres.
CHEEKS. Jungle cock.
HACKLE. Ginger cock, wound as a collar.
HEAD. Black varnish.

Ball of Malt (Salmon Fly)
TAG. Round silver tinsel.
TAIL. Golden pheasant crest, and tippet fibres.
BODY. Flat silver tinsel.
RIB. Oval silver tinsel.
BODY HACKLE. Yellow.
THROAT HACKLE. Blue.
WINGS. Underwing of golden pheasant tippet fibres, with main wing of brown bucktail.
HEAD. Black varnish.

Assassin
TAG. Round silver tinsel.
TAIL. Golden pheasant crest.
BODY. Flat silver tinsel.
RIB. Oval silver tinsel.
BODY HACKLES. Rear half lemon hackle. Front half coch-y-bondhu hackle.
THROAT HACKLE. Blue Jay or dyed blue guinea fowl feather.
WING. Grouse tail strips.
HEAD. Black varnish.

Brown Turkey
TAIL. Golden pheasant crest.
BODY. First half yellow seal's fur, front half claret seal's fur.
RIBS. Flat or oval silver tinsel.
HACKLE. Natural brown cock.
WINGS. Tippet in strands, with strips of cinnamon turkey tail each side.
HEAD. Black varnish.

Usk Grub
TAG. Round silver tinsel.
TAIL. Golden pheasant red breast wound as a hackle.
BODY. First half yellow or orange seal's fur. Second half black floss.
RIBS. Oval silver tinsel.
VEILING. Tips of dyed red hen hackles.
CENTRE HACKLE. Light furnace.
FRONT HACKLE. Light furnace, longer in fibre than centre hackle.
"WINGS." Two jungle cock feathers back to back.
HEAD. Black varnish.

Prince Philip
TAIL. Fibres of red Ibis substitute.
BODY. Purple floss silk.
RIB. Oval or lace gold tinsel.
HACKLE. Claret.
WING. Two strips of yellow goose, with two strips of oak turkey either side.
EYES. Jungle cock.
(Dressing of trout version is the same except for outer wings which are grey mallard wing quill).

Rhy Ness (Salmon Fly)
TAG. None.
TAIL. Tippet strands and teal flank fibres in equal lengths.
BODY. White floss silk.
RIB. Oval silver tinsel with one turn under the tail.
HACKLE. Greenish blue.
WING. White goose or turkey tied on flat, with a jungle cock feather tied flat on top of wing.
HEAD. Black varnish.

SECTION 6

THE INTRODUCTION OF
NEW PATTERNS

INTRODUCTION

ONE WOULD THINK that with the vast number of patterns available to the fly fisherman it would be almost impossible to evolve a new one with better fish-taking qualities than its predecessors. This is certainly not the case, thank goodness, or enthusiasm for progressive fly tying would have waned long ago!

I do not say that some of the new flies do not approximate other and older patterns in appearance, but where this is the case it usually means that some dedicated and enthusiastic angler and fly tyer has produced a fly that will consistently take fish from the particular water he fishes.

A haphazard list of fly patterns conveys little to even quite experienced anglers, but this is altogether different when it is indicated where and when to use it.

This field, of course, has been covered before by such masters as the late Roger Woolley in his *Modern Trout Fly Dressing*, and the late A. Courtney Williams with *A Dictionary of Trout Flies*. C. F. Walker gave us an entirely new approach to still-water flies with *Lake Flies and their Imitation*, as did T. C. Ivens with *Still Water Fly-Fishing*.

In addition to those who manage to put their researches and knowledge into book form are the many individual anglers who have studied their craft and who now and again come up with patterns which they have evolved after much painstaking work on the waters they fish.

It does not matter that a pattern so carefully brought into existence might only have a brief success; it merely means that there is more interesting work to be done to improve the pattern or find a new one. If anyone ever finds a pattern or material which will take fish under any circumstances, fly fishing will lose most of its appeal, I am sure, the greatest losers being the inventors of future "Greenwell's Glory's", "Dogsbody's", "Grey Duster's", "Blue Upright's", and "Wickham's Fancy's", all now famous patterns evolved in the way I have described.

I am very pleased, therefore, to devote a small section of this book to the enthusiasts who have produced worthwhile patterns or improved on old ones, but my limited scope must not be overlooked. I mean that it should not be forgotten that *every* fly pattern in existence was the result of work and observation by someone who had the interests of other fly fishermen at heart, and who saw that the result of his or her labours was recorded and passed on. Not forgetting, of course, those whose work has been carried out in territories far removed from our own waters, and I have given some details of these in the sections of this book devoted, in particular, to the Commonwealth countries.

I hope the few I have been able to mention, and the results they have achieved, will encourage others to take an interest in this fascinating aspect of fly fishing.

I would add that any comments or tying instructions are also the work of those who evolved the flies.

PATTERNS

PETER DEANE

Mr. Deane has contributed much to angling, and fly tying in particular. Although he lost completely the use of both legs during World War II, this has not prevented him taking an active part in fishing, as well as conducting a progressive fly-tying business.

His flies are very much in demand, particularly those he has evolved himself, and as he specialises in tying flies to a client's particular requirements, he has accumulated a fund of knowledge which must be of value to us all. Some of the patterns he has produced or helped to produce are now accepted as standard, and it gives me great pleasure to give the following list, including Mr. Deane's personal comments.

Beacon Beige (dry-fly)

Designed as far as I know by the late Lord Dulverton and the late Fred Tout, who kept the local tackle shop at Dulverton, Somerset. Fred Tait gave me the pattern to copy when I first started tying in 1948—he called it the "Beige". I experimented with the fly on the Culm and found it floated even better when dressed with a very springy Indian red-game hackle (dark), rather long in the fibres. It's by far the best olive dun I've come across—good anywhere, and like Terry's Terror now a firm favourite on the chalk streams. I rechristened it "Beacon Beige" as the water I first fished it on, the River Culm at Hemyock, was dominated by Culmstock Beacon, one of the warning beacons for the approach of the Armada.

WHISKS. Four fibres from a Plymouth Rock (Grizzle) cock hackle. Good stiff ones.

BODY. Well-marked stripped peacock quill from "eye".

HACKLES. Plymouth Rock with a dark Indian game cock wound through it.

Dress as lightly as possible.

Claret Sherry Spinner (dry-fly)

This Sherry Spinner was given to me by a client who had experimented with the artificial Sherry for years, and found this simple pattern best of all.

WHISKS. Three fibres from a Plymouth Rock (Grizzle) cock hackle.

BODY. Claret wool or seal fur—lightly dressed.

HACKLE. Plymouth Rock cock, four turns at the most.

Leckford Professor (dry-fly)

An excellent pattern, especially when trout are selective. Given to a friend of mine by Ernie Mott, keeper of the Leckford water on the River Test.

Tie fly in "reverse", i.e. with hackle at bend of hook.

TAIL. None.

BODY. Fur from hare's ear.

RIB. Fine flat gold tinsel.

HACKLES.

FIRST (nearest to body). Bright red-game cock.

SECOND. A good stiff white cock hackle.

Terry's Terror (dry-fly)

This wonderful fly was devised by that first-class fly fisherman Dr. Cecil Terry of Bath, the doyen of Hungerford, and the late Ernest Lock of Andover. It represents several stages of an "Olive Hatching Nymph", "Dun and Spinner", and dressed small is well taken for an "Iron Blue Dun". Tied on Size 3 (new scale) and upwards, it is good for sedges. Excellent throughout the season on any water. Seldom dressed as a sunk pattern, but on one occasion when tied on a Size 2 Limerick Double killed the following Loch Neagh trout for Comm. R. Martin in a morning at Shanes Castle: $1\frac{1}{2}$ lb., $9\frac{1}{2}$ lb., six at $\frac{1}{2}$ lb., and finally one of $7\frac{1}{2}$ lb.

TAIL. Equal parts of orange and yellow goat hair, cut short to make a stiff "tag".

BODY. Bronze peacock herl—one strand only.

RIB. Fine flat copper tinsel.

HACKLE. Medium red game (as near fox-red as possible). The bottom half of the hackle may be trimmed, but this is optional.

SIZES. Any.

Camasunary Killer (sea-trout fly)

I was sent this fly by a client, Francis Williams, of Melrose, Roxburghshire, in 1961. As I liked its appearance, I dressed a number and sent them to clients of mine up and down the country. The result in practically every case was an outstanding success. One rod in Sutherland took two grilse and twenty-one sea trout in an afternoon's fishing and did well the following day with it. It was equally effective in Ireland, particularly at Waterville. The year 1962 was a repetition of 1961—one rod in the Isle of Lewis had six salmon and twenty-three sea trout with it in three days, and it did equally well in Ireland again.

It was originally designed by Stephen Johnson of Jedburgh (the "Blue Fly"), but how the variation came about is beyond me. The fact still remains that it is without any doubt the most successful wet-fly I've come across. Salmon take it as freely as sea trout, and in small sizes it is an excellent lake pattern. As good in Scotland and Ireland as it is in the south and west country.

TAIL. Royal blue wool.

BODY. Two equal halves. The tail half royal blue wool, followed by red "Fire-brand" D.F.M. wool.

RIB. Oval silver tinsel, rather broad in the large sizes.

HACKLE. Black cock, rather long in fibre. Use plenty of turns on the bigger sizes, two hackles if necessary.

Blue Fly (sea-trout fly)

As stated, this is the original of the "Camasunary Killer". Designed by Stephen Johnson. Very killing and ideal for the monster sea trout of the Isle of Skye. A tip-top all-round pattern.

TAG. Flat silver tinsel.

TAIL. None.

BODY. Royal blue seal's fur or wool.

RIB. Oval or flat silver tinsel.

HACKLE. Three turns of black cock hackle, rather long in fibre.

SIZE. No. 5 (new scale) and upward.

Bright Boy (sea-trout fly)

An ideal fly for low water and very bright conditions, and also another of Stephen Johnson's patterns. Stephen Johnson, incidentally, was the author of that excellent book *Fishing from Afar*.

TAG. None.

TAIL. None.

BODY. Smooth flat gold tinsel—no ribbing.

HACKLE. Two—scarlet cock hackle followed by a black hen's hackle, both doubled.

WING. Teal flank, rather slim, reaching to bend of hook.

Old Charlie (salmon fly)

A first-class all-round hair-wing salmon fly designed by Douglas Pilkington of Stow on the Wold. Equally good as a low-water fly, and does very well on the Spey and many other rivers.

TAG. Flat gold tinsel.

TAIL. Golden pheasant crest.

BODY. Claret floss silk.

RIBBING. Oval gold, rather wide.

HACKLE. Hot orange cock hackle.

WING. Natural brown bucktail, with black tips if possible.

SIDES. Jungle cock.

HEAD. Red varnish.

Rhy Ness (low-water salmon)

A fly of Norwegian origin, and becoming very popular in this country. I have seen variations using golden pheasant tippets instead of the crest as a tail, and a silver body instead of the white floss. Both can be very good.

TAG. Flat gold tinsel.
TAIL. Golden pheasant crest.
BODY. White floss silk.
RIB. Oval silver tinsel.
HACKLE. Dyed blue cock hackle.
WING. From white duck wing quill.
SIDES. Small jungle cock, tied close to head.
HEAD. Black varnish.
Tied in the usual low-water style.

Deane's Spinning Jenny (low-water salmon)

Designed by myself as a low-water salmon fly, and it has done extremely well on occasions. I find it equally good for sea trout, and took my first big one with it.

TAG. Flat gold tinsel.
TAIL. Golden pheasant crest.
BODY. Purple seal's fur.
RIB. Flat silver tinsel.
HACKLE. Black hen's hackle.
WING. From grouse tail.
SIDES. Small jungle cock, tied close to head.
HEAD. Black varnish.

THE JOHN GODDARD DRY-FLIES

John Goddard spends most of his time in the realm of angling, as both his business and personal interests lie in this direction. Not only has he devoted much time and study to the improvement of the equipment used by anglers of every kind, sea angling has called upon him competitively, and much of his spare time is spent by the riverside, where he has acquired an entomological knowledge that few of us can emulate.

He has studied aquatic life in its natural surroundings, and has produced a complete series of coloured photographs of the life-cycle of the insects we try to copy, which is the finest I have ever seen. It is not possible for me to give full details of all his work, as it is to be produced in a volume of its own, but I am very pleased to pay tribute to his remarkable skill with the camera.

Any pattern produced with this background of knowledge and attention to detail must be worth consideration, and I can vouch for the five I am giving by the excellent results I have had personally.

The "Nevamis" Mayfly

This is a very killing and lifelike pattern designed to overcome the bad hooking aspect of most artificial mayflies due to the large hackles used. To compensate for the loss of buoyancy caused by using a small main hackle, the body hackle is tied "palmer" and clipped. Also, a hackle-fibre wing is used, which, in my opinion, is the best method of portraying the gossamer-like quality of the natural insect. The dressing is as follows:

TYING SILK. Yellow.

HOOK. Long shank fine wire No. 8.

TAIL. Three fibres from a cock pheasant's tail.

BODY. Natural unbleached baby seal's fur tied fairly thickly.

RIB. Oval gold tinsel—fine.

BODY HACKLE. Honey cock. Tied "palmer" fashion from tail to shoulder, and then clipped back to within $\frac{1}{4}$ in. at shoulder and tapering to $\frac{1}{8}$ in. at tail. Because of the clipping, the size of hackle is immaterial.

WINGS. A pale blue dun cock hackle with all the fibres set in the upright position with the usual figure of eight tying. When complete the wing fibres should be about $\frac{7}{8}$ in. long.

HACKLE. A furnace cock hackle (red with black centre) with fibres under $\frac{1}{2}$ in. long.

Last Hope (Pale Watery)

This pattern was developed on the Itchen and the Test rivers, and designed to imitate the Pale Watery Dun. The secret of its success is that it is tied on a very small hook, and by using a hackle that is very short in the fibre. When this type of hackle is not available, a clipped hackle can be used as an alternative.

This fly can also be used as a very small general pattern, and has been accepted by smutting trout on a great number of occasions when they had refused all other patterns.

TYING SILK. Pale Yellow.

HOOK. Up Eye Fine Wire, No. 18.

TAIL. Four to six fibres from a honey dun cock hackle.

BODY. Natural (stone or buff coloured) condor herl.

HACKLE. Cream cock, very short in fibre.

Cream Spinner

This is a tying to represent the male spinners of the small and large spurwings, as these are two male spinners which fall spent on the water in fair quantities on some occasions. A small hook—o or oo (15 or 16) is suggested for the small pattern and a No. 1 (14) for the larger.

TYING SILK. Cream.

TAIL. Pale blue dun cock hackle fibres.

BODY. Baby seal's fur—cream.

WINGS. Tips of two small pale blue dun cock hackles, or hackle fibres, tied spent.
HACKLE. Cream cock hackle—two turns only.

Pink Spinner

Another pattern which represents the spinner of the large female spurwing. A rather uncommon fly, but a very useful pattern to have at the right time.

HOOK. 0 or 1 (14 or 15).
TAIL. Fibres from a white or cream cock hackle.
BODY. Cellulite floss No. 219, pink.
RIB. One D.F.M. fluorescent filament—orange.
WINGS. Tips of two small pale blue dun cock hackles, or hackle fibres, tied spent.
HACKLE. Pale blue dun cock hackle—two turns only.

Large Spurwing Dun

Although this fly is not very common, when hatches do occur a representative pattern such as this can be of great assistance. It should be noted that a natural characteristic of this dun as it floats down is a tendency to spread its wings slightly. Therefore tying instructions for wings should be followed carefully.

HOOK. 0 or 1 (14 or 15).
TYING SILK. Cream.
TAIL. Fibres from a pale blue dun cock hackle.
BODY. Cream seal's fur.
WINGS. Palest starling wing, tied split to form a definite "V".
HACKLE. Pale olive cock hackle.

DEREK MOSELEY'S IRISH MAYFLIES

The advent of the mayfly hatch on the Irish Loughs is anticipated as eagerly each year as the hatch in England. One great difference, however, is that whereas the artificial fly has long been the recognised lure for the English streams, it has been customary to use the natural fly on the Loughs.

I personally have had no experience in Ireland, but Mr. Moseley, of W. Wickham, Kent, who has fished year after year in Ireland, has evolved three flies which kill fish on the Loughs, even when the natural is being refused.

He has very kindly passed on the dressings of these flies, together with the method of tying and the way to fish them.

Green Mayfly (Sub-imago): "Ginger"

This pattern has been used on all ordinary occasions when the greenfly is hatching, with definite success since 1939. It is appreciated that, to the human eye at any rate, this fly does not resemble a mayfly, but the fact remains that it is taken, apparently with relish, by trout during a greenfly hatch when other patterns are refused.

HOOK. No. 9 or 10 long shank.

TYING SILK. Olive.

WHISKS. Three cock pheasant tail fibres tied in cocked up at 45 deg. and varnished, and separated (1 in.).

BODY. Natural cream or white raffia, with gold rib.

BODY HACKLE. Deep golden dun cock.

WING HACKLES. One each, dyed deep golden dun cock and natural deep red cock.

Tie in body and body hackle as for "Female Spinner" (see below).

Prepare one of each type of the wing hackles, *including* some of the lower part where they go soft and dull. Lay the two hackles together with the red on top and tie in at eye. Wind tying silk back to body so that hackles are wound over it. Wind the two hackles together till the body is reached. Carry tying silk back through hackles and build up head and finish off. Varnish head. Part and trim the hackles underneath as for "Female Spinner", i.e. 90 deg.

Notes: In all the patterns the wing hackles will go on better if a layer of tying silk is wound on first. All hackle points not needed are, of course, cut off, after fastening down. The two hackles on the Green Mayfly will mix themselves as they are wound on, but it is better to make the golden hackle wider than the red.

Female Spinner (Imago): "Jimmy R"

Used with consistent results since 1935. Used when there is a genuine "fall" of spinner in the evenings, when the females blow or fly out from the bushes on their last journey, and are fully fertilised. This fly will float in quite a "chop"—often a necessity, as the flies sometimes go out quite a distance and do not always choose a flat calm to do it.

HOOK. No. 9 or 10 long shank.

WHISKS. Three cock pheasant tail fibres, tied in flat and varnished (1½ in.).

BODY. Natural cream or white raffia, with gold rib.

BODY HACKLE. White cock.

WING HACKLE. Rusty black cock hackle or dark iron blue cock hackle.

The body should be varnished with clear Cellire before winding the body hackle. Leave a good ⅛ in. between body and hook eye. The wing hackle is tied in at the eye and wound to the body. Finish off tying silk at eye; form a good "head", which should be well varnished. The hackle is then trimmed *underneath* the hook-shank to form a parting of 90 deg. The top half of the hackle is left untrimmed.

Male (Cock) Mayfly Spinner (Sub-imago): "Purple Tail"

This pattern has been used from 1948 onwards, and will also kill when a "fall" is taking place. Its main use, however, comes when on hot days or in sheltered corners during the day, the cock imago flies down to drink and gets trapped in the scum, generally well into the mayfly season. These flies get gathered in patches and when a fish finds them he will eat the lot, but will *not*, as a rule, look at any normal artificial. This fly is often quite good the morning after a big fall of spinner, when some of the previous night's spinner, utterly drowned and floating just under the surface, blow back into some spot and accumulate enough to attract a fish. The fly floats, or should be trimmed to float, *absolutely flush with the surface*, and for that reason is obviously unsuitable for use in open water when there is a good "lip" on the water, unless the light is very good or the angler has exceptional sight.

HOOK. No. 9 long shank.

WHISKS. Three cock pheasant tail fibres dyed purple, tied in flat, separated and varnished with clear Cellire ($1\frac{1}{2}$ in.).

BODY. Cream or white raffia with mauve waxed silk rib.

WING HACKLES. Two very large Andalusian or similar rusty brown cock hackles —with fibres about $\frac{3}{4}$ in. in length on each side of the stalk; i.e. $1\frac{1}{2}$ in. overall.

TYING SILK. Black or chocolate.

The two hackles should be wound and fixed in the "spent" position and they should occupy $\frac{1}{8}$ in. of the hook-shank. The fibres must be at absolute right-angles to the hook-shank, so that the fly floats flush with the water, held up by whisks and hackles.

THE W. J. GOLDING "WONDER WING" FLIES

These unusually winged flies were first brought to my notice by an article in the American magazine *Outdoor Life* in the April 1953 issue. Its author, Mr. William J. Golding, and the editor of the magazine, Mr. William E. Rae, very kindly gave their permission to bring this new method before the fly tyers of the U.K. through the columns of the *Fishing Gazette*. The article was published by the *Fishing Gazette* in August 1953.

I discovered consequently that several tyers in the U.K. knew of the method, but none denied the fact that it was Mr. Golding who introduced it. He first tied these flies in 1934, but it was not until 1953 that the results obtained by him and other anglers prompted him to let all anglers benefit from the idea.

The "Wonder Wings" has several unusual features. It can be fished with the wings in either the upright or the spent positions, the change being made simply by pressing the wings up or down. It can be fished wet and switched back to a dry fly with one or two false casts. The wings are remarkably sturdy; no amount of casting will split or fray them, and without the aid of a special hook the hackle can be wound in a plane parallel to the shank—"parachute" fashion.

My first impression after tying several of these flies was that the wings would be too stiff to be taken by a delicately feeding fish, but after trying out different kinds of feathers I came to the conclusion that by using the right mediums—durable, natural and "takeable" wings could be made. Moreover, they are simple to tie, and the following instructions, together with the drawings, should be quite sufficient to put the idea across.

Mr. Golding advocated the use of mallard breast and flank feathers for wings, dyed and undyed, and although as I said previously, they make a rather stiff wing, they are excellent feathers with which to practice, and should make very good mayfly wings.

The feathers used must have fibres of equal length each side of the centre quill, and they are prepared as is usual, by stripping off the fluffy fibres at the base. The fibres immediately below the part of the feather which forms the wing are also cut off, not stripped. This latter operation makes it easier to tie in and "cock" the wings. Fibres sufficiently far up the quill are then pulled downwards, so that the feather should now be as Fig. 1. When two feathers have been prepared in this manner they are held back to back to form a pair of wings as shown in Fig. 2. They are then tied in on top of the hook as are the wings of any other dry-fly, as Fig. 3. It is the tying of both the quill and the fibres which gives the "Wonder Wing" its remarkable strength.

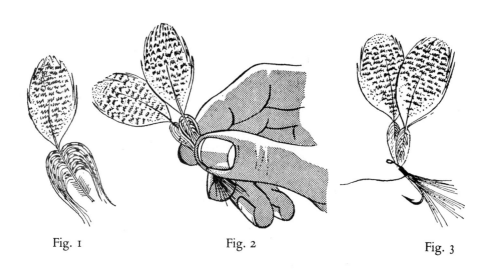

Fig. 1   Fig. 2   Fig. 3

To set the wings in the upright position, raise them up with the forefinger and thumb of the left hand, and then put several turns of silk round their base in a plane parallel to the shank. Another couple of turns close up to them, but this time round the hook itself, will ensure that they stay upright. The part of the feathers above the tied-in fibres are then cut off, and after forming the body, hackle and tail as required, the finished fly should be as Fig. 4.

Fig. 4

For a "parachute" type of fly, the hackle is wound round the base of the wings instead of the hook shank, making the fly appear as Fig. 5.

Fig. 5

For a wet fly, the feathers are tied in curving inwards instead of outwards, and left to slope over the body of the fly.

To make the wings less rigid, the part of the quill which is normally tied in with the fibres can be cut off, so that only the fibres are tied in. This wing is not as strong, of course, but is ideal for small dry-flies and wet-flies.

If the wings are wanted in the spent position, they are pressed between the finger and thumb. They can be put back to the upright position by pressing them together again.

Now for materials for these wings. The best ones to use are those with a fine centre quill and long fibres. One of the best I have used is the largest of the partridge flank feathers, which range from 2 to 4 in. in length. When used as near to the tip as possible, a fine mottled wing results, ideal for a "March Brown" and also for mayflies when dyed. The realistic veined appearance is highlighted by the transparency of the centre that runs through the wing vertically, with the stem showing through this.

Surprisingly enough, the centre quills of hens' hackles are often stiffer than those of cocks, especially in the very large sizes. The best ones come from capes of hackles taken from cocks which have not reached full maturity. They are found at the back of the cape, intermixed with the largest pointed hackles, and although they look very much like hens' hackles, they are much softer in the quill. These feathers are ideal, of course, if dyed colours are required for wings of the "Blue Dun", "Iron Blue", etc.

No doubt many fly tyers have feathers in their collections which they may consider even more ideal for this type of wing, and I quote Mr. Ray Bergman, fishing editor of *Outdoor Life*, and taken from his comments on the "Wonder Wing". "Some fine new designs should result from the introduction of the 'Wonder Wing'. Even if you belong to the school of anglers who think that wings are unimportant, I believe you will find that these wings do make the fly look different to the fish as well as to the angler."

Since the *Fishing Gazette* published the article there have been several items of correspondence with regard to these flies, none of which had anything detrimental to say about the results obtained. There also appeared another article in *Outdoor Life* in June 1954, giving a graphic account of the successes obtained with these flies on Irish lake and sea trout.

On one of the occasions described one "Royal Coachman" accounted for twenty-three trout and one pike, before wear and tear on one wing put it out of commission.

JOHN JOE HALPIN'S "HALPIN"

This fly shared first prize in a fly-tying competition in Eire, not only for the way it was tied, but also on its merit as a killing pattern.

Although mainly a salmon fly it is good in all sizes down to size 12 for trout, and is particularly good in peaty-coloured conditions.

TAG. Oval silver tinsel.

TAIL. None.

BUTT. Red wool teased out, or seal's fur.

BODY. Black floss silk.

RIB. Oval silver tinsel.

BODY HACKLE. Dyed bright red cock.

FRONT HACKLE. White cock.

WING. Fibres from a cock pheasant tail, with grey mallard flank over.

HEAD. Red varnish.

THE REV. E. POWELL'S SERIES OF FLIES FOR ROUGH STREAMS

Although these patterns were not sent to me personally, it would be amiss to leave them out from a selection of dressings such as this. I get many requests for the dressings, so I am very happy to make a permanent record of them here.

The flies were designed for use in even the roughest of waters, and to attract non-rising fish. Therefore they should be tied as a good "mouthful", and with plenty of hackling to keep them afloat. The patterns are meant to impersonate groups of insects rather than a specific one, and in all cases the hook is size 16 long shanked.

No. 1: "The Paragon" (suggesting sedge flies)

BODY. From rabbit's face.

RIB. Fine oval gold tinsel.

HACKLES. Two dark red hen's hackles, the dark liver colour found in some specimens. About ten turns—well pressed together.

TAIL WHISKS. Four fibres from a stiff natural dark red cock hackle, preferably from a spade feather.

No. 2: "The Doctor" (suggesting Coleoptera or beetles).

BODY. Black rabbit fur from tail or foot.

RIB. None.

TAG. Fibres from a swan primary dyed yellow, or any fur dyed yellow.

HACKLE. One large Coch-y-bondhu hackle, at least ten turns. The diameter of the hackle should be about 1 in. when wound.

TAIL. Fibres from a stiff Coch-y-bondhu hackle.

No. 3:

Same as "The Doctor", but with black hackle and tail whisks, and a hot orange tag.

No. 4: "The Black Spot" (suggesting gnats and midges)

BODY. A roundish bead of black rabbit fur no longer than $\frac{1}{4}$ in., and wound close up to the hackle.

HACKLE. Fairly long cock (white), dyed dark green drake colour.

No. 5: The "Ermine Moth" (suggesting the Lepidoptera or moths)

This dressing is given on page 129, as are several other good moth representations. It is also illustrated between pages 80 and 81.

No. 6: The "Small Harry" (suggesting the lesser crane fly)

TAIL. Fibres from a red cock hackle.

BODY. Rabbit's face or hare's ear.

RIB. Fine gold oval tinsel.

HACKLES. First—a stiff natural red cock's hackle, with a brown partridge back feather in the front.

This is also a good dressing for a "March Brown".

THE FRANK SAWYER NYMPHS

Frank Sawyer, through his broadcasting, books, and articles in the angling press, must be one of the best-known "moderns", and has produced several original patterns which are now regarded by many as standard. He is the keeper on a well-known stretch of the Wiltshire Avon, and has made a lifetime study of the trout stream.

He is best known for his series of nymph patterns, which are outstanding in simplicity, and with his kind permission I have much pleasure in giving his dressings here.

The "Pheasant Tail" Nymph

Undoubtedly the best known and most successful of the series, and primarily a pattern for rivers.

HOOK. 16–12.

Material for tails, body and wing cases—cock pheasant centre tail fibres, and fine copper wire. The cock pheasant tail should be from a mature bird with the edges of the tail as deep a red as possible. The wire should also approximate this colouring.

Construction: the copper wire is wound on to the hook to form a core for the body, and should represent the shape of the nymph, i.e., a hump to represent thorax, and then tapering to the tail. This acts as ballast and general appearance.

Take four fibres from the cock pheasant tail, and tie them in with wire so that the tips of the fibres form the tail whisks. Now wind both wire and feather fibres evenly up to the eye of the hook. Fasten with one turn of the wire, then lap the feather fibres backwards—forwards—then backwards again, to form the characteristic nymph "hump at the thorax". The wire is not used during the lapping, but should be kept separate from the fibres and just brought backwards or forwards as the case may be, to secure each lap of the fibres. The finish should be made with two half hitches of the wire behind the eye of the hook.

No hackle is used, and it will be observed that it is possible to make this pattern without the use of tying silk either! In spite of its simplicity this is one of the most popular and successful patterns ever evolved.

Pale Watery Nymph

HOOK. No. 15.

TAIL FIBRES. Four or five fibres of ginger cock hackle.

BODY. Fawny pink darning wool (about one-third of a strand) and plain (unvarnished) copper wire.

THORAX. Wood Pigeon primary feather.

Construction: as for "P.T." nymph, except that the feather fibres for the thorax must be added after the wool and wire have been wound to the eye of the hook.

"Spurwing" Nymph

HOOK. 16–14.

TAIL FIBRES. Tips of fibres used for body.

BODY. Three fibres of browny-yellow condor wing, and same colour wire as used for "P.T." nymph.

THORAX. Same fibres as used for body, but the copper wire should be cut off at completion of body and replaced with gold wire.

Finish off with about twelve windings of the gold wire, then cut off all spare as usual.

"Grey Goose" Nymph

HOOK. 15–12.

TAIL. Tips of fibres used for the body.

BODY. Pale grey goosefibres and same copper wire as used for "P.T." nymph. The correct shade of grey goose feather is very rare, so Mr. Sawyer recommends that the wing feathers of swan be used—dyed light grey. Use four or five fibres.

Construction: exactly the same as "P.T." nymph.

"S.S." Nymph

This was evolved for use on the lakes in northern Sweden, and has proved to be a very good pattern elsewhere also. "S.S." stands for "Sawyer Swedish" or as an abbreviation of the Latin name of the nymph S. Spinosis.

HOOK. 13–10.

TAIL. Tips of fibres used for body.

BODY. Dark grey goose and same copper wire (red) as used for "P.T." and "G.G." nymphs.

Construction: exactly the same as for these two nymphs.

"Grayling Lure"

The simplest of the patterns. This "bug" was evolved for killing grayling on the Avon, where it proved very deadly, and is very good indeed for reservoir fishing.

HOOK. 13–12 for rivers—up to 10 for reservoir fishing.

TAILS. None.

BODY. Fawny-pink darning wool (Chadwick's 477), and fuze wire, using a thickness of wire most suited to the hook size.

Construction: first a double layer of wire as ballast, then a treble layer of the wool lapped on very tightly. Finish by making a treble winding at the hook end, which will ensure a neat and secure finish.

Comment: all the nymphs change colour when wet, with strong translucent effects. The hairy fibres of both the feathers and wool retain tiny air bubbles when submerged, and in this respect alone the imitations appear very natural when sinking or moving horizontally through the water. When natural nymphs are moving through the water the legs are held close to the body, and this is the reason the hackle is omitted in these patterns. The tails however, although short, should be fairly substantial, as the tail of the nymph is its propulsion unit.

THE TONY LEIGH PATTERNS FOR RESERVOIR FISHING

Tony Leigh is a director of a progressive plastics manufacturing plant, and it will be observed from his dressings that he has applied his knowledge in this field to the making of his fishing flies.

He has been a fisherman most of his life, strictly for trout since the late 1950's, and his experiments for these patterns were carried out on Blythfield reservoir.

He began fishing the reservoir, like most of us, with standard lake patterns, but discovered (also like most of us) that there were many days proving blank when conditions were absolutely right, including rises.

The three patterns given are for use under completely different conditions which are as follows:

1. Chironomid hatch—imitation of *chironomus tentans* or "shushmak" as it is sometimes called ("Copper Lad").
2. When there is no rise at all and something is required to draw the fish from the bottom ("Black Sambo").
3. When trout are attacking fry ("Leigh's Fry").

Copper Lad

HOOK. No. 11 round bend.

BODY. Black tying silk foundation of approximately .050 in. average thickness and slightly tapered, and dressed half-way round bend.

RIB. Copper "Lurex" tinsel wound with a gap of approximately $\frac{1}{64}$ in. between the turns. The body is then covered with plastic skin (obtainable from any chemist), and rubbed over with Sanford's orange marker pen No. 500. These pens are felt tipped.

THORAX. This is a ball of black turkey tail herl about .10 in. in diameter, using about three strands tied in point first. Twist with tying silk and wind into true ball shape. Hold the ball shape by tying it in two or three times over with figure-of-eight windings.

HACKLE. Black hen with fibres about $\frac{1}{2}$ in. long. Strip hackle along one side and make one turn only, so that you get nine or ten fibres. Twist these fibres vigorously between thumb and forefinger so that you get a "knees and ankles" effect which is most lifelike.

Comment: I don't know why this fly is so successful, because it is not a correct colour, but I have caught over a hundred trout with it this year at Blythfield during "shushmak" rises; when much more exact imitations on the same cast have caught only occasional fish. I believe it is the fact that just before the chironomids hatch, the pupa takes air into its shuck and becomes "iridescent banded"; it may be this that is so irresistible. This is more particularly a killer in the early part of the season, as later on the trout seem to prefer a more exact imitation.

The "Copper Lad", as with all nymphs, should not be tugged through the water in the traditional loch manner, but allowed to fall naturally like the real pupa descending to the bottom again after an abortive attempt to hatch. It is only good when cast speedily to a rising fish.

"Copper Lad"

Black Sambo

This is a "stoat tail" tube fly with a jungle-cock throat, and is dressed as follows:

BODY. $\frac{1}{2}$ in. or $\frac{3}{4}$ in. plastic tube, left plain.

WING. Stoat tail hairs—$1\frac{1}{4}$ in. long on $\frac{1}{2}$ in. tube, $1\frac{3}{4}$ in. long on $\frac{3}{4}$ in. tube. The hairs should be tied on to a bed of tying silk so that they cock right, i.e. if the bed is too small you get a triangle of hairs which is unnatural, and if it is too big the hairs are too parallel with the body. Something in between is required.

CHEEKS. Small jungle-cock feathers.

Comment: I have fished it seems, for ever "into the Blue", but if trout are not rising you can't win with artificial insects—I think you have to do something desperate to draw them off the bottom. Black Sambo is very successful in doing this. It is not a new fly to salmon fishing, but not many use it for trout, which they should, for it's a good fly when nothing is rising; it's good to smutting fish and also when they are taking fry on the surface at dusk. In fact, it is the best all-rounder I know.

"Black Sambo"

Leigh's Fry

HOOK LENGTHS. $\frac{1}{2}$ in., $\frac{3}{4}$ in., and 1 in. long shank down eye.

Procedure:

1. Grip the bend of the hook in a pair of hackle pliers.
2. Hold it for about five seconds one or two inches over the top of a gas cooker flame.
3. Plunge the hook into Polythene Sintering Powder just short of the hackle pliers (so you do not fill them with plastic also).

4. Return to one or two inches above the flame and turn it about so that it does not catch fire. (If it does catch fire, withdraw the hook and blow it out.) Carry on over the flame until the plastic is shiny, more or less smoothed and obviously melted.

5. Return to the powder and do this two or three times until the hook is sufficiently covered, and make sure that it adheres evenly.
   Note: If the body is now not transparent but "smoky" it has been burnt in the flame. If the plastic coating is uneven it needs more heat treatment.

6. While the body is still hot, drop it on to a sheet of P.T.F.E. plastic material. Bend the sheet over and gently mould to shape—more or less oval, but bigger in silhouette at the head than the tail. This is the time you get the shape of the "fry", and the operation should be carried out slowly, so that the plastic body has time to harden. Leave to cool for about three minutes and then take it out of the P.T.F.E. sheet.

7. With a razor blade cut the shape more perfectly and clean the "eye" of the hook and about one tenth of the shank at the front.

8. Return to gas flame to smooth cut edges.

9. Wind on white tying silk at the front and tie on small jungle-cock feathers to simulate the head of the fry. See illustration. A drop of tacky varnish should be put on each shoulder to ensure that the jungle-cock lies flat.

10. Varnish the tying silk with clear varnish.

"Leigh's Fry"

Comment: "Leigh's Fry" will consistently take trout when they are attacking fry. The best way to recognise this distinctive rise is to observe when the trout rise recklessly for five seconds or so and then disappear altogether for a couple of minutes. The reason for this peculiarity is that the fry sun themselves in the surface film and when a sufficient number have spread themselves out, the trout rush at them and disperse them.

If one or two artificials are thrown to them they should be left to drop naturally and not tugged through the water.

"Leigh's Fry" does not seem to me to be any good at any other time except when the trout are taking fry, but it really works like magic about June and July, fished round the reed margins to rising fish.

Final comment: Tests carried out with these three patterns under circumstances detailed at the beginning, resulted in 235 fish from forty-eight visits—usually evenings only, and not full-day sessions.

L. R. N. GRAY'S "SILVER INVICTA" FOR SALMON AND SEWIN

Mr. Gray must be one of the most experienced salmon fishermen in the West Country, and has made many contributions to our knowledge through the columns of the angling press.

Consequently, his "Invicta" dressing for salmon and sewin, and the notes on its use, must be of interest to anglers when they come up against the conditions he describes.

"In the recent high water in Towy—I have been doing well with large sewin and the odd salmon—fishing a No. 4 Low-Water 'Silver Invicta' tied long, and lightly. Fish are scarce where I fish (they run through) and anglers are many, but it is 'fly only'.

"My best hour with this fly in highish clear water between 10 and 11 a.m. was one salmon 13 lb., and four sewin 3–5 lb. on a 10 ft. trout rod with *ungreased* forward taper line to sink fly well. I carry this line on a spare reel and use it with this fly when fish are not showing—fished deep and slowly. It does very well by day in high or fairly high water, and also at night after dusk when fish go down. Of course, I fish the dusk rise with a semi-floating line and the usual sea-trout flies.

"A short dressed low-water hook is not too good, except in fairly fast water. Ditto an ordinary salmon hook of equal length. Although the latter will fish deeper—it would not fish level some of the time when fished slowly in slowish water. A No. 4 low-water hook dressed long and slinky seems the most useful size —sometimes varied with a No. 2 or a No. 6."

TAG. Four turns of fine silver tinsel above barb, or at least over hook point.

TAIL. Golden pheasant crest and tip of an Indian crow feather.

BODY. Flat silver tinsel—as slim as possible.

RIB. Fine oval silver.

BODY HACKLE. Rhode Island Red cock hackle. Stripped one side, and starting about one-third up body from tail.

SHOULDER HACKLE. Two turns of the body hackle. Do not slope the fibres back more than slightly, and they should project well out from the sides.

NO. 2. FRONT HACKLE. Turn fly upside down and tie in a $\frac{1}{4}$ in. wide web of blue jay feather. (A "false hackle" as described on page 37.) Adjust the web to a fan shape and cut off surplus. Half-hitch and turn fly back right way up. The fibres of the shoulder hackle will keep the jay fibres splayed out.

WING. A $\frac{1}{4}$ in. width is now taken from each side of a hen pheasant centre tail and then divided in half. The four halves are then placed on top of each other to form a flat wing $\frac{1}{8}$ in. wide. This is now placed on edge and tied on top of the hook in the usual way. It should lie as close to the body as possible, and the tip should reach to the tip of the tail.

When using a No. 2 low-water hook it is usually found that the hen pheasant tail fibres are not long enough to reach the tip of the tail. The wing is then varied by including a very slim tuft of grey squirrel tail as a core to the wing already described using single strips only. This size is only used in highly coloured water, and can be improved by adding small jungle-cock cheeks—tied in to stick out slightly to resemble gill coves.

The head, of course, is the usual black varnish.

H. WESTMORLAND'S THREE FOR RIVER, LAKE AND SEA TROUT

1. Kingsmill

TAIL. Golden pheasant crest.
BODY. Black ostrich herl.
RIB. Silver wire.
HACKLE. Black cock.
WING. From rook wing quill, rolled and tied low over body.
CHEEKS. Jungle cock.
Topping over all—golden pheasant crest.

2. Claret Bumble

TAIL. Golden pheasant tippet fibres.
BODY. Claret seal's fur.
RIB. Oval gold tinsel.
BODY HACKLES. Black cock and claret cock, wound together.
FRONT HACKLE. Blue jay, slightly longer in fibre than the body hackles.

3. Black Robin

TAG. Fine flat gold tinsel.
No body, but a black cock hackle wound "palmer" which is then trimmed like a bottle brush.
This is fished dry on hot summer days.

RICHARD WALKER'S HATCHING MAYFLY NYMPH

There can be few anglers who have not heard of Richard Walker and his valuable contributions to the "know-how" of carp catching. His record-breaking 44-pounder is still swimming happily in the London Zoo at the time of writing.

What some of them are not aware of is his work in the field of fly fishing and fly design, particularly where mayflies are concerned.

One unusual pattern he designed which has been tried, tested, and found good, is an imitation of the mayfly emerging from its nymphal shuck, and is included here as a tribute to his work in general and his ingenuity in particular.

HOOK. Down eye, long shanked, fine wire, No. 10.
TYING SILK. Olive.
TAIL. Three short fibres from a cock pheasant tail.

BODY AND THORAX. Four strands of Cellulite rayon floss, shades 228 and 229. Do not paint hook-shank white as is customary with this type of floss.
RIBS. Fine gold wire, round body only.
WING CASES. (Over thorax.) Fibres from a black hen wing quill.
WING. Equal quantities of fibres from large white hen hackles which have been dyed pale green and blue dun.
THROAT HACKLE. A small grouse hackle.

The hackle-fibre wing should be tied in before the wing cases are tied down at the head of the fly, and all the fibres brought above the hook-shank and fixed by making figure-of-eight turns underneath the hook-shank. The wing cases are then divided in the middle, and each half taken round the outside of the upright wing. Tie in wing cases at eye and cut off surplus.

The result is a nymph pattern as we usually know it, with a "shaving brush" tuft of hackle fibres protruding from the wing cases to give the emerging nymph effect.

H. A. J. FETHERSTONHAUGH'S B.W.O. SPINNER ("SHERRY SPINNER")

This is a killing pattern of fly that we all find very difficult to imitate, and it will also take fish at other times.
WHISKS. From cream badger cock hackle, with black tips.
BODY. Claret fur dubbed very lightly, and put loosely on silk so that it spreads and is really translucent.
HACKLE. Badger cock with lightly marked centre—and not more than two turns.
TYING SILK. Orange.
HOOK. 14–16.

THE DAVID JACQUES "BLUE WINGED OLIVE"

As all chalk-stream dry-fly anglers know, the "Blue Winged Olive" and Skues' "Orange Quill" have been synonymous for years, but in view of the fact that this pattern was so unlike the natural fly, David Jacques spent many seasons studying this phenomenon. He came to the conclusion, after much painstaking research, that the "Orange Quill" was taken for the sherry spinner, and when the sherry spinner is absent from a B.W.O. rise the "Orange Quill" is always refused.

This describes the position but briefly, and a full account of the work of Mr. Jacques was given in *The Field* of 18 December 1958, under the heading "Challenge to the Orange Quill".
TAIL. Fibres from a dark dirty olive cock hackle.
BODY. Clear plastic dyed in picric acid over ostrich herl dyed light yellow.
WINGS. Two pairs from wing feathers of a coot.
HACKLE. Dark dirty olive cock hackle.

TYING SILK. Hot orange.

HOOK. No. 14.

The plastic sheet should be immersed in the acid for about an hour, and then cut into thin strips about ⅛ in. wide. The end to be tied in should be tapered to prevent "bunching" and the strip stretched lengthwise to narrow it still further.

ALEC ILES "BREATHERLIZER"

Mr. Iles developed this fly specially for Chew Valley lake, and freely admits that it was of Canadian origin. It is supposed to represent the stickleback, and when seen actually in the water, it is as fair an imitation as one would want to see.

The fly must be fished fast, casting a long line and stripping as fast as one can—a long retrieve with one's left hand, holding the line on the rod handle with the right index finger. It is not necessary to fish the fly deep, but no doubt this would produce results if no fish were showing.

To obtain the best results, a "Worm Fly" should be used on the bob, either a "Silver Invicta" or a "Dunkeld" on the middle dropper, and the "Breatherlizer" on the tail *always*.

Included with the instructions Mr. Iles sent me was a photograph of seventeen fish taken at Chew Magna on 1 August 1960, 1 Brown of 3 lb. 4 oz., the remainder Rainbows ranging from 2½ lb. to 3 lb.

TAIL. Fibres from a soft black cock or hen's hackle.

BODY. Flat silver tinsel.

RIB. None.

WINGS. Two hot orange cock hackles, with two Green Highlander hackles outside, streamer style.

"EYES". Jungle cock tied close to head.

HACKLE. Badger. Wound as a collar as above.

HEAD. Black varnish.

HOOK. No. 6–8 down eyed.

A. J. HAYTOR MIDGE PUPA DRESSINGS

Mr. Haytor gave the following four dressings in an article he wrote containing details of fishing at Sutton Bingham reservoir. I have used them myself on water far removed from Sutton Bingham, and can vouch for them from personal experience. I had two fish over two pounds in less than an hour, at Ham Bridge Lake, the Piscatorial Society's water near Newbury.

The dressings are quite simple, but the underbody of silver is essential, and the thorax should be made large and round.

Black Pupa
HOOK. 12–14.
TYING SILK. Black.
UNDERBODY. Flat silver tinsel.
BODY. Black floss.
RIB. Silver wire.
THORAX. Black seal's fur.
HACKLE. Peacock herl with long "flue".

Olive Pupa
HOOK. 16–13.
TYING SILK. Olive.
UNDERBODY. Flat silver tinsel.
BODY. Olive floss.
RIB. Gold wire.
THORAX. Olive seal's fur, with a little brown wool mixed in.
HACKLE. Olive ostrich herl.

Brown Pupa
HOOK. 12–14.
TYING SILK. Brown.
UNDERBODY. Flat silver tinsel.
BODY. Brown (lightish) floss silk.
RIB. Gold wire.
THORAX. Orangy-brown seal's fur.
HACKLE. Orangy-brown ostrich herl.

Red Pupa
HOOK. 12–14.
TYING SILK. Scarlet.
UNDERBODY. Flat silver tinsel
BODY. Scarlet floss.
RIB. Gold wire.
THORAX. Red and brown seal's fur mixed.
HACKLE. Brown ostrich herl.

THE A. B. BOURNE "PINK PERIL"

The dressing of the dry-fly was introduced to me by Mr. Bourne in 1958, and no doubt readers would be interested in his comments. "Certainly mention the 'Pink Peril' in your new book. You know how I tried some and thought the colouring *too* awful. How, when I could not move a fish on my little chalk stream, I tried one and immediately got rises *and* fish. Whether even with flies, it pays to have one that advertises itself, I do not know. Anyhow it catches brown trout and sea trout—between 900 and 1,000 to date!!

"It is essential that the fly be tied with a fat succulent body, and plain D.F.M. silk seems to be more attractive than silk to which varnish has been applied. The fly has also been tied tube style using varnished raffia instead of cork. Both solid cork and strips of cork have been used. It may be that there is some better base material for the fat body?"

HOOK. No. 14 fine wire, long shank.
TAIL. Ibis or substitute.
BODY. Fat cork body covered with pink D.F.M. floss.
HACKLE. Light red-game cock.

THE LATE WILLIAM BANNERMAN COLLECTION OF PATTERNS

In addition to the very interesting and constructive contribution to the section on fluorescent materials, Mr. Bannerman placed a very fine list of trout, sea-trout and salmon flies at my disposal.

Some of them were the result of Mr. Bannerman's long experience as a fisherman and fly tyer, and some from an old notebook which once belonged to a retired gillie who spent all his days on a beat on the middle reaches of the River Spey. The dressings in the book were given to the gillie's father and himself by various personalities very well known in the angling world, and when this applies the name is given alongside the dressing concerned. Although some of these patterns have familiar names, it will be observed that most of them differ in some detail from the accepted standard patterns.

I am giving the patterns here exactly as they were listed by Mr. Bannerman, and with no alteration whatsoever.

SEA-TROUT AND TROUT PATTERNS

Grey Monkey
TAIL. Teal fibres long.
BODY. First third gold wool remainder grey monkey fur or grey wool, rough spun.
RIB. Gold oval.
HACKLE. Light grey dun hen.
WING. Lightest starling or few strands of inside widgeon secondary.
CHEEKS. Jungle cock.
HOOK. 14–12 doubles.

Green Monkey
TAIL. G.P. topping short.
BODY. One turn green wool remainder grey monkey fur or wool.
RIB. Gold oval.
HACKLE. Green Highlander.
WING. Lightest starling.
CHEEKS. Jungle cock.
HOOK. 14–12 doubles.

Murray's Bluebottle Spider
TAIL. Black hackle fibres.
BODY. Green Lurex flat.
HACKLE. Black hen.
HOOK. 16–12 singles.

Double Black and Silver (or Delphi)
TAIL. Two very small jungle cock back to back.
BODY. Flat silver tinsel.
HACKLES. Black hen tied in at head and half-way down body.
HOOK. From 12 singles and doubles upwards.

Variations. Equally effective in gold floss silk or tinsel, orange floss silk, etc. Double hackle flies can be made in many variations; practically all hackle patterns lend themselves to this method of tying.

SALMON FLY PATTERNS

Stoat's Tail
BODY. Black floss.
RIBS. Silver or gold oval tinsel (silver preferably).
HACKLE. Black cock hackle tied underneath only, sparse.

WING. Stoat's tail or black squirrel.
HEAD. Black.
HOOK. All sizes.

Stoat Tail Variations
As above with silver or gold wire tag.

Stoat Tail Variations

As above with topping and silver or gold wire tag.

As above, but with dark claret floss silk body. Claret becomes nearly black when wet.

As above, but with the black silk rolled in fine particles of D.F.M. which gives the body an olive flash.

Stewart's Killer

TAIL. 5 or 6 R.I. Red Hackle fibres, long and sharp.

BODY. Flat silver tinsel ribbed gold wire.

HACKLE. R.I. Red hackle fibres, sparse and tied underneath only.

WING. Stoat's tail or black squirrel.

CHEEKS. Jungle cock.

HEAD. Black.

HOOK. From 12 L.W. doubles upwards.

Stewart's Killer Variations

As above, but with hot orange hackle.

As above, but with blue hackle.

As above, but with green Highlander hackle.

As above, but with yellow hen hackle.

The Original Stewart's Killer Tie may be as follows: Tail, G.P. topping—Body, flat silver tinsel ribbed silver wire—Hackle, R.I. Red hen—Wing, bronzed mallard —J.C. cheeks.

Hairy Mary

TAIL. G.P. topping.

BODY. Black floss silk.

RIB. Silver oval or gold oval.

HACKLE. Mid or dark blue hen hackle tied underneath only.

WING. Bucktail natural.

HEAD. Black.

HOOK. All sizes from 12 L.W. upwards.

(There is a Hairy Mary tie used on the Nith and Tweed districts quite different from above.)

Professor Cash

TAIL. Bronze mallard long (four strands).

BODY. Hare's lug and brown flax mixed.

RIB. Fine flat gold (or silver).

HACKLE. Medium R.I. Red.

WING. Well-marked woodcock.

HOOK. Size 12 upwards.

Bourach

BODY. Embossed silver tinsel.

HACKLE. Blue bucktail light or mid shades.

WING. Yellow or primrose bucktail.

HOOK. Size 6 singles or larger.

Bill's Olive

TAIL. Ibis three strands.

BODY. Yellow wool or seal's fur.

RIB. Gold oval.

HACKLE. Yellow hen "palmer" tied.

WING. Mink or dun shade of squirrel.

CHEEKS. Jungle cock, long.

HOOK. Sizes 6 and larger.

Olive Drab

TAG. Gold wire.

TAIL. Three strands of teal sloping downwards.

BODY. Well-teased-out olive brown wool or seal's fur.

RIB. Gold oval tinsel.

HACKLE. Black.

WING. Bronzed mallard.

HOOK. Size 8 doubles upwards.

Tugnet
BODY. Black floss silk thinly applied.
RIB. Gold oval tinsel.
HACKLE. Few strands of hot orange hackle covered with golden olive hen hackle, tied underneath only.
WING. Black squirrel or stoat's tail.
HEAD. Black.
HOOK. 12–10 L.W. doubles.

Dallochy
TAIL. G.P. topping.
BODY. Golden olive seal's fur or rough wool, dubbed and twisted round.

RIBS. Gold tinsel, tinsel showing irregularly.
HACKLE. Light blue full length of body.
WING. Darkest bronzed mallard with G.P. crest over.
HEAD. Black.
HOOK. Size 6 singles and larger.

Bill's Badger
BODY. Black silk thinly spun on shank.
RIB. Narrow flat silver evenly spaced.
HACKLE. Dark blue underneath only.
WING. Well-marked badger hair wing full length of body.

PATTERNS FROM NOTEBOOK

The Black Doctor (Wright)
TAG. Silver twist and yellow silk.
TAIL. Topping and chatterer.
BUTT. Scarlet Berlin wool.
BODY. Black silk ribbed oval silver tinsel.
HACKLE. Blue from second turn of tinsel.
THROAT. Blue jay.
WINGS. Tippet in strands, pintail, dark mottled turkey, blue and yellow swan, red macaw, gallina, golden pheasant tail, mallard with topping over all.
HORNS. Blue macaw.
CHEEKS. Chatterer.
HEAD. Scarlet Berlin wool.

The Blue Charm (W. Brown)
TAG. Silver twist.
TAIL. Topping.
BODY. Scarlet silk ribbed oval silver tinsel.
THROAT. Blue hackle.
WINGS. Broad strips of mallard covered strips of teal, topping over all.
HEAD. Black wool.

The Bruce (Colonel Bruce)
TAG. Silver twist, full.

TAIL. Topping.
BUTT. Black herl.
BODY. Silver tinsel, ribbed oval silver.
HACKLE. Claret from second turn.
THROAT. Gallina.
WINGS. Silver mottled turkey, golden pheasant tail.
HORNS. Blue macaw.
HEAD. Black wool.

The Butcher (Jewhurst)
TAG. Silver twist and yellow silk.
TAIL. Topping, teal and blue macaw.
BUTT. Black herl.
BODY. Seal's fur; light red claret; light blue; dark red claret; and dark blue.
RIBS. Silver tinsel.
HACKLE. Black from light claret.
THROAT. Yellow hackle and gallina.
WINGS. Tippet; golden pheasant breast feathers, back to back; veiled with teal; golden pheasant tail; gallina; bustard; peacock; yellow parrot and swan; mallard.
HORNS. Blue macaw.
CHEEKS. Chatterer.

The Candlestick Maker (Holbrow)

TAG. Silver tinsel, fine oval.
TAIL. Ibis and summer duck.
BODY. Three turns of black silk followed by black seal's fur.
RIBS. Silver tinsel.
HACKLE. Dark fiery brown from second turn.
WINGS. Double jungle cock and two toppings.
HEAD. Black wool.

The Carron Fly

BODY. Orange Berlin wool short.
RIBS. Silver tinsel.
HACKLE. Black heron from end of body.
WINGS. Mallard showing brown points and light roots.

The Chalmers (David Murray)

TAG. Silver twist and yellow silk.
TAIL. Topping.
BUTT. Black herl.
BODY. Magenta silk.
RIBS. Silver tinsel equally spaced.
THROAT. Magenta hackle.
WINGS. Two strips of dark mottled turkey showing white tips, and topping.
CHEEKS. Jungle cock.
HEAD. Two turns of magenta silk.

The Clark (W. Garden)

TAG. Silver Twist.
TAIL. Topping.
BUTT. Black herl.
BODY. Dark blue silk.
RIBS. Oval silver tinsel.
THROAT. Teal and gallina.
WINGS. Tippet fibres; mallard with two narrow strips of summer duck above.

The Cluny (W. Garden)

TAG. Silver twist.

TAIL. A topping and scarlet ibis.
BODY. Black silk.
RIBS. Oval silver tinsel.
THROAT. Gallina.
WINGS. Teal.

The Cromarty (Holbrow)

TAG. Silver twist and yellow silk.
TAIL. Toucan.
BUTT. Black herl.
BODY. Black silk.
RIBS. Silver tinsel.
HACKLE. Black from second turn.
THROAT. Gallina dyed blue.
WINGS. Two tippets back to back; veiled with bustard; mallard and topping.
SIDES. Yellow and blue dyed swan.
HEAD. Black wool.

The Dallas Fly (Dallas)

BODY. Three turns of yellow Berlin wool, followed by black wool.
RIBS. Silver tinsel, gold tinsel, narrow oval, red and blue silk, all equal distances apart.
HACKLE. Black cock's.
THROAT. Red golden pheasant's breast.
WINGS. Two strips of plain cinnamon turkey.
HEAD. Orange wool picked out.

The Duke (Kelson)

TAG. Silver twist and yellow silk.
TAIL. A topping.
BODY. Light red fiery brown seal's fur.
RIBS. Silver tinsel.
THROAT. Widgeon and jay.
WINGS. Strands of tippet; grey mallard; summer duck; mallard and topping.
SIDES. Jungle cock.
HEAD. Black herl.

The Dunkeld (W. J. Davidson)

TAG. Gold twist and orange silk.

TAIL. Topping and point of jungle cock.
BUTT. Black herl.
BODY. Gold tinsel.
RIBS. Gold tinsel oval.
HACKLE. Orange second turn.
THROAT. Jay.
WINGS. Two strips of peacock wing, mallard and topping.
HORNS. Blue and red macaw.
CHEEKS. Chatterer.

The Durham Ranger (G. S. Wright)

TAG. Silver twist and yellow silk.
TAIL. Topping and Indian crow.
BUTT. Black herl.
BODY. Two turns of orange silk, two turns of dark orange seal's fur, the rest, which is about half, black seal's fur.
RIBS. Silver lace and silver round tinsel.
HACKLE. A white Coch-y-bondhu dyed orange, running along the furs.
THROAT. Light blue hackle.
WINGS. Four tippets overlapping (two on each side) and enveloping two projecting jungle cock (back to back) and a topping.
CHEEKS. Chatterer.
HORNS. Blue macaw.
HEAD. Black Berlin wool.

The Dusty Miller (Jewhurst)

TAG. Silver twist and yellow silk.
TAIL. Topping and Indian crow.
BUTT. Black herl.
BODY. Silver tinsel embossed two thirds: orange silk.
RIBS. Silver tinsel oval.
THROAT. Gallina.
WINGS. Two strips of black turkey white tipped, golden pheasant tail, bustard, pintail, gallina, mallard and one topping.
SIDES. Jungle cock.
HORNS. Macaw.

The Gold Judge (Turnbull)

TAG. Gold twist and yellow silk.
TAIL. Topping and blue chatterer.
BUTT. Peacock herl.
BODY. Gold tinsel.
RIBS. Gold tinsel oval.
HACKLE. Olive green, second turn.
THROAT. Fiery brown, jay.
WINGS. Cinnamon turkey, pintail, swan, yellow and red, summer duck, and two toppings.
HORNS. Blue macaw.
HEAD. Black herl.

The Gold Riach (Riach)

BODY. Orange Berlin wool three turns, followed by black wool.
RIBS. Gold tinsel narrow, gold and silver twist towards head and equal distance apart.
HACKLE. A red spey hackle from end of body, root instead of point crossing over the ribs the whole way.
THROAT. Teal two turns.
WINGS. Two short strips of mallard. Brown mottled points and grey mottled roots.

The Green Highlander (Grant)

TAG. Silver twist and canary silk.
TAIL. Topping and teal.
BUTT. Black herl.
BODY. Two turns of yellow silk and green seal's fur.
RIBS. Silver tinsel.
HACKLE. Green from yellow silk.
THROAT. Yellow hackle.
WINGS. Two tippets (back to back) veiled with bustard, golden pheasant tail, dark mottled turkey, swan green, mallard and topping.
HORNS. Blue macaw.

The Green King (S.S.)
BODY. Dull shade of green composed of Berlin wools green, brown and yellow.
RIBS. Gold tinsel narrow, silver tinsel narrow, and light olive green thread reverse way, thread is put on with hackle.
HACKLE. Red spey cock usual way.
THROAT. Teal two turns.
WINGS. Two strips of mallard, B.M. points, G.M. roots.

The Green Peacock (Murdoch)
TAG. Silver twist and yellow silk.
TAIL. A topping.
BODY. Light blue silk.
RIBS. Oval tinsel.
THROAT. Light blue hackle.
WINGS. Peacock herl, sword feather, double hooks 7, 8, 9, good sun fly.

The Inver Green (C. Austin Leigh)
TAG. Gold twist.
TAIL. A topping.
BUTT. Black herl.
BODY. Light olive green silk.
RIBS. Gold embossed tinsel.
HACKLE. Light olive green second turn.
WINGS. Two strips of tippet bustard, pintail, swan crimson, golden pheasant tail and mallard.
HORNS. Blue macaw.
HEAD. Black herl.

Jeannie (W. Brown)
TAG. Silver twist.
TAIL. Topping.
BODY. One third yellow silk followed by black.
RIBS. Silver tinsel.
THROAT. Black hackle natural.
WINGS. Mallard.
SIDES. Jungle cock.

Lady Caroline (G.S.)
TAIL. Golden pheasant breast.
BODY. Two parts brown, one part green Berlin wool.
RIBS. From separate starting points, gold tinsel narrow, gold and silver twist usual way.
HACKLE. Grey heron from point, along gold tinsel.
THROAT. Golden pheasant red breast.
WINGS. Two strips of mallard showing brown points and light roots.

The Lemon Grey (Jewhurst)
TAG. Silver twist and yellow silk.
TAIL. Topping.
BUTT. Black herl.
BODY. Silver monkey.
RIBS. Silver tinsel oval.
HACKLE. Irish grey second turn.
THROAT. Yellow hackle.
WINGS. Tippet in strands teal gallina, mallard and topping.

The Logie (W. Brown)
TAG. Silver twist.
TAIL. Topping.
BODY. Dark claret silk.
RIBS. Silver tinsel oval.
THROAT. Light blue hackle.
WINGS. Two strips of dyed swan yellow, veiled with broad strips of mallard.
SIDES. Jungle cock.

March Brown (G.S.)
TAG. Gold twist.
TAIL. Topping.
BODY. Silver monkey's fur and a little dirty orange seal's fur, mixed.
RIBS. Gold tinsel oval.
THROAT. Partridge hackle.
WINGS. Hen pheasant tail. Small double hooks.

Mar Lodge (John Lamon)
TAG. Silver tinsel.
TAIL. Topping and two small jungle above back to back.
BUTT. Black herl.
BODY. Silver, black, silver.
THROAT. Gallina.
WINGS. Underwing, swan yellow red and blue, strips of peacock wing, summer duck, grey mallard, dark mottled turkey, golden pheasant tail and topping.
SIDES. Jungle cock.
HORNS. Blue macaw.
HEAD. Black wool.

Miss Grant (John Shanks)
TAG. Silver twist.
TAIL. Teal in strands.
BODY. Two turns of orange silk followed by olive green Berlin wool.
RIBS. Silver tinsel.
HACKLE. Grey heron, second turn.
WINGS. Two strips of golden pheasant tail.

The Mystery (Michael Maher)
TAG. Silver twist and gold silk.
TAIL. Topping.
BUTT. Black herl.
BODY. Gold silk.
RIBS. Silver tinsel oval.
HACKLE. Blue dun second turn.
THROAT. Claret hackle.
WINGS. Two strips of swan dyed yellow and a topping.
HORNS. Red macaw.
CHEEKS. Chatterer.

Pitcroy Fancy (Turnbull)
TAG. Silver twist.
TAIL. Topping and strands of tippet.
BUTT. Scarlet wool.
BODY. Silver tinsel.
RIBS. Silver tinsel oval.

HACKLE. Grey heron from centre.
THROAT. Gallina.
WINGS. Tippet large strips, light mottled turkey, pintail, mallard and topping.
SIDES. Jungle cock.
HEAD. Scarlet wool.

The Rough Grouse (Cruickshank)
TAIL. Few fibres of yellow macaw's hackle.
BODY. Black Berlin wool.
RIBS. Silver tinsel.
HACKLE. Grey heron, from second turn.
THROAT. Black and white speckled turkey.
WINGS. Black and white speckled turkey strips.

The Little Inky Boy (Kelson)
TAG. Silver twist and one turn of crimson Berlin wool.
TAIL. Topping.
BODY. Black.
THROAT. Badger dyed yellow.
WINGS. A few tippet strands, two strips of unbarred summer duck and topping.

Thunder and Lightning (Wright)
TAG. Gold twist and yellow silk.
TAIL. Topping.
BUTT. Black herl.
BODY. Black silk.
RIBS. Gold tinsel oval.
HACKLE. Orange second turn.
THROAT. Jay.
WINGS. Mallard and topping.
SIDES. Jungle cock.
HORNS. Blue macaw.
HEAD. Black wool.

The Sailor (W. Brown)
TAG. Silver twist.
TAIL. Topping.
BODY. Yellow seal's fur and blue seal's fur equally divided.

RIBS. Silver tinsel oval.
HACKLE. Blue from yellow fur.
WINGS. Teal and topping.
CHEEKS. Chatterer.
HEAD. Blue wool. Dressed on small double hooks.

Sir Percy (Sir Percy Dyke)
TAG. Gold twist and gold silk.
TAIL. Topping and chatterer.
BUTT. Black herl.
BODY. Two turns of claret silk, two turns of claret seal's fur, followed by black seal's fur.
RIBS. Gold tinsel oval.
HACKLE. Natural black from claret fur.
THROAT. Jay.
WINGS. Tippet strands, two strips of mallard and topping.
SIDES. Jungle cock.
HEAD. Black herl.

The Silver Blue (W. Brown)
TAG. Silver twist.
TAIL. Topping.
BODY. Silver tinsel.
RIBS. Silver tinsel oval.
THROAT. Blue hackle.
WINGS. Two broad strips of teal.
HEAD. Blue wool.
Dressed on small double hooks.

The Silver Doctor (Wright)
TAG. Silver twist and yellow silk.
TAIL. A topping sometimes chatterer.
BUTT. Scarlet wool.
BODY. Silver tinsel.
RIBS. Silver tinsel oval.
THROAT. Blue hackle and gallina.
WINGS. Strands of tippet, summer duck, pintail, gold pheasant tail, swan yellow and blue, bustard, mallard and topping.
HORNS. Blue macaw.
HEAD. Scarlet wool.

The Silver Grey (Wright)
TAG. Silver twist and yellow silk.
TAIL. Topping, two strands of blue macaw and unbarred summer duck.
BUTT. Black herl.
BODY. Silver tinsel.
RIBS. Silver tinsel oval.
HACKLE. Silver Coch-y-bondhu.
THROAT. Widgeon.
WINGS. Golden pheasant tippet and tail in strands, bustard, swan yellow, amherst pheasant, gallina, powder blue macaw, mallard, grey mallard and topping.
HORNS. Blue macaw.
SIDES. Jungle cock.
HEAD. Black Berlin wool.

Green Heron (John Cruickshank)
TAG. Silver twist.
TAIL. Golden pheasant red breast feather.
BUTT. Black herl.
BODY. Mohair two parts yellow and one part green mixed together.
RIBS. Gold tinsel flat.
THROAT. Gallina short.
WINGS. Golden pheasant tail.
Dressed on small double hooks.

The Gordon (Cosmo Gordon)
TAG. Silver twist and yellow silk.
TAIL. Topping.
BUTT. Black herl.
BODY. One-third yellow and claret silk remainder.
RIBS. Silver lace and silver tinsel.
HACKLE. Claret from yellow.
THROAT. Jay hackle.
WINGS. One tippet backed with sword feather of golden pheasant, peacock herl, bustard, swan light blue, light green and claret red, amherst tail and topping.
SIDES. Jungle cock.
HEAD. Black wool.

The Brora

TAG. G.P. Topping.

TAIL. Topping and two chatterer.

BODY. One half oval tinsel, second half black silk.

RIBS. Oval tinsel, butted in centre with toucan.

THROAT. Black heron.

WINGS. Peacock wing, covered by teal, blue and white swan.

STEWART'S "DOUBLE PATTERN" FLIES FOR SEA TROUT

Mr. K. Stewart, of Stevenston, Ayrshire, is a progressive angler and fly tyer with whom I have had much enlightening correspondence.

He gave me the full coverage for his "Slim Jim" flies, but as the mount on which they are dressed is the same as that used for the Waddington Elverine Lures, which are under patent at the time of writing, it is not possible for me to give full details here.

The "double pattern" flies were designed to eliminate some of the time wasted in changing flies when endeavouring to find out the preferences of the fish on any particular day. As the name suggests, each fly is really two flies of a similar type, and made up by giving two bodies to the same wing. In other words a "Mallard and Claret" and a "Mallard and Yellow" are made into one fly by having the rear half of the body yellow, and the front half claret. The two bodies are divided by a hackle of the type one would use for the rear body, in this case a ginger or a yellow one. The front hackle would be the one used by the front body, in this case a claret or a black one.

As one can see, a multitude of patterns can be produced in these combinations of two, and this system can also be applied to the tandem hook lures which are so popular for sea trout.

Although I said earlier that I could not give full coverage to Mr. Stewart's "Slim Jim" flies, I feel sure that some of his excellent dressings could be applied to tube flies for trout and sea-trout fishing, and I have given a list of these in the tube fly section on pages 105–109.

Terry Thomas Sedge Flies

No. 1. Standard

HOOK. 14–4 as required.

BODY. Fibres from a dark cock pheasant tail, wound as thickly as possible.

BODY HACKLE. Ginger cock.

WING. Grey deer body hair tied on flat with cut ends to the rear, and splayed out.

FRONT HACKLE. Ginger cock, wound over wing roots.

No. 2. Light Sedge

HOOK. 14–4 as required.

BODY. Fibres from a light cock pheasant tail wound on as thickly as possible.

BODY HACKLE. Ginger cock.

WING. Brown deer body hair tied on as No. 1.

FRONT HACKLE. Ginger cock.

No. 3. Dark Sedge
HOOK. 14–4 as required.
BODY. Black wool or chenille.
BODY HACKLE. Black cock.

WING. Black deer hair tied as for Nos.
1 and 2.
FRONT HACKLE. Black cock.

DANISH DRY-FLY PATTERNS
EVOLVED BY PREBEN TORP JACOBSEN

Mr. Jacobsen and I have corresponded for many years, and I know him to be one of the most knowledgeable and dedicated of fly tyers. Furthermore, although he is self-taught, the sample patterns he has sent me on various occasions have been exquisite examples of the fly tyer's art.

He is working at this moment on a book on dry-fly fishing for his home country, and when I say that it will cover Fly Tying, Entomology, Anatomy and Physiology of Trout, Fish Diseases and Parasites, you will understand that I am not exaggerating when I say that I think his book will become the standard work on dry-fly fishing in Denmark.

His versatility also includes deftness on the drawing-board, which must add to the value of his book, as I know from the many descriptive line drawings with which he has often profusely illustrated his many letters to me.

Following are the concluding lines of the letter he wrote to me when sending the dressings I am giving here: "My flies are used in two good trout streams in the north of Jutland, Simested a and Binderup a (a or aa is the Danish name for stream or river), and my friends and I have good success with them. The streams are slow flowing, meandering through meadows and with a strong growth of weeds. Water ranunculus, ribbon weed, water parsnip, curly pondweed are the most common weeds. Denmark is a lowland and all our streams are of this type; only the surroundings change. Most meadows are without trees and woods, but in the centre of Jutland there are beautiful streams bordered with woods. On the meadow-streams we are exposed to the full force of the wind, but luckily in the summer we have most often wind from the west, and as our streams run north-south or westward, we can always find a reach where it is not necessary to struggle against the gods of the winds."

Large Dark Olive Dun

HOOK. No. 13.
TYING SILK. Amber.
TAIL. Ginger cock hackle fibres.
BODY. Two natural blue heron herls and two of the same dyed in picric acid, all four twisted together before winding up hook.
RIB. Fine silver wire.

HACKLES. Watery olive cock (medium size) and ginger cock (small size) mixed together, and a larger dark rusty dun cock in front.

Medium Olive Dun

HOOK. No. 14.

TYING SILK. Yellow—waxed with brown wax, and a few turns left exposed at tail end.

TAIL. Natural dun cock hackle fibres.

BODY. Watery olive seal's fur.

RIB. Fine silver wire.

LEG HACKLE. Pale watery olive cock.

FRONT HACKLE. Dun cock hackle.

Simulium Hatch

HOOK. No. 16–18.

HACKLE. Black cock tied parachute.

BODY. Black condor herl behind and in front of hackle.

Or a "Black Jassid" the only pity being that the jungle-cock "eye" feathers are lost by the least crack of the fly.

[The "Jassids" are flies which incorporate a small jungle-cock tied flat over the body. J.V.]

Addendum re dressing:

Hackle Point Wings. "I don't pluck the fibres from the hackle stem but cut them off so that the remaining stumps make the fastening of the hackle stems more secure. I press the two wings together after they are tied in and cut them to shape."

"Hackle Point Wings"

Dubbing Bodies. "After making the turn of silk and dubbing which actually secures the dubbing to the body, I give the dubbing some further twists to make the body firmer."

Spent Spinners. "I tie them with either a parachute hackle or an ordinary hackle with a figure-of-eight tying of the silk underneath the body. This forces the hackle fibres sideways and upwards and very little downwards, to mitigate the landing of the fly on the water."

Watery Olive Dun

HOOK. No. 15.

TYING SILK. Primrose—with a few turns left exposed at tail.

TAIL. Buff Orpington cock hackle fibres.

BODY. Natural blue-grey heron herl. Two fibres twisted round the tying silk.

RIB. Lime-coloured fluorescent (D.F.M.) nylon.

LEG HACKLE. Buff Orpington cock hackle.

FRONT HACKLE. Dun cock hackle.

Iron Blue Dun

HOOK. No. 15.

TYING SILK. Blue-grey.

TAIL. Dark blue dun cock hackle fibres.

BODY. Brown olive seal's fur.

RIB. Fine silver wire.

WING. Two dark blue dun cock hackle tips, cut to shape.

HACKLE. Pale watery olive cock.

Little Claret Spinner (Vangsgaard's design)

HOOK. No. 15.

TYING SILK. Brown.

TAIL. Dun cock hackle fibres.

BODY. Condor herl dyed red-brown.

RIB. Fine gold wire.

WING. Tips of two rusty blue dun cock hackles, cut to shape and tied "half spent".

HACKLE. Brown olive and greenish olive cock—mixed.

B.W.O. Dun

HOOK. No. 14.

TYING SILK. Brown.

TAIL. Brown olive cock hackle fibres.

BODY. Two natural heron herls, and two dyed in picric acid, all twisted together.

RIB. Fine silver wire.

WING. Two blue dun cock hackle tips, cut to shape.

HACKLE. Dun and olive dun mixed together.

Large Dark Olive Spinner

HOOK. No. 14.

TYING SILK. Primrose—left exposed at tail end of body.

BODY. Seal's fur dyed red-brown.

RIB. Fine gold wire.

HACKLE. Brown olive cock, with figure-of-eight turn of silk underneath body, so that the hackle fibres project at sides and upwards only.

(Alternative hackle: Steely blue cock.)

No wings.

Caenis rivulorum hatch—small "white midges"—(evening). "Grey Duster" tied on No. 16 hook with the badger hackle tied parachute fashion. See page 127 for dressing of "Grey Duster".

Knotted Midge version:

TAIL. Fibres from a white cock's hackle.

BODY. Cream condor herl.

HACKLE. Badger cock—one in the centre of the body and one in the front.

Besides good floating capacity, the taking results of this fly have been excellent.

SECTION 7

AUSTRALIAN AND TASMANIAN, NEW ZEALAND, AND SOUTH AFRICAN PATTERNS

INTRODUCTION

To watch the development of the artificial fly in countries overseas has been a most interesting experience, for it must be obvious to the most casual observer that the breakaway from orthodox U.K. patterns has been different in each sphere, due, of course, to the local conditions that prevail.

The most notable instance of this is shown in the New Zealand patterns, which in the main are produced to imitate the small fish that the trout of the lakes and big rivers rely on for their food. Orthodoxy is maintained in the dry fly and nymph section, as will readily be seen.

The South African Patterns show a definite boldness of approach, and it will also be observed that in some instances similar types have been produced as those in New Zealand. See "Mrs. Simpson" and "Walker's Killer".

Australia and Tasmania give a much different picture, in that instead of imitations that arouse the canabalistic instincts of the trout, we have flies that have been produced to imitate the insect life living on or near the waters. In other words, the path has followed the British style much more closely.

The development of these patterns was not achieved by accident, of course, and the fly fishermen of the Commonwealth owe much to the enthusiastic amateur and professional fly tyers (who are, of course, fishermen also) who have taken so much trouble to produce the flies most suitable for their particular territory.

I am most fortunate in my particular sphere of business to have the opportunity of cultivating the acquaintance of these people, and it is to them that the main credit for this collection should go.

ACKNOWLEDGMENTS

Australia and Tasmania

Elsa Lowry, J. M. Gillies, Rice Jackson, Canon D. M. Wallace, A. R. Peacock, the late R. H. Wigram, the late Howard Joseland, A. R. Burk.

New Zealand

Don Page, the late R. H. Wigram, Mr. and Mrs. Arthur Brett, C. H. Kendrick, R. Sanderson, A. M. McDonald, the late Michael Foster.

South Africa

Q. E. Carter, Dr. McShane, E. V. Evans, Mrs. Helen B. Hilliard, Col. W. Park Gray, R. S. Crass, B.Sc., F. Bowker, H. G. Place, Alan Yates, Mr. Friel, the late J. Spranger Harrison, W. W. Small, Dr. Drew, Chris Hieber, G. B. Mackenzie, Derek Thorneville, Lionel M. Walker, and Jack Blackman, who supplied the patterns for the coloured illustrations.

INDEX

AUSTRALIAN AND TASMANIAN FLIES

NEW ZEALAND FLIES

SOUTH AFRICAN FLIES

AUSTRALIAN AND TASMANIAN FLIES

Bogong Moth
BODY. Black or grey chenille.
WINGS. Two small round feathers from front of crow wing, tied back to back.
HACKLE. Natural red cock, wound as collar.

Bredbro (Grasshopper)
BODY. Orange floss.
RIB. Oval gold tinsel.
HACKLE. Brown partridge back.
WING. (Fairly long.) An underwing of golden pheasant tippet fibres, and an overwing from brown speckled hen wing quill feather.

Burrinjuck Wonder (wet or dry)
TAIL. Tips of two grizzle cock hackles dyed orange.
BODY. Bronze peacock herl.
HACKLE. Claret cock, mixed with natural red cock.

Black Nymph
TAIL. Three fibres from black cock hackle.
BODY. Black seal fur.
RIB. Silver tinsel.
WING CASE. Any black fibres from tail or wing quills, such as crow.
HACKLE. Short fibred black cock.

Brown Nymph
TAIL. Three fibres from natural red cock hackle.
BODY. Dark chocolate brown fur wool. Tease out wool and mix thoroughly with fur, and spin on brown silk.
RIB. Flat copper tinsel.
LEGS. Pick out fur at head.

Butler's Killer
TAIL. Three or four strands of tippet fibres.
BODY. Bronze peacock herl.
HACKLE. Two trimmed quail breast feathers.

Caddis Nymph
HOOK. No. 13 or 14.
BODY. A piece of hackle quill tied to shank with black silk. About $\frac{1}{4}$ in. to protrude at bend, and about $\frac{1}{8}$ in. at eye of hook. The whole is then wrapped with olive raffia, building it up into nymph shape.
HACKLE. Black cock—one turn.
HEAD. Built up with black tying silk.
Complete length to be about $\frac{3}{4}$ in.

Clear Water Nymph
TAIL. Four fibres from a bright red cock hackle.

BODY. Pale brown seal's fur spun on bright red silk.
HACKLE. Pick out fur at head.

Cocky Spinner
TAIL. Three fibres from natural red cock hackle.
BODY. Two strands of red macaw tail wound round shank.
RIB. Oval gold tinsel.
HACKLE. Grizzle cock and natural red cock wound together, and separated into "spent" position by figure-of-eight tying.

Dr. Brandon's Claret (dry)
HOOK. No. 10.
TAIL. Golden pheasant tippet fibres cocked well up.
BODY. Claret mohair ribbed gold oval tinsel-short, stout and well shaped.
HACKLE. At least three stiff black cock hackles.

Eildon Shrimp
BODY. Tail half, flat gold tinsel, front half claret wool, fairly thick.
HACKLE. First. Long-fibred red game cock over tinsel body. Second. Long-fibred black cock at body joint.

Early Nymph (Ouse Fancy)
TAIL. Three fibres from red game cock hackle.
BODY. Grey wool teased out and mixed with blue underfur of rabbit.
RIB. Oval gold tinsel.
Pick out fur at head, and make complete fly look rough.

Garrett's Marong (dry)
HOOK. No. 10.
TAIL. Golden pheasant tippet fibres.

BODY. Furnace cock hackle wound very thickly up body.
HACKLE. Bright orange.
(This is a bi-visible type of fly.)

Great Lake Beetle
BODY. Black cock hackles wound closely, and then clipped to shape (tapering from) shoulder to tail end until stiff like bristles.
WINGS. Clipped grizzle cock hackles tied spent, and sloping backwards at about 45 deg. to hook-shank.
HACKLE. Grizzle dyed orange.

Hopper Hackle (Grasshopper)
TAIL. Fibres from claret cock hackle.
BODY. Natural raffia.
HACKLE. Golden pheasant tippet feather, mixed with brown partridge back feather fairly long in fibre.
HOOK. No. 8–10.

Hair Fibre Nymph
TAIL. Fibres from brown partridge back feather.
BODY. Blue under-fur from hare or rabbit very lightly dubbed.
RIB. Oval silver tinsel.
THORAX. Hare's fur, picked out at sides to form legs.
WING CASE. Fibres from brown partridge (speckled) tail or back feathers.

Hair Silver Nymph
TAIL. Fibres from brown partridge back feather.
BODY. Silver twist tinsel.
THORAX. Hare's fur from ear.
WING CASE. Fibres from speckled brown partridge tail or back feathers.
HACKLE. Brown partridge back.

Joseland's Favourite (wet)
TAIL. Fibres from claret cock hackle.
BODY. Buff seal's fur.
RIB. Oval gold tinsel.
HACKLE. Dark claret.
WING. (Fairly long.) Underwing of two white and black feathers from front of mallard wing, dyed yellow, and tied in back to back. Overwing consisting of two strips from speckled turkey (oak) wing quills, each side of duck feathers.

Joseland's Favourite (dry)
TAIL. Three *tips* from dyed claret cock hackles.
BODY. Brown mohair ribbed with a brown hackle which is clipped to give body a shaggy appearance.
HACKLE. Two brown hackles tied in reverse so as to stand out well over eye.

Murrumbidgee Wonder (Yellow Dog)
TAIL. Fibres from dyed scarlet duck quill.
BODY. $\frac{1}{4}$ in. at tail end of yellow silk, remainder yellow seal's fur.
RIB. Oval gold tinsel.
HACKLE. No. 1: Pale ginger cock wound over seal's fur. At head: Pale ginger cock, longer in fibre than body hackle.

Pale Watery Olive
TAIL. Fibres from pale olive yellow cock hackle.
BODY. Horsehair dyed pale lemon.
WING. From starling wing quill.
HACKLE. Pale olive yellow cock.

Penstock Brown
TAIL. Three fibres from furnace cock hackle.
BODY. Natural coloured silk (ash or dun).
RIB. Stripped quill from peacock "eye" tail.

WING. Brown speckled turkey wing quill, tied upright.
HACKLE. Furnace cock, fairly long in fibre.

Red Bug
TAIL. Scarlet wool.
BODY. Red wool, two-thirds of hook.
RIB. Oval gold tinsel.
HACKLE. Front one-third of hook, stiff red game cock hackle, closely palmered.

Shannon Moth (Male)
BODY. Cream and blue-grey fur, mixed together.
WING. Strands of barred teal feather tied in at shoulder to lie low over body.
HACKLE. Light partridge breast or hen pheasant neck, clipped short.

Shannon Moth (Female)
BODY. Fawn fur or wool.
WING. Strands of brown mallard shoulder feather tied in at shoulder to lie low over body.
HACKLE. Two brown partridge back feathers, clipped short, or a short-fibred grizzle cock hackle.

Smart's Hopper (Grasshopper)
TAIL. Fibres from a claret cock hackle.
BODY. Natural raffia.
HACKLE. Brown partridge back.
WING. (Fairly long.) Married strips of bright green goose and brown turkey feathers, the green to be on top.

Smart's Yellow Tail
TAIL. Golden pheasant crest.
BODY. Yellow seal's fur.
RIB. Gold wire.
BODY HACKLE. Honey cock.
FRONT HACKLE. Rear one apple green, middle one grey partridge breast, front one pure white.

Spring Olive
TAIL. Three fibres from dark brown olive cock hackle.
BODY. Medium olive seal's fur, very lightly dubbed.
RIB. Fine gold wire.
WING. Blackbird, tied forward.
HACKLE. Dark brown olive cock.

Styx Special
TAIL. Tips of three black cock hackles.
BODY. Black cock hackles wound closely and clipped to shape.
HACKLE. Furnace cock.

Tarana (Grasshopper)
TAIL. Four golden pheasant tippet fibres.
BODY. Natural raffia.
HACKLE. Brown partridge back feather.
WING. (Long.) Two strips of dyed yellow duck or goose feathers as underwing, with two strips of brown (oak) turkey wing quill each side.

Ti-Tree Beetle (Wet)
BODY. Black wool—beetle shape.
HACKLE. Few strands of soft black hen hackle.
WING CASE. Fibres from brown hen wing quill feather tied in at bend and brought down over body and hackle and tied in at head.

Ti-Tree Beetle (Dry)
BODY. Black ostrich herl.
RIB. Black quill.
WING CASE. Fibres from brown hen wing quill feather tied in at bend and brought down to lie flat over body, and tied in at head.
HACKLE. Black cock.

Wallace Fancy
BODY. Strand of dyed red horsehair.
HACKLE. Red game and blue dun wound together and tied "spent" with figure-of-eight tying.

Yarrongobilly
BODY. White chenille.
HACKLE. Ginger.
WING. From grey speckled turkey wing quill feathers.

NEW ZEALAND FLIES

Albino
BODY. White chenille, floss, or wool.
RIB. Oval silver.
WING. Two white cock hackles, back to back, and tied down on top of hook with ribbing tinsel.
HACKLE. White cock, wound as a collar.
HEAD. Black varnish.

Awahou Special
TAIL. Cock pheasant rump fibres.
BODY. Red, yellow or green chenille.
RIB. Oval silver tinsel.
WING. Two pairs of cock pheasant rump feathers tied in to lie alongside body.
HEAD. Black varnish.

Black Phantom
TAIL. Black squirrel tail fibres.
BODY. Black chenille.
RIB. Oval silver tinsel.
WING. Six pairs of black pukeko feathers tied in to lie alongside body as in Mrs. Simpson. (Small dyed black heron feathers could be used as a substitute.)
HEAD. Black varnish.

Basket Moth (New Zealand)

HOOK. 10–6.

BODY. Five or six alternate turns of yellow and black floss—fine.

HACKLE. Rather long-fibred speckled guinea fowl—about four turns.

(A good fly when moth are on the water.)

Black and Yellow (Devil)

TAIL. Black bucktail fibres.

BODY. Two equal parts of black and yellow mohair.

JOINT. Black cock hackle trimmed to about $\frac{1}{4}$ in.

HEAD HACKLE. Black cock.

Blondie

TAIL. Bunch of white or cream mohair cut off flat, about $\frac{3}{4}$ in. long.

BODY. Flat silver tinsel.

WING. Another bunch of white mohair tied in at head and cut off level with end of tail.

A good example of a whitebait or smolt lure.

Blue Dun Smelt

BODY. Blue floss silk.

RIB. Oval silver tinsel.

WING. Two light blue dun cock hackles, back to back, and tied down on top of body with ribbing tinsel.

HACKLE. Light blue dun cock, wound as a collar, and fairly long in fibre.

HEAD. Black varnish.

Claret Jessie

TAIL. Claret hackle fibres.

BODY. Bronze peacock herl—tied thickly.

HACKLE. Claret cock or hen.

WING. Grouse tail.

Craig's Nighttime

TAIL. Red wool.

BODY. Black chenille.

RIB. Oval silver tinsel.

WING. Three blue pukeko feathers tied on to lie flat over body, plus a single jungle cock feather also tied on flat over the pukeko feathers. (Small heron feathers dyed blue could be used as a substitute for the pukeko.)

THROAT HACKLE. Black cock.

HEAD. Black varnish.

Dad's Favourite

TAIL. Red cock hackle fibres.

BODY. Red floss, seal's fur or chenille.

RIB. Gold wire.

HACKLE. Dark furnace.

WING. Starling, or grey duck in the larger sizes.

HOOK. No. 10–14.

Dorothy *See* "Yellow Dorothy".

Dunham (Dry)

TAIL. Fibres from golden pheasant red breast feather.

BODY. Two blue-yellow macaw tail fibres wound together.

HACKLE. Long and sparse. Coch-y-bondhu, with a grizzle cock dyed blue, in front.

Ewe Wasp

TAIL. Yellow hackle fibres.

BODY. Yellow and black chenille.

RIB. Oval silver tinsel.

WING. Split speckled partridge tail.

THROAT HACKLE. Black cock.

HEAD. Black varnish.

Ewe Wasp (Barred)

TAIL. Yellow hackle fibres.

BODY. Alternate bands of black and yellow chenille.

RIB. Oval silver tinsel.
WING. Split grouse tail.
HACKLE. Black cock.
HEAD. Black varnish.

Ferris
BODY. Yellow mohair.
RIB. Oval gold tinsel.
WING. Two bright red cock hackles, back to back, and tied down on body by winding ribbing tinsel over hackle stem.
HEAD. Black varnish.

Fruit Salad
TAIL. Red wool.
BODY. Four sections of chenille, yellow, black, yellow, black.
RIB. Oval silver tinsel.
WING. Three blue pukeko feathers tied down flat over body, with orange hackle fibres over.
THROAT HACKLE. Orange cock.
HEAD. Black varnish.

Fuzzy Wuzzy
TAIL. Black squirrel tail fibres.
BODY. Red, yellow, green, orange or black chenille.
RIB. None, but the body is divided in half by a black cock hackle.
HACKLE. Black cock, longer in fibre than centre hackle.
HEAD. Black varnish.

Golden Demon
TAIL. Ibis or substitute.
BODY. Flat gold tinsel.
RIB. Oval gold tinsel.
HACKLE. Bright orange.
WING. Brown mallard shoulder feather.
CHEEK. Jungle cock.

Gregg's Nighttime. *See* Craig's "Nighttime".

Green Matuka
BODY. Green chenille, wool, or seal's fur.
RIB. Oval silver tinsel.
WING. Two badger hackles back to back, tied down on body by ribbing tinsel.
HEAD. Black varnish.

Green Orbit
BODY. Green chenille.
RIB. Oval silver tinsel.
WING. Two honey grizzle (cree) cock hackles dyed light olive or light green, and tied in "Matuka" style, i.e. on top of body with ribbing tinsel.
HACKLE. Light green, wound as a collar.
HEAD. Black varnish.

Grey Ghost (N.Z.)
TAIL. None.
BODY. Flat silver tinsel.
RIB. Oval silver tinsel.
WING. Two light grey cock hackles, bound down on to body by ribbing tinsel.
HEAD. Black varnish.
A light grey head hackle is sometimes added.

Hairy Dog
TAIL. Black squirrel tail fibres.
BODY. Any one of following colours: red, yellow, green, black chenille, or silver or gold tinsel.
RIB. Oval silver tinsel.
WING. Black squirrel tail fibres.
HACKLE. Black cock.
HEAD. Black varnish.

Ihi Green
TAG. Silver tinsel.

BODY. Green seal's fur or chenille.

RIB. Flat silver tinsel.

WING. Four black cock hackles, tied in as two pairs, back to back.

HACKLE. Black cock.

HEAD. Black varnish.

Ihi Red

Same as "Ihi Green" except for red body.

Invicta Jay

TAIL. Red ibis or substitute.

BODY. Yellow mohair or floss.

RIB. Oval gold tinsel-fine.

BODY HACKLE. Dyed yellow cock.

HEAD HACKLE. Blue jay, or natural black cock.

WING. From hen pheasant wing quill.

Jack Sprat

TAIL. None.

BODY. Flat silver tinsel.

RIB. Oval silver tinsel.

WING. Two badger hackles, back to back and tied down on to body by ribbing tinsel.

HEAD. Black varnish.

A badger head hackle is sometimes added.

Jessie

BODY. Peacock herl—tied thickly.

HACKLE. Black or dark furnace cock.

WING. Brown mallard shoulder feather, tied low over body.

Kakahi Queen

TAIL. Fibres from grey mallard flank feather.

BODY. Well-marked stripped quill from peacock "eye" tail.

HACKLE. Furnace.

WING. Slate grey wing quill, with a strip of dyed yellow mallard flank either side.

Leslie's Lure

Sometimes called "Ohahau".

TAIL. Fibres from brown barred squirrel tail.

BODY. Red, yellow or green chenille.

RIB. Oval silver tinsel.

WING. Two pairs of hen pheasant wing front or body feathers, tied in to lie close alongside body.

HEAD. Black varnish.

Lord's Killer

TAIL. Black squirrel tail fibres.

BODY. Yellow, red, green, or orange chenille—any one of these colours.

WING. Six pairs of woodcock breast feathers to lie alongside body.

HEAD. Black varnish.

An oval silver or gold rib is optional.

Love Lure

TAIL. Good bunch of peacock green sword, tail fibres.

BODY. Bronze peacock herl—tied thickly.

RIB. Scarlet floss.

WING. Any black feathers, which should be set in the upright position if the fly is to be dressed as a dry fly.

HACKLE. Black cock.

Mallard and Yellow

TAIL. Brown squirrel tail fibres.

BODY. Yellow chenille.

WING. Two pairs of grey mallard flank feathers tied in each side of body.

HEAD. Black varnish.

Bodies of orange, green, red, etc., can also be used.

Manuka Beetle

BODY. Light yellow floss.

WING CASE. Light green floss, tied in at tail, brought down over body and tied in at head.

HACKLE. Red game, underneath body only.

HEAD. Black silk—varnished.

Matukas (or Matukus)

The variations of these dressings are too numerous for all to be included here. The red and green matukas, however, are illustrated, and the dressings given. They will give a good idea of the general appearance. Body colours can be varied, red, yellow, orange, etc., and the wings can be either of hackles tied back to back, or split tail feathers of partridge (most popular), grouse, or turkey, all tied in the same manner, i.e. with the solid stem of the hackle or the quill of the tail feathers tied down on top of the body with the ribbing tinsel. This method is illustrated in the dressings of "Parson's Glory", "Tiger Ross" (hackles), and "Tamiti", "Turkey and Green", "Orange Partridge", and "Ewe Wasp" (split tail feathers).

Jungle cock feathers, tied in close to head of fly, are sometimes added, and matukas tied with this addition are known as "Imperials".

Metaura Midge

TAIL. Three fibres from a stiff red hackle.
BODY. Dark stripped quill from peacock tail.
WING. Tips of two red-brown cock hackles, set upright.
HACKLE. Red-brown.
HOOK. No. 14–18.

Mrs. Simpson

TAIL. Black squirrel tail fibres.
BODY. Yellow, red or green chenille.
WING. Six pairs of green cock pheasant rump feathers, tied alongside body.
HEAD. Black varnish.

Nimmo's Killer (Dry)

HOOK. No. 10–14.
TAIL. Three or four tippet fibres.
BODY. Half red, and half black, floss.

RIB. Fine flat silver.
HACKLE. Dark furnace. Two should be used if extra buoyancy is required.

N.Z. Coch-y-Bondhu

TAIL. Three fibres of Coch-y-bondhu cock, hackle.
BODY. Tail end, dark stripped quill remainder, light stripped quill.
WING. Tips of two Coch-y-bondhu or dark brown cock hackles, set upright.
HACKLE. Coch-y-bondhu.
HOOK. No. 12–14.

N.Z. Red Tip Governor

TAIL. Fibres of red game cock hackle.
BODY. Rear end scarlet silk, remainder stripped quill from "eye" of peacock tail.
WING. Tips of two red game cock hackles, set upright.
HACKLE. Red game cock.
HOOK. No. 11–14.

Ohahau. *See* "Leslie's Lure".

Old Nick (1)

HOOK. No. 6–8.
TAIL. Golden pheasant tippet fibres.
BODY. Dark claret mohair or seal's fur.
RIB. Oval gold tinsel.
WING. Black-brown barred skunk or squirrel tail fibres.
HACKLE. Red game cock.
CHEEK. Jungle cock.
HEAD. Black varnish.

Old Nick (2)

TAIL. Ibis or substitute.
BODY. Red wool.
RIB. Oval gold tinsel.
HACKLE. Medium red.
WING. (Under) red goose or ibis. (Over) speckled partridge tail.

Orange Hawk

TAIL. None.
BODY Orange chenille.
RIB. Oval silver tinsel.
WING. Two cream with brown centre hen
hackles, back to back, and tied on
"Matuka" style, or hawk feathers if
available.
HEAD. Black varnish.

Orange Partridge

TAIL. Yellow hackle fibres.
BODY. Orange chenille.
RIB. Oval silver tinsel.
WING. Split partridge tail.
HACKLE. Red cock hackle, natural.
HEAD. Black varnish.

Another pattern where the body colours
may be varied, i.e. "Yellow Partridge",
"Green Partridge", etc.

Parson's Glory

TAIL. Orange hackle fibres.
BODY. Yellow chenille.
RIB. Oval silver tinsel.
WING. Two honey-grizzle (cree) cock
hackles back to back, and tied down on
top of body with ribbing tinsel.
HACKLE. Red game or cree, wound as a
collar.
HEAD. Black varnish.

This is another pattern which can have
variations of body colour.

Pukeko and Red

As "Taihape Tickler", but without the
yellow hackle fibres.

Rabbit

TAIL. Red wool.
BODY. Chenille—any colour from red,
yellow, green, orange or black.
RIB. Oval silver tinsel.
WING. A strip of skin from a rabbit's pelt,
about $\frac{1}{8}$ in. wide and tied down in the
same manner as "Matuka" wings, i.e.
on top of body with ribbing tinsel.
HEAD. Black varnish, except for green-
bodied fly, when red varnish is used.

Red-bodied Waipahi

TAIL. Black cock hackle fibres.
BODY. Red silk.
WING. Tips of two black cock hackles,
set upright.
HACKLE. Black cock.
HOOK. No. 14–18.

A black silk body turns this into the
"Black-bodied Waipahi".

Red Matuka

BODY. Red chenille, or wool.
RIB. Oval gold tinsel.
WING. Two black hen hackles back to
back, and tied down on top of body
with ribbing tinsel.
HEAD. Black varnish.

Sam Slick

TAIL. Tippet fibres.
BODY. One third at tail of yellow floss,
remainder of brown seal's fur.
RIB. Oval gold tinsel.
HACKLE. Brown partridge back feather.
WING. Speckled partridge tail feather.
Smolt or smelt flies. See "Whitebait".

Scotch Poacher

TAIL. Black hackle fibres.
BODY. Light orange or golden yellow
chenille, halved in the centre by an
orange hackle.
HACKLE. Orange and black mixed.
WING. Black hackle fibres (black hair in
larger sizes), strips of teal either side, and
a golden pheasant crest over.
HEAD. Black varnish.

Split Turkey

TAIL. Golden pheasant tippet fibres.
BODY. Claret chenille.
RIB. Oval gold tinsel.
WING. Mottled brown turkey tail feather
"split". See below.
CHEEK. Jungle cock.
HACKLE. Wound in front of wings—
claret.

HEAD. Black varnish.

The instructions apertaining to the Matukas also apply to the Turkey series of patterns. See "Turkey and Green" in illustrations.

Syd's Ginger
BODY. Yellow mohair or floss.
RIB. Oval gold tinsel.
HACKLE. Four ginger cock hackles, tied on in the "Matuka" style.
HEAD. Black varnish.

Taihape Tickler (Deadly Dick)
TAIL. Red wool.
BODY. Red chenille.
RIB. Oval silver tinsel.
WING. Three blue pukeko feathers tied flat over body, with yellow cock hackle fibres over. (Small heron feathers dyed blue could be used as a substitute.)
THROAT HACKLE. Red cock.
HEAD. Black varnish.

Tamiti
TAIL. Yellow hackle fibres.
BODY. In sections—red, yellow, black, yellow, chenille.
RIB. Oval silver tinsel.
WING. Split partridge tail.
THROAT HACKLE. Natural red cock.
HEAD. Black varnish.

Tamiti (Full dressing)
TAG. Silver tinsel and red floss.
TAIL. Golden pheasant crest.
BODY. In sections as above, and each section butted with a natural red game hackle.
RIB. None.
WING. Strips of dark mottled turkey tail, tied in salmon fly style, i.e. in strips without the quill.

THROAT HACKLE. Natural red game cock hackle, tied under eye in salmon-fly style.
CHEEK. Jungle cock.
HEAD. Black varnish.

Taupo Tiger
BODY. Yellow chenille or mohair.
RIB. Oval gold tinsel.
WING. Badger hackles tied in the "Matuka" style.
CHEEK. Jungle cock.
HACKLE. Badger, wound as a collar.
HEAD. Red varnish.

Te Tauiwha
HOOK. No. 1. Long shank.
BODY. Pale lemon chenille.
WING. Pale grey mohair tied in at intervals along the body and extending beyond the bend of the hook.
HEAD HACKLE. Badger cock.
HEAD. Brown varnish.

Tiger Ross
TAIL. Orange hackle fibres.
BODY. Yellow chenille.
RIB. Oval silver tinsel.
WING. Badger hackles back to back, tied down on top of body, "Matuka" style.
HEAD. Red varnish.

This is another pattern where the body colour may be varied, also the tail colour, and on some patterns a badger hackle wound as a "collar" is also added. Jungle cock cheeks are also a popular addition to this pattern.

Tinopai
TAG. Round silver tinsel.
TAIL. Red ibis or substitute.
BODY. Two equal parts—of yellow and red mohair or chenille.

RIB. Oval gold tinsel.

HACKLE. Brown partridge back feather.

WING. Brown mottled turkey feather, with a strip of red goose over.

HEAD. Black varnish.

Turkey and Green

TAIL. Red game hackle fibres.

BODY. Green chenille.

RIB. Oval silver tinsel.

WING. "Split" turkey tail—brown mottled.

HACKLE. Red game, tied as a collar.

The wings of the "Turkey" series can also be tied in the orthodox salmon style, i.e. without the quill.

Turnip Fly

HOOK. No. 12–10.

TAIL. Fibres of black cock hackle.

BODY. Black thread, with crimson thread behind wings, approx. half and half of body for each colour.

WING. Grey mallard wing quill.

HACKLE. Black cock.

TYING SILK. Crimson.

Twilight Beauty (Dry)

TAIL. Fibres of natural medium red cock hackle.

BODY. Black tying silk.

WING. Starling wing feather.

HACKLE. Natural medium red cock hackle.

Waipahi—Red or Black

See "Red-bodied Waipahi". "Waipahi Black", is the same, but with a black body.

Whitebait Flies

This is another series with multiple variations, some of which are listed in the Index. I refer to "Albino", "Blondie", and "Blue Dun Smelt", which are illustrated, and also "Te Tauiwha", "Dorothy", "Grey Ghost" and "Jack Sprat".

The following selection will no doubt also be useful to the tyer who wishes to build up a collection of this series.

No. 1

TAIL. White ostrich herl.

BODY. Flat silver tinsel.

WING. White mohair extending to end of tail.

HACKLE. White, tied underneath only, salmon fly style.

HEAD. Black varnish.

No. 2

BODY. Yellow mohair.

RIB. Flat gold tinsel.

WING. Badger hackles in any of the light colours, ranging from pure white to deep cream, and tied on "Matuka" style.

HEAD. Black varnish.

No. 3

TAIL. White and green mohair.

BODY. Flat silver tinsel.

WING. In three layers—white, green, white mohair.

HEAD. Black varnish.

No. 4

TAIL. Red mohair.

BODY. Flat gold tinsel.

WING. White or cream mohair.

HEAD. Brown varnish.

No. 5

BODY. Grey seal fur or wool.

RIB. Oval silver tinsel.

WING. Two grizzle (Plymouth Rock) cock hackles, tied on "Matuka" style.

THROAT. A short tuft of red wool.

HEAD. Black varnish.

No. 6
BODY. Flat silver tinsel.
RIB. Oval silver tinsel.
WING. Two grizzle cock hackles dyed orange, and tied on "Matuka" style.
HACKLE. Red cock, wound as a collar. (Dyed bright red.)
HEAD. Black varnish.

No. 7
Same as No. 6, but with flat gold tinsel body, and oval gold rib.

No. 8
BODY. Orange floss silk.
RIB. Oval gold tinsel.
WING. Two badger cock hackles dyed bright yellow, and tied on "Matuka" style.
HACKLE. Dyed bright red cock, wound as a collar.
HEAD. Red varnish.

White Moth
BODY. White or yellow mohair.
RIB. Flat silver tinsel.
HACKLE. Light red cock, or white cock.
WING. White goose or duck strips.
HEAD. Black varnish.

William's Wonder
TAIL. Fibres from stiff natural red cock hackle.
BODY. Herl from a cock pheasant tail with a good red tinge.
WING. Tips of two brown cock hackles, set upright.
HACKLE. Natural brown.
HOOK. No. 14–18.

Yellow Dorothy
TAIL. Orange hackle fibres.
BODY. Yellow chenille.
RIB. Oval silver tinsel.
WING. Grizzle (Plymouth Rock) cock hackles tied in the "Matuka" style, i.e. back to back, and tied down on top of body by the ribbing tinsel.
HEAD. Black varnish.
Alternative bodies: Red chenille, silver or gold tinsel.

SOUTH AFRICAN FLIES

African Belle
HOOK. No. 10–6.
TAIL. Golden pheasant tippet.
BODY. Red seal fur or mohair.
THORAX. Golden yellow seal fur or mohair.
RIB. Gold tinsel.
HACKLE. Guinea fowl.
WING. Turkey rump feathers, dark brown, and with cinnamon tips.

Black and Silver
HOOK. No. 10–6.
TAIL. Red ibis or wool.
BODY. Black wool.
RIB. Flat silver tinsel.
HACKLE. Black hen hackle.
WING. Hadeda ibis green-black secondaries, or English magpie tail.

Bungalow Black
HOOK. 10–16.
TAIL. Three long whisks dyed olive cock hackle.
BODY. Black floss.
RIB. Gold wire.
HACKLE. Ginger/black hen.
WING. Starling wing quill dyed green olive.

Carter's Pink Lady
HOOK. No. 10–6.
TAIL. Bunch of fibres from soft speckled hen feather. (Either back or wing front feathers.)
BODY. Pink wool.
HACKLE. Soft speckled hen wing feather as used for tail.

Cox's Fancy
TAIL. Yellow wool.
BODY. Bronze peacock herl.
WING. Guinea fowl wing quill, dyed blue.
HACKLE. None.

Dark Ferrash
HOOK. No. 10–6.
TAG. Three to four turns flat gold tinsel.
TAIL. Golden pheasant crest, with tips of two Indian crow feathers each side.
BODY. Bronze peacock herl, ribbed with scarlet floss.
BODY HACKLE. Red cock hackle (natural), tied palmer.
KICKER. Quill points of black ostrich herl with herl cut close to quill.
ANTENNAE. Tips of bronze peacock herl.

Emerging Nymph
TAIL. Cock pheasant tail, three strands. (Centre tail feather preferred.)
BODY. Bronze peacock herl.
RIBBING. Flat gold tinsel.
WING. Coch-y-bondhu cock fibres tied bunched and standing up vertically from the hook-shank.
WING CASE. Magpie tail, tied in two slips to lie with the sheen side outermost around the wing roots and over the thorax.
THORAX. Bronze peacock.
LEG. Brown partridge, tied spent.
HACKLE. Hen, cinnamon and black sparse.
HOOK. No. 12–8.

Evans's Chameleon
So called because after being in the water a few minutes the blue changes to green and imitates a grasshopper.
TAIL. A few whisks of any yellow feather.

BODY. Orange and green silk in alternate bands. (Alternative—black ribbed with silver.)
WING. Two peacock blue breast feathers rolled and tied in streamer fashion.
HACKLE. One side of budgerigar tail feather, stripped. (Alternative: Blue kingfisher tail feather.)

Friel's Fancy
HOOK. No. 10–6.
TAIL. Two strands peacock herl.
BODY. Black cock hackle wound Palmer and ribbed with silver tinsel. (Variations: ribbed with yellow or red floss silk.)
HACKLE. Black. Wound as a collar.
WING. Guinea fowl wing quill, with well marked white spots.

Game and Green
HOOK. No. 4–6.
TAG. Four to six turns of oval or round gold tinsel.
TAIL. Bunch of brown mallard shoulder feather fibres. (Thick and fairly short.)
BODY. Dyed green seal's fur or mohair, ribbed with scarlet floss.
HACKLE. Brown partridge back.
WING. English hen pheasant centre tail, well marked.

Guardsman
HOOK. No. 4–8.
TAG. Four to six turns round silver tinsel.
TAIL. Six paired fibres from black crow wing quill, fairly long, with Indian crow feather over.
BODY. Tail one-third golden yellow floss, remainder scarlet seal's fur, wool or mohair.
RIB. Embossed silver tinsel.

HACKLE. A bunch of fibres stripped from black feather of cock golden pheasant, tied in under shank of hook at throat, to reach point of hook. These feathers are red at the base and gold at the tip.

WING. Four whole feathers from partridge shoulder. (These are brown speckled with a white stripe down centre.) Tied in pairs, two each side, reaching just beyond bend of hook.

TOPPING. Golden pheasant crest.

HEAD. Several turns of bronze peacock herl.

Gorbenmac

HOOK. No. 12–8.

TAIL. Golden pheasant tippet.

BODY. Peacock herl.

RIB. Scarlet floss.

HACKLE. Jay, blue lesser covert.

WING. Mallard drake, blue secondaries.

Grizzle Hackle

HOOK. No. 12–10 up eyed.

TAIL. Three strands from red game hackle.

BODY. Well-marked stripped peacock quill from "eye".

HACKLE. Two grizzle (Plymouth Rock) cock, tied bushy. (Alternative: Red game cock hackle at rear, grizzle in front.)

Harrison's Bluebottle

HOOK. No. 10–12.

TAG. Two to three turns gold thread, followed by three turns overlapping, of scarlet floss.

BODY. Bronze peacock herl from "eye" part of tail.

HACKLE. Black hen.

WING. S.A. yellowbill duck wing quills. (Substitute: English Teal.)

Heiber's Fancy

HOOK. No. 9–7.

TAIL. Golden pheasant tippet fibres.

BODY. Crimson floss.

RIB. None.

BODY HACKLE. Grizzle (Plymouth Rock) ribbed up body, from shoulder to tail.

WING. Guinea fowl wing or tail quill.

HEAD. Black.

Heiber's Sgebenga

HOOK. Large.

TAIL. Brown mottled bustard tied wing-wise—small.

BODY. Flat gold tinsel.

WING. Brown mottled bustard tied very small and short.

HACKLE. The long-fibred neck hackle of the bustard, tied to sweep back beyond tail.

THROAT HACKLE. Ginger cock.

Hilliard Special

BODY. Bronze peacock herl.

RIB. Flat silver tinsel.

HACKLE. Black cock.

WING. (Streamer.) A bunch of bronze peacock herl. (The fine bronze-green from the "eye" part of the tail.)

SHOULDER. Two strips of scarlet duck wing quill, about one-third length of wing.

CHEEK. Jungle cock, with "eye" part close to head of fly.

Ivor's Special

TAIL. A good bunch of brown mallard, grouse or partridge fibres.

BODY. Bronze peacock herl, thick.

RIB. Pink silk or wool.

HACKLE. Brown partridge back.

WING. Brown mallard, grouse tail or turkey tail.

Jindabyne

TAIL. Light ginger hackle fibres.

BODY. Bright yellow floss silk.

RIB. Black silk.

HACKLE. Light ginger.

WINGS. Teal flank.

Katamayo Killer

HOOK. Any size preferred.
TAIL. Black cock hackle fibres.
BODY. Black wool.
WING. Black crow.
HACKLE. Black cock.
HEAD. Red tarnish.

Kenya Bug

TAIL. Black whisks—sometimes blue guinea fowl.
BODY. Black wool thick, ribbed with silver tinsel.
HACKLE. Large soft black cock.
WING. Nil.
HEAD. Black varnish.

Kerr's Special

TAIL. Fibres of brown mallard.
BODY. Peacock bronze herl, very thick.
HACKLE. Natural red hen.
WING. Brown mallard, tied in a bunch low over body, or grey mallard, dyed medium olive.

King Butcher

HOOK. No. 8–11.
TAIL. Golden pheasant tippet fibres, with tip of Indian crow feather above.
TAG. Flat silver tinsel which is continued to form body.
RIB. Oval silver tinsel.
HACKLE. Black hen.
WING. From secondary feathers of wing lilac breasted roller royal blue outermost. (Substitute: Blue-white tipped mallard.)

Little Redwing

HOOK. No. 10–11.
TAG. Three to four turns round gold tinsel.
TAIL. Three paired strands white duck quill, dyed golden yellow.

BODY. Mole fur.
RIB. Yellow floss.
HACKLE. Brown partridge back.
WING. From wing secondaries of S.A. redwing partridge. (Substitute: Woodcock.)

March Brown Variant

TAIL. Three or four whisks from speckled hen feather.
BODY. Yellow and red wool in alternate bands.
HACKLE. Soft speckled hen feather.
WING. Speckled hen wing quill feather.
HOOK. No. 12–16 (old).

Mooi Moth

TAIL. Several fibres of medium blue dun cock hackle.
BODY. Well-marked peacock quill.
HACKLE. Medium blue dun cock.
WING. From grey mallard duck wing quill.

Mountain Swallow

TAIL. Blue and orange cock hackle fibres.
BODY. Orange wool.
RIB. Flat gold tinsel.
HACKLE. Mixed orange and blue cock hackles.
WING. Two strips of dyed blue duck wing quill, with two married strips of orange duck quill on top.

Musson's Mephistopheles

HOOK. No. 12–9.
BODY. Yellow silk.
RIB. Red silk.
HACKLE. Guinea fowl.

Nut Brown Beetle (two versions)

HOOK. No. 10–11.

No. 1. Beetle contemplating flight.

Wing tips protruding beyond shell, the tips of two golden pheasant crest feathers laid back to back, on top of and at right-angles to bend of hook.

BODY. Bronze peacock herl.

HACKLE. (Legs.) Coch-y-bondhu.

WING CASE. Red golden pheasant breast feather fibres, tied in at tail and brought over body and tied in at head. Best side uppermost.

No. 2. Beetle in flight.

TAG. Three to four turns round gold tinsel.

BODY. Bronze peacock herl.

HACKLE. (Legs.) Coch-y-bondhu.

WING. Hackle tips from breast of brown francolin, tied fanwise, at right-angle to body (i.e. spent).

SHELL. Two medium-sized jungle cock feathers tied fanwise in front of wings and having a slight forward sweep.

Outspan Coachman

TAIL. Tuft of white D.F.M. floss or wool.

BODY. Bronze peacock herl.

RIB. Scarlet "Lurex".

HACKLE. Natural brown.

WING. From any white feather, usually white duck quill.

Pirie Green

TYPE. Salmon, but used for large brown and rainbow trout.

TAIL. Golden pheasant crest.

BODY. Orange wool or seal's fur.

RIBBING. Flat gold tinsel.

HACKLE. Hot orange.

WING. The dark green shiny wing feather of the Egyptian goose, tied horizontal.

SIDE. Narrow strip either side of the black barred white feather from the wing of the Egyptian goose, dyed orange.

HEAD. Black varnish.

HOOK. No. 6–7–8.

Popeye the Prawn

HOOK. No. 6–8.

WHISKERS. Bunch of black buck tail—graduated.

THROAT. Bunched red breast feathers from cock golden pheasant.

EYES. Jungle cock.

HEAD. Shoulders, legs, duiker buck fur, or brown part of bucktail.

BODY. Sand-coloured floss, ribbed gold tinsel, and two applications of clear varnish over.

TAIL. Points of two broken partridge back feathers.

Notes: The prawn swims backwards, so the hooks are dressed in reverse. The body should be dressed very thickly.

Prince Charming

HOOK: No. 12–8.

TAIL. Golden pheasant tippet fibres.

BODY. Bronze peacock herl each end with flat silver tinsel in centre. (Three equal parts.)

HACKLE. Blue jay wing feathers.

WING. Blue part of white-tipped quill from mallard duck wing.

Rector's Fancy

TAIL. Golden pheasant tippet.

BODY. Embossed silver tinsel.

HACKLE. Bright orange.

WING. Mallard drake, blue secondaries.

HOOK. No. 10–7.

Ricky's Mole

TAIL. Claret web. (Variation: Black and white web-ibis or guinea fowl.)

BODY. Mole skin.
HACKLE. Black, cock, long.
HOOK. No. 9–6.

Silver Knight
HOOK. No. 10–6.
TAIL. Golden pheasant tippet.
BODY. First two-thirds from tail—flat silver. Remaining one-third—seal's fur dyed scarlet.
RIBBING. Silver wire.
HACKLE. Brown partridge.
WING. Corncrake; or bustard; barred.

Small's Green Nymph
TAIL. Partridge or hen pheasant tail, two or three strands.
BODY. Olive green wool, fairly heavily tapered.
RIBBED. Oval gold tinsel.
HACKLE. Brown-red (R.I.R.) or honey, sparse.
HOOK. Long ($\frac{3}{4}$ in.) shank-straight eye, modified as required for individual waters.
Good for deep, still pools or dams. Allow to sink naturally, and retrieve very slowly near the bottom.

Staple Diet
BODY. Black wool.
HACKLE. Black crow feather, soft.

Swazi Queen
HOOK. No. 12–9.
TAG. Gold, round tinsel.
TAIL. Golden pheasant crest.

BUTT. Peacock, bronze herl.
BODY. Floss silk, pale olive green.
RIB. Gold, round tinsel.
HACKLE. Partridge, brown, back or shoulder.
WING. Duck, silver-grey satins.
HEAD. Peacock, bronze herl.

Tanager
TAIL. Fibres of plain blue vulturine guinea fowl feather.
BODY. Yellow floss.
WING. Tips of two yellow tanager feathers, back to back, with blue vulturine guinea fowl fibres over.
No hackle.

Walker's Black Widow
HOOK. No. 6. Long shank.
BODY. Red floss.
RIB. Oval silver tinsel.
HACKLE. Black cock.
WING. Two black cock hackles back to back, tied down on top of body by winding ribbing tinsel over stem of hackle.
HEAD. Black varnish.

Walker's Green Nymph
TAIL. Bunch of black cock hackle fibres.
BODY. Green chenille.
RIB. Flat gold tinsel.
HACKLE. Black cock hackle.
WING CASE. Two partridge striped shoulder feathers, tied in at side to envelope front half of body.
TYING SILK. Green.
HEAD. Clear varnish over tying silk.

Walker's Killer

In an earlier edition of this book, the fly shown as Walker's Killer in a colour plate was incorrect. Three sets of partridge feathers have to be used as shown in the plate, but the tips of all three sets should meet as shown in the black and white illustration.

"Walker's Killer"

I apologise to all concerned for the mistake, particularly as this is one of the most successful flies now used in African waters. I am therefore including the report on the evolution of the fly, sent to me in October 1962 by Lionel Walker, and give it here verbatim:

"I am frequently asked why I made the 'Walker's Killer', and because of its success, I think it a good idea to put on paper my reasons for doing so.

Firstly, let me give the correct dressing of this fly. It should be made on a No. 4 hook. The body is of red chenille, tail a bunch of black hackle fibres. Over the chenille body, eighteen tips of English Partridge heckles, either speckled or striped are tied. These are put on in three layers of three feathers each, on each side of the body. The first layer is placed one-third of the way up the shank and extends to the bend. The second layer about two-thirds up the shank and completely covers the first layer. The final layer tied in at head covering all, but tied not too close to the eye of hook, the idea being to give the head a torpedo shape appearance which helps to give the fly a good entry. That is, it should come through the water in an upright and natural position not on its side or upside down as many flies do, and not making any undue disturbance.

I have always been one to look for the bigger fish, and I wanted a fly that would look more like their staple diet than those generally used for wet fly fishing. From my observations the bigger fish generally like a secluded spot in deepish pools, near a tree or some large boulders, near a bank where there is plenty of overhanging vegetation or in a backwash, and such places, and they prefer to obtain their food with the least possible exertion. They also like a good big morsel and feed mostly on the various nymphs and larvae, tadpoles and the like.

During my many years of fishing, I have learned a little about entomology and aquatic insects, a study of their life cycle, a most fascinating subject. I have never been happy about fishing a winged fly under water as it is most unnatural. A winged fly does not swim under water and so my fly had to be something that would look more like a nymph and more natural. It had to be a good mouthful and it had to be made with the ordinary fly tying materials. I chose red for the body as I believe that a red body has more appeal to the trout than any other colour. I decided on chenille because it gives a good fat body and also soaks up a lot of water quickly, helping the fly to sink. The fly had to have a sleek appearance and keep its shape with the feathers sticking well down on the sides when wet, hence the idea of three layers of feathers. If the feathers were tied in at the head only, but covering the body, although tied on the sides, these would still be the ordinary wet fly effect, but by putting the under layers, each layer sticks firmly on the other when wet and it will maintain its shape however much false casting may be done. A good bunch of fibres in the tail of the fly, I believe, gives balance and movement.

Partridge hackles were chosen because they more generally represent the colour of the various nymphs, and they blend well with the body colour. For best results this fly should be fished rather deep, retrieved with a fairly fast jerky action at the same time aiding the movement with the tip of the rod."

Durham

30th October 1962

Walker's Red Nymph
Same as Green Nymph, but with red chenille body.

Walker's Special
HOOK. No. 6–8.
TAIL. Golden pheasant tippet fibres.
BODY. Black chenille or seal's fur.
RIB. Flat silver tinsel.
HACKLE. Black cock.
WING. Bronze peacock herl from "eye" part of tail, clipped short above bend of hook.
HEAD. Black varnish.

Walker's Yellow Nymph
TAIL. Bunch of natural brown cock hackle fibres.
BODY. Yellow chenille.
RIB. Flat gold tinsel.
HACKLE. Natural medium red cock hackle.

WING CASE. Two partridge-striped shoulder feathers, tied to envelope front part of body.
TYING SILK. Yellow olive.
HEAD. Clear varnish over tying silk.

Wizard
HOOK. No. 10–6.
TAG. Several turns flat silver tinsel.
TAIL. Brown mallard shoulder fibres, fairly long, with any scarlet fibres each side.
BODY. Red or yellow wool or chenille tied thick, and then heavily overlaid with strips of any long-fibred coarse mottled or speckled fur.
HEAD. Black.
WHISKERS. Black bucktail or goat main.
(The finished article looks like a small mouse or water shrew.)

Yates' Stand-by

TAIL. Nil.

BODY. Peacock herl, bronze.

UNDER-HACKLE. Cinnamon and black hen, medium size (Variation: Cree hen.)

HACKLE. Coch-y-bondhu type, cock, large.

HOOK. No. 11-8.

Yates' Silver

HOOK. No. 10-7.

UNDER-BODY. Tinned copper. (10-amp. fuse wire will do.)

TAIL. Fibres from jay blue wing feather.

BODY. Flat silver tinsel.

RIB. Round silver.

HACKLE. Coot lesser wing covert.

WING. From crow wing quill.

Kemp

Suitable for both Kenyan and Rhodesian trout.

HOOK. 10-6 long shank.

TAIL. Golden pheasant crest.

BODY. Flat gold or copper tinsel.

UNDER HACKLE. Golden pheasant crest tied to lie back along and below the body.

HACKLE. Grey partridge back feather.

UNDERWING. Light brown hair fibres.

WING. Bronze peacock herl.

CHEEKS. Jungle cock.

SECTION 8

―――――――

CANADIAN AND U.S.A. PATTERNS

*Sixty illustrated in colour
between pages 80 and 81*

*Patterns for the Coloured
Plates supplied by
Mr. C. G. Joudry of Montreal*

Broadbent
TAIL. Golden pheasant tippet.
BODY. Yellow floss.
RIB. Flat gold tinsel.
HACKLE. Yellow cock.
WING. Guinea fowl wing quill.

March Brown Silver
TAIL. Two strands as hackle.
BODY. Flat silver tinsel.
RIB. Oval silver tinsel.
HACKLE. Brown partridge back feather.
WING. Hen pheasant wing quill.

Quebec Partridge
TAIL. Strands golden pheasant tippet.
BODY. Dark green wool.
RIB. Narrow flat gold tinsel.
HACKLE. Light red game cock.
WING. Brown speckled turkey wing quill.

Alder
TAG. Flat gold tinsel.
TAIL. Fibres as wing.
BODY. Peacock bronze herl.
HACKLE. Black cock.
WINGS. Brown speckled turkey wing quill
   or speckled hen.

Grasshopper
TAG. Flat gold tinsel.
BODY. Yellow wool.
HACKLE. Furnace cock.
WING. Speckled grey turkey wing quill.

Chantry
BODY. Peacock bronze herl.
RIB. Flat gold tinsel.
HACKLE. Red game cock.
WINGS. Mottled brown turkey wing quill
   or speckled hen.

Grizzly King
TAIL. Scarlet duck quill.
BODY. Green floss.
RIB. Flat gold tinsel.
HACKLE. Grizzle cock.
WINGS. Grey mallard flank.

Green Drake
TAIL. As hackle.
BODY. Green wool.
RIB. Flat gold tinsel.
HACKLE. Red game cock.
WING. Green mallard flank.

Queen of Waters
TAG. Flat gold tinsel.
TAIL. Golden pheasant tippet.
BODY. Orange floss.
RIB. Flat gold tinsel.
HACKLE. Light red game cock.
WING. Grey mallard flank.

King of Waters
BODY. Crimson floss.
RIB. Flat gold tinsel.
HACKLE. Brown cock.
WING. Grey mallard flank.

Yellow May
TAIL. Yellow mallard.
BODY. Yellow floss.
RIB. Black tying silk.
HACKLE. Yellow cock.
WING. Lemon yellow mallard flank.

Professor
TAIL. Scarlet duck quill.
BODY. Yellow floss.
RIB. Flat gold tinsel.
HACKLE. Light red game cock.
WINGS. Grey mallard flank.

Royal Coachman
TAIL. A few strands of golden pheasant tippet.
BODY. Divided roughly into thirds. The two outer thirds of bronze peacock herl and the centre of scarlet floss.
HACKLE. Natural light red cock.
WINGS. White duck wing quill.

Jenny Lind
TAIL. Fibres as wing.
BODY. Yellow floss.
RIB. Flat gold tinsel.
HACKLE. Scarlet cock.
WING. Bright blue duck wing quill.

Parmachenee Belle
TAIL. White duck and scarlet as for wings.
BODY. Yellow floss.
RIB. Flat gold tinsel.
HACKLE. Scarlet cock.
WING. White duck wing quill with a stripe of scarlet on each side. The scarlet should be about one-third the width of the white.

Colonel Fuller
TAIL. Scarlet as wing.
BODY. Yellow floss.

RIB. Flat gold tinsel.
HACKLE. Scarlet cock.
WING. Strips of yellow and scarlet duck wing quill.

Scarlet Ibis
TAIL. Scarlet as wing.
BODY. Scarlet floss.
RIB. Flat gold tinsel.
HACKLE. Scarlet cock.
WING. Scarlet duck wing quill.

Yellow Sally
BODY. Yellow wool.
RIB. Flat gold tinsel.
HACKLE. Light red game cock.
WING. Yellow duck wing quill.

Butcher
TAIL. Scarlet duck quill.
BODY. Flat silver tinsel.
HACKLE. Black cock.
WING. Blue feather from mallard duck.

Tippet and Silver
TAIL. Golden pheasant tippet.
BODY. Flat silver tinsel.
RIB. Silver wire.
HACKLE. Badger.
WING. Golden pheasant tippet.

Alexandra
TAG. Scarlet floss.
TAIL. Peacock herl and scarlet as wing.
BODY. Flat silver tinsel.
HACKLE. Black cock.
WING. Peacock sword herl and scarlet duck wing quill.

McGinty
TAIL. Three strands as hackle.
BODY. Black and yellow four-joint chenille.

HACKLE. Red game cock.
WING. White tip feather from mallard duck or turkey rump.

Annoncia
TAIL. Strands golden pheasant tippet.
BODY. Scarlet wool, picked out.
RIB. Flat silver tinsel.
HACKLE. Scarlet cock.
WING. Cock pheasant brown breast feather with dark tip.

Bee
BODY. Black and yellow chenille.
HACKLE. Furnace cock.
WING. Grey mallard wing quill.

Grouse and Yellow
TAIL. Golden pheasant tippet.
BODY. Yellow wool.
RIB. Flat gold tinsel.
HACKLE. Yellow cock.
WING. Speckled grouse tail feather.

Bustard and Orange
TAIL. Golden pheasant tippet.
BODY. Orange wool.
RIB. Flat gold tinsel.
HACKLE. Red game cock.
WING. Brown speckled turkey wing quill or speckled hen.

Mallard and Claret
TAIL. Golden pheasant tippet.
BODY. Claret wool.
RIB. Flat gold tinsel.
HACKLE. Claret cock.
WING. Brown mallard.

Light Montreal
TAIL. Scarlet duck quill.
BODY. Scarlet wool.
RIB. Flat gold tinsel.
HACKLE. Scarlet cock.
WING. Light brown speckled turkey wing quill or speckled hen.

Dark Montreal
TAIL. Scarlet duck quill.
BODY. Claret floss.
RIB. Flat gold tinsel.
HACKLE. Claret cock.
WING. Dark brown speckled turkey wing quill or speckled hen.

Quebec
TAIL. Golden pheasant topping.
BODY. Three turns orange floss, remainder claret wool.
RIB. Flat gold tinsel.
HACKLE. Claret cock.
WING. Two strips purple goose covered with two strips brown mallard.

Bradshaw's Fancy
TAIL. Scarlet wool, and carry through to top of head.
BODY. Peacock herl.
HACKLE. Blue grey cock, as collar.

Dyson
TAIL. Scarlet duck quill.
BODY. Peacock herl.
HACKLE. Brown cock, as collar.

Orange Fish Hawk
BODY. Orange floss.
RIB. Flat gold tinsel.
HACKLE. Light badger cock.

Black Woolly Worm
TAIL. Scarlet wool.
BODY. Black chenille not too thick.
RIB. Flat silver tinsel.
HACKLE. Grizzle cock—eight turns along the hook-shank and tied so that the fibres point forward.

Red Tag
TAG. Scarlet floss.
BODY. Peacock bronze herl.
HACKLE. Red game cock.

Zulu
TAIL. Scarlet wool.
BODY. Black wool.
RIB. Flat silver tinsel.
HACKLE. Black cock.

NORTH AMERICAN PATTERNS
WET-FLIES

Buck Caddis (light)
BODY. Deep yellow wool, or seal's fur.
HACKLE. Natural brown, palmered.
WING. Fibres from light brown bucktail.
HEAD. Black varnish.

Buck Caddis (dark)
BODY. Orange wool.
HACKLE. Natural brown—palmered.
WING. Fibres from dark brown bucktail.
HEAD. Black varnish.

Carey Special
TAIL. Fibres from cock pheasant rump feather.
BODY. Brown wool—short—about one third of tail end of hook.
The remainder of the hook is taken up by winding several cock pheasant rump feathers hackle-wise. The fibres of the hackles should slope well back over body.
HEAD. Black varnish.

Carey Coloured
Example: "Carey Red".
TAIL. Fibres of cock pheasant rump feather.
BODY. Red wool—wound as for "Carey Special".
The remainder of the hook is taken up as for the "Carey Special", but one or two of the rear hackles should be long-fibred cock hackles dyed red.
Other coloured variations can be: Green, yellow, blue, orange, etc.

Chimo
BODY. Orange wool or seal's fur.
RIB. Oval gold tinsel.
HACKLE. Blue jay, or spotted guinea fowl dyed blue.
WING. Dark moose body hair or dyed bucktail.
HEAD. Black varnish.

Claret Gnat
TAIL. Fibres from dull hen's hackle.
BODY. Claret floss or seal's fur.
HACKLE. Dull black hen.
WING. From grey mallard wing quill.

Cosseboom (salmon fly)
TAIL. Green floss or green cock hackle fibres.
BODY. Green floss or seal's fur.
RIB. Oval or flat silver tinsel.
WING. Grey squirrel tail.
HACKLE. Yellow—wound as a collar.
HEAD. Black varnish.

Dappled Dog (Canadian shrimp fly for salmon)
TAIL. Fibres of grey squirrel tail, and a strand of red fluorescent wool.
BODY. Lime green fluorescent wool, divided in centre with a grizzle hackle.
HACKLE. Grizzle, longer in fibre than centre hackle.

Dolly Varden
TAG. Gold tinsel.
TAIL. Brown hackle fibres.
BODY. White floss.
RIB. Gold tinsel.
WINGS. Brown mottled turkey wing quill.
(Oak turkey quill.)
HACKLE. Brown cock or hen.

Grasshopper
TAIL. Few fibres of red golden pheasant
body feather.
BODY. Apple green floss.
RIB. Oval silver tinsel.
WING. A few strands of brown bucktail,
covered with two segments from oak
brown turkey wing quill.
HACKLE. Wound in front of wings—
natural dark brown, and an English
brown partridge hackle in front of that.

Grey Moth
BODY. Grey floss silk.
RIB. Gold oval tinsel.
HACKLE. Dun.
WING. Widgeon wing quill.

Gunnison
TAIL. Fibres from grey mallard flank
feather.
BODY. Green floss silk.
RIB. White floss silk.
HACKLE. Natural brown.
WING. From white-tipped blue mallard
wing quill.

Haggart
TAIL. Fibres from brown mallard shoulder
feather.
BODY. Orange seal's fur.
RIB. Oval gold tinsel.
HACKLE. Woodcock breast or wing front
feather.
WING. From woodcock wing quill. (Variation: Yellow seal's fur.)

Jerry-Ma-Didler
TAIL. Scarlet duck wing quill.
BODY. Green wool, fur or floss.
RIB. Gold tinsel.
HACKLE. Claret.
WINGS. Brown mottled turkey tail, with
strip of scarlet duck wing quill each side.
HEAD. Black varnish.

Last Chance
TAG. Gold tinsel.
TAIL. Scarlet hackle fibres.
BODY. Yellow floss silk.
RIB. Black silk floss.
HACKLE. Natural red.
WING. Black wing quill feather.

Lord Baltimore
TAIL. Black and green wing quill fibres—
married.
BODY. Tan floss.
RIB. Black floss.
HACKLE. Dun.
WING. Black wing quill feather.
CHEEKS. Jungle cock.

Magalloway
TAG. Silver tinsel.
TAIL. Fibres from dyed yellow wing quill.
BODY. Brown wool.
HACKLE. Furnace.
WING. Peacock sword herls.

Magee
TAIL. Fibres of dark red cock hackle
(natural).
EGG SAC (just in front of tail). Yellow
chenille.
BODY. Bronze peacock herl.
HACKLE. Natural dark red cock.
WING. From guinea fowl spotted wing
quill.

HEAD. Yellow chenille.

(The colours of the egg sac and head may be varied—red, green, etc., and the wing should extend well beyond bend of hook.)

Maxwell Blue
TAG. Silver tinsel.
TAIL. Blue hackle fibres.
BODY. Grey wool or fur.
RIB. Oval silver tinsel.
HACKLE. Dyed blue.
WING. From white-tipped blue mallard wing quill.

McAlpin
TAG. Gold tinsel.
TAIL. Fibres from dyed scarlet wing quill feather.
BODY. Claret seal's fur.
RIB. Gold tinsel.
HACKLE. Guinea fowl.
WING. Green peacock herl.
SIDES. Ibis, or substitute.

Montana Nymph
TAIL. Fibres from black hen hackle, about $\frac{1}{4}$ in. long.
TAIL HALF OF BODY. Black ostrich herl, which is then brought over front half and tied at head.
FRONT HALF OF BODY. Yellow chenille.
HACKLE (over front half only). Good stiff black cock hackle.
HORNS. Section from any black wing quill feather, divided into two (about $\frac{1}{2}$ in. long).
HOOK. No. 7 long shank.

Nation Silver Tip
TAIL. Tippet fibres.
BODY. Tail end two or three turns of silver tinsel, remainder black floss.
RIB. Oval silver tinsel.

WING. Fibres of golden pheasant tippet, with strips from grey speckled turkey wing quill each side.
SIDES. Two narrow strips of scarlet ibis or substitute.

Orvis Grey
TAIL. Dun hackle fibres.
TAG. Gold tinsel.
BODY. Olive seal's fur.
RIB. Oval gold tinsel.
HACKLE. Dun.
WING. White-tipped turkey rump feather.

Pembina
TAIL. Fibres of scarlet and yellow dyed duck wing quill.
BODY. Scarlet wool or floss.
RIB. Oval silver tinsel.
HACKLE. Scarlet.
WING. Brown speckled hen wing quill, with married strips of scarlet and yellow duck each side.

Salmon Pink
TAIL. Fibres from grey partridge hackle.
BODY. Black wool or fur.
RIB. Oval silver tinsel.
HACKLE. Grey partridge.
WING. From hen pheasant tail.

Skinnum
TAIL. Fibres from blue dun cock hackle.
BODY. Stripped peacock quill, or grey floss with a black silk rib.
HACKLE. Pale blue dun, very sparse.
WING. From woodcock wing quill.
Sometimes used as a dry-fly.

Swiftwater
TAIL. Fibres from grey mallard flank feather.
BODY. Alternate bands of bronze peacock herl and orange floss.
HACKLE. Natural brown.
WING. Any white wing quill feather.

Tooley Special
TAIL. Section of dyed red duck wing quill.
BODY. Light claret or crimson wool.
RIB. Gold tinsel.
HACKLE. Natural brown.
WING. Two or more cock pheasant rump feathers tied, rolled or flat on top of hook, depending on how heavy a fly is required.
HEAD. Black varnish.

Yellow Helfly
TAIL. Two black cock hackle tips tied back to back.
BODY. Yellow chenille.
RIB. Oval silver tinsel.
HACKLE. Bright yellow wound full.
Sometimes dressed as a dry-fly.

Yellow Spinner
TAIL. Yellow hackle fibres.
TAG. Round gold tinsel.
BODY. Yellow ostrich herl.
HACKLE. Scarlet.
WING. Any black wing quill feather.

Mitchell. Small salmon fly.
TAG. Fine oval tinsel and yellow floss.
TAIL. Golden pheasant crest and any bright blue feather fibres.
BUTT. Red floss.
BODY. Black floss.
RIB. Rine oval silver tinsel.
HACKLE. Mixed—black and golden pheasant crest.
UNDERWING. Bright blue strip.
WINGS. Black, golden pheasant crest over.
CHEEKS. Jungle cock.
HEAD. Red varnish.

NORTH AMERICAN PATTERNS
DRY-FLIES

Brown Palmer
BODY. Brown wool.
RIB. Flat gold tinsel.
HACKLE. Brown cock.

Black Palmer
TAIL. Scarlet hackle fibres.
BODY. Black wool.
HACKLE. Black cock.

Grey Palmer
BODY. Grey wool.
RIB. Flat gold tinsel.
HACKLE. Grizzle cock.

Partridge Spider
TAIL. Brown partridge fibres.
BODY. Dark brown wool.
RIB. Flat gold tinsel.
HACKLE. Brown partridge.

Red Spider
BODY. Flat gold tinsel.

HACKLE. Natural dark red cock.

Black Spider
BODY. Black chenille.
HACKLE. Black cock.

Blue Dun
TAIL. Blue dun hackle fibres.
BODY. Blue dun wool.
WING. Blue dun duck wing quill.
HACKLE. Blue dun cock.

Mosquito
TAIL. Grey mallard fibres.
BODY. Light grey floss.
RIB. Flat silver tinsel.
WING. Grizzle hackle tips.
HACKLE. Grizzle cock.

Mosquitoes (coloured)
Same as Mosquito, but with hackle and tail fibres dyed various colours—yellow, green, orange, etc.

August Dun
TAIL. Dark brown hackle fibres.
BODY. Light brown floss.
RIB. Yellow tying silk.
WING. Hen pheasant wing quill.
HACKLE. Dark brown cock.

Black Gnat
BODY. Black chenille.
RIB. Flat gold tinsel.
WING. Starling wing quill.
HACKLE. Black cock.

Hardie's Favourite
TAIL. Golden pheasant tippet.
BODY. Claret floss.
RIB. Bronze peacock herl.
WINGS. Woodcock wing quill.
HACKLE. Grey partridge breast.

Wickham's Fancy
TAIL. Red cock hackle fibres.
BODY. Flat gold tinsel.
RIB. Gold wire.
WING. Starling wing quill.
HACKLE. Red game cock.

NORTH AMERICAN PATTERNS
DRY-FLIES

Bradford
TAIL. Tips of two grizzle hackles dyed yellow.
BODY. Bronze peacock herl.
WING. Tips of two grizzle cock hackles, dyed yellow.
HACKLE. Grizzle dyed yellow, wound in front of wings.

Cap Davis
TAIL. Grey squirrel tail fibres.
BODY. Light grey wool.
RIB. One strand of bronze peacock herl.
WING. Grizzle hackle tips.
HACKLE. Mixed grizzle and furnace.

Dark Sedge
BODY. Chocolate-coloured wool.
BODY HACKLE. Brown—tied palmer.
WING. Two partridge striped shoulder feathers, one each side of hook shank and in line with it.
FRONT HACKLE. Brown.

Dark Trinity (dapping fly)
TAIL. Golden pheasant tippet fibres.
BODY. Black raffia—lacquered.

WINGS. Two matched pairs of cock pheasant brown neck feathers.
HACKLE. Yellow cock or hen.

David James (T or S)
TAIL. Crimson hackle fibres.
BODY. Water rat or seal's fur dyed black.
RIB. Fine oval silver tinsel.
WING. Black bucktail, tied forward.
HACKLE. Black cock, wound behind wings.

Dry Bucktail
TAIL. Fibres of red game cock hackle.
BODY. Orange floss.
BODY HACKLE. Red game cock.
WING. Fibres from natural brown bucktail, the stiffer the better.

Irresistible
TAIL. Caribou hair fibres.
BODY. Deer hair, wound on shank and cut short.
WING. Caribou hair, tied upright.
HACKLE. Blue dun cock, tied behind wing.

Orange Sedge
TAIL. Orange hackle fibres.

TAG. Gold tinsel.
BODY. Brown wool.
RIB. Gold tinsel.
BODY HACKLE. Ginger.
WING. Dyed orange wing quill feather.
HEAD HACKLE. Ginger.

Rat Faced McDougal
TAIL. Brown bucktail fibres.
BODY. Deer body hair (grey), clipped to shape.
WINGS. Badger hackle tips.
HACKLE. Ginger.

NORTH AMERICAN PATTERNS
HAIR WING AND STREAMER FLIES

Blue Damsel
TAIL. Golden pheasant tippet.
BODY. Bronze peacock herl.
HACKLE. Blue cock tied as collar.
WING. Blue goose wing quill.

Black Demon
BODY. Flat gold tinsel.
HACKLE. Scarlet cock tied as collar.
WING. Black goose wing quill.

Ashdown green
TAIL. Two strips scarlet duck or goose quill.
BODY. Claret wool.
RIB. Flat gold tinsel.
HACKLE. Claret cock.
WING. White goose wing quill.

Old Gold
TAIL. Golden pheasant topping.
BODY. Dark yellow wool.
RIB. Flat gold tinsel.
HACKLE. Furnace cock.
WING. Scarlet goose, covered by bronze mallard.

Joe's Hopper
TAIL. Scarlet hackle fibres.
BODY. Yellow ostrich herl.
BODY HACKLE. Red game cock.
FRONT HACKLE. Grizzle cock dyed yellow.
WING. Light brown speckled turkey wing quill.

Fingerling
TAIL. Tip of scarlet cock hackle.
BODY. Embossed gold tinsel.
HACKLE. Red game cock.
WING. Four golden pheasant tippets back to back to show three bars.
CHEEKS. Scarlet goose wing quill with green peacock herl overall.

Red Badger
TAIL. Scarlet duck or goose quill.
BODY. Scarlet wool.
RIB. Flat gold tinsel.
HACKLE. Badger cock as collar.
WING. Two badger hackles back to back.

Titian
TAG. Orange floss.
BODY. Bronze peacock herl.
RIB. Orange floss.
HACKLE. Brown wound as collar.
WING. Fronds of bronze peacock herl with brown cock hackle each side, to be twice the length of body.

Grey Mare
TAIL. Scarlet duck or goose quill.
BODY. Flat silver tinsel.
RIB. Oval silver tinsel.
HACKLE. Brown cock.
WING. Two grizzle cock hackles back to back.

Red Abbey

TAIL. Scarlet goose or duck quill.
BODY. Scarlet floss.
RIB. Flat gold tinsel.
HACKLE. Brown cock.
WING. Brown bucktail.

Black and White Bucktail

TAIL. Scarlet goose or duck quill.

BODY. Flat silver tinsel.
WING. White bucktail with black on top.

Mickey Finn

BODY. Flat silver tinsel.
RIB. Oval silver tinsel.
WING. Scarlet and yellow bucktail, in three bands of colour, with red in centre. Upper yellow band is twice the size of lower.

NORTH AMERICAN PATTERNS
HAIR WING AND STREAMER FLIES

Androscoggin

BODY. Claret floss.
RIB. Flat silver.
HACKLE. White bucktail tied underneath, and reaching to bend of hook.
WING. Two green hackles, back to back.
HEAD. Black varnish.

Black Dog

TAIL. Black and yellow cock hackle fibres.
BODY. Black floss.
RIB. Oval silver.
THROAT. Short piece of yellow wing quill feather.
WING. Dun hackles—streamer style.
EYES. Jungle cock.
HACKLE. Black cock, wound as a collar.
HEAD. Black varnish.

Black Silver Tip

TAIL. None.
TAIL THIRD OF BODY. Flat silver tinsel.
BODY. Black floss silk.
RIB. Oval silver tinsel, over floss only.
HACKLE. A few fibres of white cock hackle at throat.
WING. Black moose hair, or dyed bucktail.

Blumarabou

BODY. Flat silver tinsel.

RIB. Oval silver.
WING. Dyed blue marabou plumes, and two grizzle cock hackles.
EYES. Jungle cock.
HEAD. Black varnish.

Brook Trout

BODY. Rear two-thirds—white floss, remainder pink floss.
RIB. Medium flat gold tinsel.
THROAT. First a bunch of hot orange hackle fibres, then a bunch of black hackle fibres, followed by a bunch of white hackle fibres.
WING. A small bunch of hot orange bucktail, over which is a pair of grizzle hackles dyed yellow, and outside of these a pair of olive green saddle hackles.
EYES. Jungle cock.
HEAD. Black varnish.

Brown Buffum

TAIL. Golden pheasant tippet fibres.
BODY. Orange floss.
RIB. Oval gold tinsel.
THROAT. Golden pheasant tippet fibres.
WING. Brown squirrel tail.
EYES. Jungle cock, tied close to head.
HEAD. Black varnish.

Cut Lips
TAIL. Tip of a blue dun cock hackle.
BODY. Pale lavender wool, tapering from shoulder to tail.
THROAT. Tip of a blue dun hackle.
WING. Two olive green saddle hackles on a small pattern (No. 8), four on any larger numbers.
EYES. Jungle cock.
HEAD. Black varnish.

Dwarf Sucker
TAIL. Fibres of light brown cock hackle.
BODY. Salmon pink floss.
RIB. Flat silver tinsel.
THROAT. Small bunch of white bucktail as long as hook-shank, and below this a small bunch of light brown cock hackle fibres.
WING. Natural brown bucktail fibres, topped with a bunch of green peacock herl.
EYES. Jungle cock.
HEAD. Black varnish.

Fletcher's Super
TAIL. Scarlet duck wing quill.
BODY. Yellow chenille.
RIB. Oval silver.
WING. White and green bucktail fibres, with two blue cock hackles.
EYES. Jungle cock.
HACKLE. Yellow.
HEAD. Black varnish.

General Ike
TAIL. Fibres from dyed scarlet wing quill (duck or goose).
TAG. Gold tinsel.
BODY. Yellow chenille.
THROAT. Scarlet cock or hen.
WING. Two brown olive cock hackles, back to back.

SHOULDERS. Strips from widgeon flank feathers, two-thirds length of wing.
HEAD. Black varnish.

G.I. Joe
TAG. Silver tinsel.
TAIL. Fibres from scarlet wing quill feather.
BODY. Olive chenille.
HACKLE. Yellow.
WING. Two green olive cock hackles, back to back.
SHOULDERS. Strips from pintail flank feathers, two-thirds length of wing.
EYES. Jungle cock.
HEAD. Black varnish.

Golden Darter
TAIL. Section from mottled brown turkey wing quill.
BODY. Golden yellow floss.
RIB. Medium flat gold tinsel.
THROAT. Tip of jungle cock body feather.
WING. Two golden badger saddle or neck hackles.
EYES. Jungle cock.
HEAD. Black varnish.

Golden Pheasant
BODY. Yellow floss or chenille.
RIB. Oval silver tinsel.
WING. Two white cock hackles.
CHEEKS. Golden pheasant tippet feathers.

Golden Sprat (S.)
TAG. Fine oval gold tinsel.
TAIL. Teal flank dyed yellow.
BODY. Flat gold over a foundation of orange floss silk.
RIB. Oval gold.
HACKLE. Cree—honey grizzle.
WING. A pair of deep yellow cock hackles back to back, with two cree hackles outside.

SIDES. Mallard flank dyed yellow.
EYES. Jungle cock.
HEAD. Red varnish.

Green's Pot
BODY. Flat silver tinsel.
RIB. Oval silver tinsel.
WING. White and green bucktail, with a green hackle either side.
EYES. Jungle cock.
HEAD. Black varnish.

Gray Ghost
BODY. Orange floss.
RIB. Flat silver tinsel.
THROAT. Bunch of bronze peacock herl fibres, tied on directly under the head, then a bunch of white bucktail, both as long as the wing. Finally a bunch of yellow cock hackle fibres or a golden pheasant crest.
WING. Four medium blue dun cock hackles, tied streamer style.
CHEEKS. Silver pheasant body feathers, or barred widgeon throat feathers.
EYES. Jungle cock.
HEAD. Black varnish.

Gray Smelt
TAIL. Golden pheasant crest.
BODY. White floss—tapered.
RIB. Flat silver tinsel.
WING. Two insect green hackles, with two grey hackles outside. These hackles can be either saddle or neck feathers.
EYES. Jungle cock.
HEAD. Black varnish.

Jessabou
BODY. Flat silver tinsel.
WING. Brown hackles and peacock herl tied streamer style.

EYES. Jungle cock.
HACKLE. Natural brown.
HEAD. Black varnish.

Ken's Special
TAG. Gold tinsel.
BODY. Black floss silk.
RIB. Oval gold tinsel.
WING. White and orange bucktail.

Light Tiger
TAIL. Fibres from silver pheasant body or wing feathers.
BODY. Bronze peacock herl.
THROAT. Fibres from dyed scarlet wing quill feather, tied in short.
WING. Yellow bucktail.
EYES. Jungle cock.
HEAD. Yellow varnish.

Little Wonder
BODY. Flat gold tinsel.
WING. Grizzle hackles over scarlet—tied streamer style.
HACKLE. Yellow.

Magog Smelt
BODY. Embossed silver tinsel.
RIB. Oval silver tinsel.
BELLY. A few white bucktail fibres.
THROAT. Two dyed red cock hackle tips.
WING. First—yellow bucktail, second purple bucktail, with three or four strands of peacock herl as a topping.
HEAD. Black varnish.

Male Dace
BODY. White floss, tapered, and built up quite full at shoulder.
RIB. Flat gold tinsel.
THROAT. Tips of two hot orange cock hackles.

WING. Two olive green cock hackles, with two golden badger hackles outside.
EYES. Jungle cock.
HEAD. Black varnish.

Marabou Special

TAIL. Tippet fibres.
BODY. Flat silver tinsel.
RIB. Oval silver tinsel.
WING. White marabou plumes, with grey mallard flank feathers two thirds of length.
SHOULDERS. Golden pheasant tippets.
EYES. Jungle cock.
HEAD. Black varnish.

Mickey Finn

BODY. Flat silver tinsel.
RIB. Oval silver tinsel.
WING. Yellow-scarlet-yellow bucktail.
EYES. Jungle cock.
HEAD. Black varnish.
(Tail of yellow and scarlet bucktail is optional.)

Miramachi

TAIL. Fibres from silver pheasant wing quill, and blue hackle fibres.
BODY. Flat gold tinsel.
RIB. Oval gold tinsel.
WING. Blue and scarlet hackles, tied streamer style.
HACKLE. Blue and scarlet mixed.
HEAD. Black varnish.

Muddler Minnow

TAIL. Segment from oak turkey wing quill.
BODY. Flat gold tinsel.
WING. Two matched segments of oak turkey wing quill, with strands of black and white impala or bucktail fibres tied sparsely on each side.
HACKLE OR NECK RUFF. A bunch of deer body hair, tied to form a "collar" and the front ends cut to represent a large burr on the front of the hook.

(The procedure given on page 57 shows how deer body hair can be spun on to the hook to form a hackle.)

Old Favourite

TAIL. Short piece bright red wool.
BODY. Flat silver tinsel.
HACKLE. None.
WING. Small bunch of white bucktail fibres, with a small bunch of brown ones over, and a few strands of peacock herl over all.
EYES. Jungle cock.
HEAD. Black varnish.

Racquette

TAIL. Yellow cock hackle fibres.
BODY. White floss, wound full, and tapered.
RIB. Flat silver tinsel.
THROAT. Small bunch of white bucktail as long as hook shank.
WING. Yellow-black-yellow bucktail, with bunch of peacock herl over.
EYES. Jungle cock.
HEAD. Black varnish.

Ramsbottom's Favourite

TAIL. Dyed red bucktail.
BODY. Yellow seal fur.
RIB. Oval gold tinsel.
HACKLE. Coch-y-bondhu.
WING. Bucktail dyed yellow, red, blue, green and brown.
HEAD. Black varnish.

Rusty Rat

BODY. Brown silk or chenille.
RIB. Oval gold tinsel.
WING. Red-brown hair
HEAD. Black, with two painted "eyes".

Shushan Postmaster

TAIL. Section from mottled turkey wing quill.
BODY. Yellow floss silk, full and tapered.
RIB. Flat gold tinsel.

THROAT. Section from red goose or duck quill (dyed).
WING. Brown barred squirrel tail fibres.
EYES. Jungle cock.
HEAD. Black varnish.

Silver Darter

TAIL. Section from silver pheasant wing quill.
BODY. White floss, full and tapered.
RIB. Flat gold tinsel.
THROAT. Three or four pieces of peacock sword herl.
WING. Two white badger hackles.
EYES. Jungle cock.
HEAD. Black varnish.

Silver Sprat

TAG. Fine silver tinsel.
TAIL. Fibres of teal or mallard flank.
BUTT. Black ostrich herl.
BODY. Flat silver tinsel over a foundation of white floss.
RIB. Oval silver tinsel.
WING. A pair of dyed blue cock hackles back to back, with two grizzle hackles outside.
SIDES. Grey mallard flank.
EYES. Jungle cock.
HEAD. Black varnish.

Sneaky Joe

TAIL. Section from dyed scarlet wing quill feather.
BODY. Black chenille.
WING. Brown barred squirrel tail fibres.
EYES. Jungle cock.
HEAD. Black varnish.

Trout Perch

TAIL. Tip of a blue dun hackle.

BODY. White floss silk, wound full and tapered.
RIB. Flat silver tinsel.
THROAT. Blue dun hackle tip.
WING. Two or three strands of pink dyed ostrich herl, with a small bunch of brown squirrel tail, and a cree cock hackle each side.
EYES. Jungle cock.
HEAD. Black varnish.

Warden's Worry

TAIL. Scarlet wing quill, fairly long.
BODY. Yellow wool.
RIB. Oval silver tinsel.
HACKLE. Yellow.
WING. Brown bucktail.
HEAD. Black varnish.

Yellow Perch

TAIL. Fibres of yellow cock hackle.
BODY. White floss, wound full and tapered.
RIB. Flat gold tinsel.
THROAT. Tips of two orange cock hackles.
WING. Two well-marked grizzle saddle hackles, with two yellow hackles outside.
TOPPING. A few strands of peacock herl.
EYES. Jungle cock.
HEAD. Black varnish

Yerxa

TAG. Round silver tinsel.
BODY. Yellow wool.
RIB. Oval silver tinsel.
THROAT. Yellow bucktail fibres.
WING. White bucktail.
EYES. Jungle cock.
HEAD. Black varnish.

SECTION 9

———

SCANDINAVIAN PATTERNS

THE NORWEGIAN TROUT AND SEA-TROUT FLIES

by John Sand

Blaka Fly
BODY. Bronze peacock herl.
RIB. Flat gold tinsel.
HACKLE. Greenwell hen.
WINGS. Brown speckled partridge tail.

Espeseth Fly
BODY. Lemon floss silk.
RIB. Red silk thread.
HACKLE. Red cock or hen hackle.
WINGS. White duck or goose dyed light blue.

Gullflua
TAIL. Three fibres of light red cock hackle.
BODY. Flat or oval gold tinsel.
HACKLE. Ginger or light red cock or hen hackle.
WINGS. Starling.

Gyllermøy
TAG. Flat gold tinsel.
BODY. Golden yellow chenille.
HACKLE. Speckled grouse back feather.

Nyleptha
TAIL. Three fibres from a red cock hackle.
BODY. Embossed gold tinsel.
HACKLE. Red cock hackle.
WINGS. Starling.

Hallingen
TAIL. Grizzled cock hackle fibres dyed lemon yellow.

BODY. Flat gold tinsel.
HACKLE. Grizzle or badger cock hackle dyed lemon yellow.
WING. Grey mallard quill feather.

Lensmannsflua
TAIL. Fibres of dark red cock hackle.
BODY. Purple tying silk
HACKLE. Dark red cock or hen.
WINGS. Brown mallard flank.

Grindalsflua
TAIL. Fibres of dyed lemon cock hackle.
BODY. Stripped peacock quill from "eye".
HACKLE. Dyed lemon cock.
WING. Starling dyed olive.

Sand's Favourite
TAG. Flat silver tinsel.
TAIL. Two or three fibres from a speckled partridge tail.
BODY. Dark fur from hare's ear.
RIB. Broad flat silver tinsel.
HACKLE. Brown partridge back.

Telemarkskongen
TAIL. Ibis.
BODY. Flat silver tinsel.
HACKLE. Light blue dyed cock or hen.
WING. Grey mallard flank.

Sorais
TAIL. Three fibres from a red cock hackle.
BODY. Embossed gold tinsel.
HACKLE. Black cock or hen.
WINGS. Starling.

Yellow Tail
TAIL. Lemon wool or floss.
BODY. Flat silver tinsel.
HACKLE. Black cock or hen.
WING. Snipe or mallard wing quill feather.

Akreflua
TAIL. Fibres of red cock hackle.
BODY. Stripped peacock quill from "eye".
HACKLE. Red cock or hen.
WING. Plain brown feather from mallard wing.

Rena Special
BODY. Pale cream floss.
RIB. Oval silver tinsel.
HACKLE. Badger cock or hen.
WING. Grey mallard flank.

Torgersen's Fancy I
TAIL. Golden pheasant tippet.
BODY. Black floss.
RIB. Silver wire or thread.
HACKLE. Black cock or hen.
WING. Ibis.

Torgersen's Fancy II
TAIL. Golden pheasant tippet.
BODY. Red floss.
RIB. Gold wire.
HACKLE. Dyed red cock.
WING. Blue mallard quill feather.

Trysilflua (Martin Holmseth)
BODY. Yellowish green wool.
RIB. Flat gold tinsel.
HACKLE. Red cock hackle.
WING. Brown mallard shoulder feather.

Quill Moth
BODY. Tail half. Stripped peacock quill from "eye". Front half: Tan ostrich herl.

HACKLE. Greenwell hen.
WING. White duck or goose.

Olsen
TAIL. Fibres of light ginger cock hackle.
BODY. Tail half: Lemon wool. Front half: Red wool.
RIB. Oval gold tinsel.
HACKLE. Light ginger cock.
WING. Woodcock wing quill feather.

Mustad's Favourite
TAIL. 6–8 strands flat silver tinsel.
BODY. Flat silver tinsel.
RIB. Round silver tinsel.
HACKLE. Red cock.
WING. Brown mallard shoulder.

Bromley, Dark
BODY. Pale brown floss.
RIB. Gold wire.
HACKLE. Light green love cock or hen.
WING. Grey mallard flank dyed light green olive.

Bromley, Light
BODY. Lemon floss.
RIB. Gold wire.
HACKLE. Dyed orange cock.
WING. Grey mallard flank, dyed light green olive.

Bromley, Orange
BODY. Pale brown floss.
RIB. Gold wire.
HACKLE. Dyed orange cock.
WING. Grey mallard flank, dyed light green olive.

Gregerson
TAIL. Red ibis.
BODY. Red floss.
RIB. Flat gold tinsel.
HACKLE. Red cock or hen.
WING. Brown mallard shoulder.

Gundersen's Special
TAIL. Three fibres from a Greenwell cock hackle.
BODY. Fur from hare's ear.
RIB. Gold wire.
HACKLE. Greenwell cock or hen.
WING. Grey mallard wing quill feather.

Klara Fly
TAIL. Red cock hackle fibres.
BODY. Lemon yellow floss.
RIB. Round gold tinsel.
HACKLE. Red cock or hen.
WING. Brown mallard shoulder feather.

Peder's Fancy
TAIL. 6–8 strands flat silver tinsel.
BODY. Embossed silver tinsel.
HACKLE. Spotted guinea fowl.
WING. Brown speckled hen wing quill feather.

Heggeli Fly
TAG. Silver wire.
TAIL. Tippet fibres.
BODY. Flat silver tinsel.
RIB. Silver wire.
HACKLE. Dark red cock or hen.
WING. Brown mallard shoulder feather.
SIDES. Jungle cock.

Palsbu
TAG. Flat gold tinsel.

TAIL. Red ibis and brown speckled turkey tail fibres.
BODY. Bronze peacock herl.
RIB. Round gold tinsel.
HACKLE. Red cock or hen.
WING. Brown speckled turkey tail.
SIDE. Jungle cock.

Sølvdokka
TAIL. Golden pheasant crest.
BODY. Flat silver tinsel.
RIB. Round silver tinsel.
HACKLE. Dyed light blue cock or hen.
WING. Married strands of yellow and red goose, brown mallard over.
SIDE. Jungle cock.

Huldra
TAIL. Golden pheasant crest.
BODY. Embossed silver tinsel.
HACKLE. Black hen hackle.
WING. Tippet fibres, sheathed with blue, red, yellow goose, brown mallard over.

Prinsessa
TAIL. Golden pheasant crest.
BODY. Embossed gold tinsel.
HACKLE. Red hen.
WING. Tippet fibres, sheathed with blue, red, yellow goose, brown mallard over.
(Both "Huldra" and "Prinsessa" are famous River Klara flies.)

NORWEGIAN SALMON FLIES

Golden Mallard
TAG. Flat gold tinsel.
TAIL. Golden pheasant crest, and tip of an Indian crow feather.
BUTT. Black floss.
BODY. First (tail) half flat gold tinsel, remainder black floss silk.

RIB. Oval gold tinsel.
HACKLE. Hot orange over black floss only.
THROAT HACKLE. Guinea fowl.
WING. Tippet fibres and cinnamon turkey tail completely covered by two broad strips of brown mallard. Topping over.
HEAD. Black varnish.

Grey Fancy

HOOK. No. 3.
TAG. Round silver tinsel.
TAIL. Golden pheasant crest and fibres of barred teal.
BODY. Grey wool.
RIB. Oval silver tinsel.
HACKLE. Cream.
THROAT HACKLE. Guinea fowl.
WING. Grey mallard flank covered by strips of dun or grey turkey tail.
HEAD. Black varnish.

Namsen

TAG. Round silver tinsel.
TAIL. Golden pheasant crest and fibres of barred teal.
BODY. Brown seal's fur.
RIB. Oval or twist silver tinsel.
HACKLE. Black cock—at throat only.
WING. White goose, with broad strips of barred teal each side. Topping over.
CHEEK. Jungle cock.
HEAD. Black varnish.

Ola

TAG. Round silver tinsel and pink floss.
BUTT. Black ostrich.
BODY. Tail half: Silver grey seal's fur. Front half: Black seal's fur.
RIB. Narrow oval and broad flat silver tinsel.
HACKLE. Front half only. Black cock.
THROAT. Spotted guinea fowl.
WING. White-tipped turkey tail, sheathed with a broad strip of blue swan or goose, brown mallard over.
TOPPING. Golden pheasant crest.
SIDE. Teal flank.
CHEEK. Jungle cock.
HEAD. Black.
TAIL. Golden pheasant crest.

Ottesen

TAG. Round silver tinsel and pink floss.
BUTT. Black ostrich herl.
TAIL. Golden pheasant crest.
BODY. White floss silk.
RIB. Red floss silk.
HACKLE. Hot orange cock.
THROAT. Widgeon hackle.
WING. Two tippets back to back, sheathed with yellow, red, blue swan or goose and brown mottled turkey tail, in that order.
SIDE. Teal flank.
CHEEK. Jungle cock.
TOPPING. Golden pheasant crest.
HEAD. Black.

Peer Gynt

TAG. Round silver tinsel and yellow floss.
TAIL. Golden pheasant crest and crimson hackle fibres.
BUTT. Black ostrich herl.
BODY. Flat silver tinsel.
RIB. Oval silver tinsel.
HACKLE. Crimson.
THROAT. Spotted guinea fowl.
WING. Brown mottled turkey tail, with brown mallard over.
TOPPING. Golden pheasant crest.
CHEEK. Jungle cock.
HORN. Blue-yellow macaw.
HEAD. Black.

Rallaren

TAG. Fine oval silver tinsel.
TAIL. Golden pheasant crest, fibres of barred teal, and strip of ibis or red goose.
BUTT. Black ostrich herl.
BODY. First half yellow floss, remainder bright green floss. The two halves separated by a black ostrich herl butt and behind this a hackle formed by a grey mallard flank feather, fairly long in fibre.

RIB. Oval silver tinsel.

THROAT HACKLES. Scarlet cock followed by barred teal flank.

WING. Strips of white-tipped turkey tail, yellow swan or goose with Amherst pheasant tail over. A topping over all.

SIDE. Barred teal flank.

CHEEK. Jungle cock.

HORN. Red macaw.

HEAD. Black varnish.

Rottenikken

TAG. Fine oval silver tinsel.

TAIL. Golden pheasant crest and fibres from speckled guinea fowl hackle.

BUTT. Black ostrich herl.

BODY. Tail third scarlet floss, remainder black ostrich herl.

RIB. Flat silver tinsel.

HACKLE. Grizzle cock hackle—over ostrich herl only.

THROAT HACKLE. Long-fibres speckled guinea fowl.

WING. Dark mottled turkey tail, with a topping over.

SIDE. Barred teal flank.

CHEEK. Jungle cock.

HORN. Red macaw.

HEAD. Black varnish.

Scarlet Pimpernel

TAG. Fine oval silver tinsel.

TAIL. Golden pheasant crest and strip of ibis or red goose.

BUTT. Black ostrich herl.

BODY. In three sections—first and third, flat silver tinsel; centre, scarlet floss.

RIB. Oval silver tinsel.

THROAT HACKLES. Large scarlet cock followed by grey mallard flank.

WING. Two strips of white-tipped turkey tail with broad strips of scarlet swan or goose each side. Topping over all.

SIDE. Barred teal flank.

CHEEK. Jungle cock.

HORNS. Blue macaw.

HEAD. Black varnish.

Sheriff

TAG. Fine oval gold tinsel.

TAIL. Golden pheasant crest and fibres from speckled guinea fowl hackle.

BUTT. Black ostrich herl.

BODY. First half flat gold tinsel, remainder black ostrich herl.

RIB. Oval gold tinsel.

HACKLE. Yellow cock over ostrich herl only.

THROAT HACKLE. Speckled guinea fowl hackle.

WING. Two strips of dark mottled turkey tail, with broad strips of brown mallard each side. Topping over all.

CHEEK. Jungle cock.

HORNS. Yellow macaw.

HEAD. Black varnish.

Stens Fancy

TAG. Round silver tinsel.

TAIL. Golden pheasant crest, barred teal fibres, and tip of an Indian crow feather.

BODY. Yellow-green wool or floss silk.

RIB. Oval silver tinsel.

HACKLE. Medium furnace.

WING. Tippet fibres, yellow, red and blue goose, barred teal flank and brown mallard over.

HEAD. Black varnish.

Thunderjet

TAG. Round gold tinsel and yellow floss.

BUTT. Black ostrich.

TAIL. Golden pheasant crest, and red crow or substitute.

BODY. First half: Pink floss. Second half: Flat gold tinsel. Black ostrich herl at joint, with tail half veiled with Indian crow or substitute.

RIB. Both halves: Oval gold tinsel.

HACKIE. Front half only: Hot orange.

THROAT. Dyed blue spotted guinea fowl.

WING. Two strips of brown mottled turkey tail, with brown mallard over.

CHEEK. Jungle cock.

TOPPING. Golden pheasant crest.

HORN. Blue-yellow macaw.

HEAD. Black.

SOME OTHER SCANDINAVIAN PATTERNS

Tumma Vaeltaja (Dark Tripper)
(Finnish salmon fly)

TAG. Fine round silver tinsel and red floss.

TAIL. Golden pheasant crest.

BUTT. Black ostrich herl.

BODY. Red floss at tail, followed by claret, dark brown and black wool.

RIB. Oval silver tinsel.

HACKLE. (Throat only.) Dark claret cock hackle.

WING. Golden pheasant breast feathers in strands, white-tipped turkey tail, golden pheasant tail, florican bustard, and brown mallard flank over. A golden pheasant crest over all.

CHEEK. Red golden pheasant breast feathers.

HEAD. Black varnish.

Atsingin Keltainen (Yellow Atsinki)
(Finnish salmon fly)

TAG. Fine round silver tinsel and yellow floss.

TAIL. Golden pheasant crest.

BUTT. Bronze peacock herl.

BODY. Two equal halves—first, yellow floss; second, grey wool.

RIB. Oval silver tinsel.

HACKLE. Orange over grey wool only.

THROAT HACKLE. A grizzle cock hackle.

WING. Tippet in strands, white-tipped turkey tail, red, yellow, blue goose, speckled bustard or substitute, golden pheasant tail, brown mallard flank over, and a golden pheasant crest over all.

HEAD. Black varnish.

Kola Fly (Finland—salmon)

TAG. Round silver tinsel and yellow floss.

TAIL. Fibres of grey mallard flank and red swan, and a golden pheasant crest.

BODY. Tail half: Yellow seal fur ribbed gold tinsel. Front half: Blue seal's fur ribbed silver tinsel.

HACKLE. Male Capercailzie body feather.

WING. Brown mottled turkey tail.

TOPPING. Golden pheasant crest.

HOOK. 2–0.

Sea-Trout Pattern (Denmark)

HOOK. Long shank No. 5.

BODY. Flat silver tinsel.

WING. (Streamer.) Two badger cock hackles.

HACKLE. (Collar.) Badger cock.

Chilimps (Shrimp) (Sweden)

HOOK. No. 3 Limerick.

BODY. Red floss silk, thick.

RIB. Embossed gold tinsel.

TAIL. Hot orange hackle tip.

HACKLE. (Tied palmer.) Hot orange.

Mauritz (Sweden)

TAIL. Tippet fibres.

BODY. Red floss.

RIB. Flat gold tinsel.

HACKLE. Dyed light blue cock.

WING. Grey mallard flank.

Hyland (Sweden)

TAG. Round silver tinsel.

TAIL. Golden pheasant crest.

BUTT. Black ostrich herl.

BODY. Purple floss.

RIB. Flat gold tinsel.

HACKLE. Black hen.

WING. (Yellow goose, grey speckled turkey wing, blue, red goose, in that order.)

SIDE. (Three-quarters length of wing.) Tips of red hen hackles.

(Both salmon flies.)

Spitfire (Norway)

TAIL. Section of turkey or goose dyed red.

BODY. Black floss or chenille.

WINGS. None.

BODY HACKLE. Medium fiery brown cock hackle wound from shoulder to tail.

RIB. Oval gold tinsel.

FRONT HACKLE. Natural speckled guinea fowl hackle.

SHOULDERS (OPTIONAL). Jungle cock.

HEAD. Black varnish.

Em-Te Flugor (Sweden)

TAG. Gold wire.

TAIL. Golden pheasant crest.

BODY. Mixed red/brown and green wool.

RIB. Flat gold tinsel.

THROAT. Black cock hackle.

WINGS. Polar Bear (Bucktail as substitute?), dyed cinnamon, with a furnace hackle either side. A few strands of peacock sword fibres over all.

HEAD. Black varnish.

SECTION 10

ADDENDUM

ADDENDUM

THE ONE SERIOUS DRAWBACK I have found when writing books of this type, is the fact that as soon as it is published it is necessary to start bringing it up to date with new material that continues to come along. This is essential of course, if we are to have progressive fly-tying, and as I am fortunate in having a very tolerant publisher in Mr. Archie Black, he has allowed me to insert this addendum. This will also be a feature of my other books as they require to be brought up to date, so that new material can be added without any serious changes of page numbering or alterations to existing indexes.

I have put the country of origin on the dressings now given, so it can be taken for granted that if no country of origin is given, it is a British fly.

I would like to take this opportunity of thanking the many fly-tyers and fly fishermen who have sent in the dressings. Some have not been included here, but this is due to their having been included in my last book *Reservoir & Lake Fishing*, or will appear in the next edition of that book.

1971
                                                              JOHN VENIARD

Assassin
TAIL. Red crow substitute fibres.
BODY. Thin black floss.
RIB. Fine oval silver tinsel.
HACKLE. Black—sparse.
No wing.

Bibio
BODY. Dark blue floss silk.
RIB. Black ostrich herl.
WING. Strips from blue mallard wing quill
as used for "Butcher."

Black Brahan (or Salmon)
TAIL. Golden pheasant crest feather.
TAG. Three turns of ribbing tinsel.
BODY. Red Lurex tinsel.
RIB. Oval silver tinsel.
HACKLE. Black cock or hen.
WING. Black squirrel tail fibres.

Cochan Lass (Welsh Pattern)
BODY. Black wool.
HACKLE. Grizzle dyed scarlet.
WING. From moorhen wing quill.

Dragon (Mayfly Nymph)
HOOK. L/shank No. 8.
BODY. Peacock herl.
TAIL. Fibres of cock pheasant tail.
WING CASES. ($\frac{1}{3}$ of body), Grey goose quill
fibres.
LEGS. Short red game cock hackle.

Green Beast (Water Beetle Larva)
BODY. Grass green floss silk, wound flat.
RIB. Finest oval silver tinsel.

TAIL. Any green-dyed feather fibre, tied
very short.
HACKLE. Brown partridge back feather.
HOOK. 8–10.

Iceberg (Mayfly)
TAIL. Cock pheasant tail fibres.
BODY. Natural raffia.
RIB. One strand bronze peacock herl, or
brown silk.
WING. Deer body hairs tied sloping for-
ward.
HACKLE. Badger.

Kingfisher Butcher (Scotch version)
TAIL. White duck or any other feather
fibres, dyed kingfisher blue.
BODY. Flat gold tinsel.
HACKLE. Orange.
WING. Blue-black feather from mallard
wing.

Kite's Hawthorn (Trout fly)
HOOK. No. 13.
TYING SILK. Black.
BODY. Peacock herl dyed plum colour.
HACKLE. Black cock hackle.

Kite's Pheasant Tail Spinner
TAIL. White cock hackle fibres.
BODY. Red silk and pheasant tail fibres
twisted together, and thicker at thorax.
HACKLE. Natural red cock hackle.

Shorthorns
Imitation of pupae of some of the small
sedge flies such as black and brown silver-

horns and the grouse wing. (Richard Walker in *Trout & Salmon* magazine, December 1970.)

HOOK. 12–14.

SILK. Dark brown

ABDOMEN. Very dark brown olive feather fibre.

RIB. Pale yellow tying silk.

THORAX. Greeny-yellow or orange fluorescent wool, tied ball-shape and twice as fat as abdomen.

WING CASE. Strip of black Lurex tinsel.

HACKLE. Brown partridge back feather, tied underneath and split into two backwards-sloping bunches.

Sun Beetle

HOOK. 12–16.

BODY. Bronze peacock herl.

HACKLE. Black cock from shoulder to tail, clipped level with point of hook.

WING. A few fibres of golden pheasant tippet.

Taylor's Green Champion (Mayfly)

HOOK. No. 6–8 Long shank fine wire.

TYING SILK. Straw.

BODY. Green floss silk.

RIB. Silver wire.

BODY HACKLE. Grizzle dyed blue dun.

SHOULDER HACKLE. Same as body hackle but longer in fibre.

WINGS. Two partridge breast feathers dyed green, sloping slightly forward.

TAIL. Fibres from amherst pheasant tail ¾ in. long, or spotted guinea fowl fibres if amherst not available.

Yellow May Dun

HOOK. No. 13.

TAIL. Ginger cock hackle fibres.

BODY. Yellow seal's fur on primrose tying silk.

RIB. Gold wire.

HACKLE. White or cream cock hackle dyed yellow.

Whiskey (Lake fly)

HOOK. Long shank.

TYING SILK. red.

BODY. Gold tinsel, showing scarlet under-silk as a rib.

HACKLE. Hot orange.

WINGS. Two hot orange cock hackle tips, extending beyond bend of hook.

"EYES." Jungle cock.

Harrison's Glory

An unusual fly for trout and salmon

Harrison's Glory was designed especially for the late Bob Harrison who fished it with success for several seasons. Using this fly in 1965, his son Robert landed a 13lb fish, identified as a sea trout and believed to be a record for the River Test. The dressing, simple though somewhat unorthodox, is as follows:

HOOK. As required, any size from 1/0 to 10 (Redditch Scale).

TAG. Two or three turns of reddish brown floss silk, same colour as body.

TAIL. Three or four herls from a cock pheasant tail feather.

BODY. Reddish brown floss silk, dressed thinly and ribbed with narrow flat silver tinsel or Lurex.

THROAT HACKLE. Two pieces, back to back, from the centre tip of a cock pheasant neck feather. This is the dark golden feather with a scalloped tip and a blue/black stripe across the end. These feathers are veiled with a few strands of cock hackle dyed Cambridge blue, which should be about one third longer than the pieces of cock pheasant neck feather.

WING. Two strips of dark grey overlaid with two narrow strips of light grey, all from wood pigeon tail or wing quills according to size of fly.

The fly can also be dressed as a streamer or lure in which case a single long shank hook is used, or two or three singles joined in the usual manner. The dressing is the same except that the wing now becomes two large cock hackle feathers dyed black and overlaid with a smaller blue dun hackle feather on each side. The cock pheasant neck feather tips are tied in as a beard and the Cambridge blue cock hackle is left as wound with two or three complete turns.

J. M. Noble,
3 Oakfields Road,
Knebworth,
Hertfordshire.

THE McGARVIE PATTERNS FOR LOW WATER SALMON FISHING

These flies were evolved by Mr. John McGarvie over a period of 25 years, and are developed from a "Brown Turkey" pattern the dressings of which are also given here.

The method of fishing is as follows: 1. Grease line. 2. Cast straight across and slightly down stream. 3. Keep the rod horizontal after casting. 4. Retrieve line by pulling in short snatches of not more than six inches at a time, until most of the line used is at your feet. 5. Make one or more false casts again, shooting out the recovered line, and repeat your cast to the far side of the pool.

The method can be varied to suit different conditions, as it is most important to get the right speed of travel for the fly. In a pool with no appreciable flow, the retrieve snatches should be as fast as possible, whereas in a quick flow as the current gives the fly speed, the jerking movement can be achieved by occasional slight pulls on the line. During the very cold weather of early Spring or late Autumn, the hand movement should be slowed considerably—to about one pull per second. Similarly in very bad light or at dusk.

The speed with which the fly is jerked back is most important, and should be varied as much as possible to stimulate the interest of the fish.

Dressings.

Standard patterns—for Water clearing after a spate, on Hook No. 2. Ordinary.

TAIL. Golden pheasant crest. Tag. Fine oval silver tinsel.

BODY. Rear third yellow seal's fur, remainder black seal's fur, well plucked out.

RIB. Flat silver tinsel.

HACKLE. For Spring and Summer—Orange. For Autumn—Claret.

WINGS. Two strips of barred teal—covered with strips of Cinnamon Turkey either side.

Low Water Patterns. 1. For water not yet down to "Low Water." No. 3. Low Water Hook.

TAIL. Golden pheasant crest. Tag. Fine oval silver tinsel.

BODY. As for standard pattern. RIB. Fine oval silver tinsel.

WING. Strip wing of hen pheasant tail—narrow.

HACKLE. Light Coch-y-Bondhu wound as a "collar over front of wing.

Low Water Patterns No. 2 & 3. For Low water with still a little colour left in it. Low water hooks No. 6.

TAIL, BODY, RIB. As for Low Water pattern No. 1.

WING. Tip of a red golden pheasant breast feather, with strips of cinnamon turkey each side.

HACKLE. Light Coch-y-Bondhu, or Light Coch-y-bondhu and orange mixed.

Low Water Pattern No. 4. For Low clear water, and the deadliest of the set. Tied on a No. 6. Low Water Hook. The dressing is exactly the same as for Pattern No. 1, except that the tail is omitted.

The reason for tying the hackle as a "Collar" on the low water patterns is that the jerking movement causes it to open and close, thus giving the fly a more lifelike appearance.

Gosling Mayfly
TAIL. 3–4 brown mallard fibres.
BODY. Yellow sea fur.
RIB. Oval gold tinsel.
HACKLES. Two turns of hot orange, with grey mallard flank in front.
HOOK. Long shank mayfly.

Green Peter (Sedge Pupae) (Irish)
BODY. Green Seal's fur, with a slip of dark green olive feather over the top.
RIB. Gold tinsel.
LEGS. Mallard scapular fibres and/or a few turns of ginger hen's hackle.

Murrough (Sedge Pupae)
BODY. Orange seal's fur mixed with a little hare's ear, and a slip of dark brown feather over.
RIB. Gold tinsel.
WING. Speckled hen wing feather.
LEGS. Mallard scapular feather fibres mixed with some ginger hen's.
HOOK. 7–8 long shank.
These sedge pupae should be dressed with the seal's fur body reaching part way round the bend of the hook (to suggest the curvature of the natural), and with a slip of some darker feather laid along the top to suggest the back. This feather slip should be tied down with the narrow ribbing tinsel to suggest segmentation which is a marked feature of most pupae. The wings should be tied so as to lie alongside the body (the true pupal position, rather than the back which is the adult position, and should reach only half way to the bend of the hook. The hackle should be sparse and soft, and all fibres should be on the underside of the hook.

Dark Peter (Sedge)
BODY. Black seal's fur.
BODY HACKLE. coch-y-bondhu.
WING. Hen pheasant wing quill.
THROAT HACKLE (wound over wing roots) Coch-y-bondhu.
HOOK. No. 9–10.

Green Peter (Sedge)
BODY. Green seal's fur.
RIB. Gold wire.
WING. Speckled hen wing quill.
HACKLE. Light red cock over wing roots. No body hackle.
HOOK. No. 11.

Murrough (Sedge)
BODY. Red-Brown seal's fur.
RIB. Gold wire.
BODY HACKLE. Coch-y-bondhu.
WING. Dark speckled hen wing quill.
THROAT HACKLE. Rhode Island Red, wound over wing roots.
HOOK. 7–8.

Perch Fry (Irish)
TAIL. None.
BODY. Flat gold tinsel.
BODY HACKLE. Golden olive.
RIB. Gold wire.
THROAT HACKLE. Natural medium red.
WING. Two hen pheasant flank feathers back to back.
CHEEKS. Jungle cock.

Sooty Olive (Irish)
HOOK. No. 10.
TAIL. Golden pheasant tippets. Very dark green seal's fur.
RIB. Fine gold wire.
WINGS. From Waterhen wing quill.
HACKLE. Black cock.

Austral (Australia)

TAIL. Light red hackle fibres.

BODY. Hare's fur ribbed with silver oval tinsel.

HACKLE. Light brown.

WINGS. Strips of dyed kingfisher wing quill, with strips of light (oak) turkey wing quill each side.

Cockchafer Beetle (Australia)

HOOK. No. 12.

TAIL. Tippet fibres.

BODY. Orange chenille, with brown chenille tied in at tail and taken over body and tied down at shoulder.

HACKLE. Furnace.

Mud Eye (**Dragon Fly Nymph**) (Australia)

BODY. Dark brown chenille.

WING. Several brown partridge feathers put on flat, so that they curve down either side of body.

HEAD. Brown chenille, with two black beads for eyes on either side.

HOOK. No. 8–10 long shank.

Purple Nymbeet (Australia)

HOOK. No. 10. 1X long.

TAIL. Fibres from a black cock's hackle.

BODY. Purple chenille.

RIB. Thin strip of clear plactic (PVC).

ELYTRA. 10–15 fibres from a large crow wing, tied in at tail end, brought down at head and tied in.

LEGS. Ends of crow fibres bent under head, and cut to form short legs after being tied in position.

HEAD. Good sized blob of clear varnish over black tying silk.

Unsinkable Grasshopper (Australia)

HOOK. Size 12.

"WING". A single plastic mayfly body tied in to ensure that it is airtight, with fibres of golden pheas tippet either side. The latter cut in sections from the quill to form a "V".

HEAD. Made as for "Muddler Minnow" but ensuring that the finer points of the deer hair fibres are left sloping backwards.

White Caddis (Australia)

HOOK. No. 10.

BODY. Green floss silk.

WING. From white duck quill.

HACKLE. Grizzle, wound as a collar.

Cricket (Dr. J. Scott-Findlay, Australia)

HOOK. No. 8–9.

BODY. Rear half black chenille, with a brown hackle wound over it.

THORAX. Fibres from a dark brown turkey tail (3 in. long), wound down on top of the hook so that the ends form legs sticking out from the middle and front of the fly. A brown hackle is then wound over the space where the turkey fibres are tied down.

WING. One white hackle tip.

HEAD. Black cock hackle.

These two flies are originals by Dr. Scott-Findlay, who must be congratulated for the originality of design and natural appearance of the two flies.

Wasp (Dr. J. Scott-Findlay, Australia)

HOOK. No. 10.

BODY. Orange and black hackles wound together and then clipped.

THORAX HACKLE. Orange.

WINGS. Two white cock hackle tips sloping over body.

HEAD. Short black cock hackle.

Emphasis should be on floatability.

Steelhead Flies (American)

Single Egg Fly
TAIL. Orange hackle feather.
BODY. Thick pink chenille, wound double.
HACKLE. White cock hackle.

Thor
TAIL. Bunch of hot orange hackle fibres.
BODY. Red chenille.
WING. White bucktail.

Skyomish Sunrise
TAIL. Red and yellow hackle fibres.
BODY. Red chenille.
RIB. Narrow silver tinsel.
WING. White bucktail extending beyond tail.

Umpqua Special
TAIL. White bucktail.
BODY. Front two-thirds red chenille, remainder (rear one-third) yellow chenille.
RIB. Wide flat silver tinsel.
WING. White bucktail with smaller bunches of red bucktail each side.

Umpqua Red Brat
TAIL. Thick bunch of mallard flank fibres.
BODY. Red chenille.
RIB. Wide flat silver tinsel.
WING. Red bucktail, thick and bushy.
HACKLE. Grey mallard flank wound long in flank, sweeping back to cover bend of hook.

All steelhead flies should be brightly coloured, should sink readily, and fairly sparsely dressed on heavy wire hooks.

KENYA–SOUTH AFRICA FLIES

Black Coachman (Kenya)
HOOK. No. 12.
BODY. Black chenille.
TAG. Flat silver tinsel taken right round bend of hook.
HACKLE. Black hen, wound as collar and sloping backwards, and behind wings.
WINGS. White duck wing quill strip tied flat over hackle.

Highmoor Lady (South Africa)
TAG. Four turns silver wire.
TAIL. Red squirrel tail fibres tied bushy.
BODY. Red chenille.
RIB. Flat silver tinsel.
HACKLE. Blue Jay.
WINGS. Two jungle cock feathers.
HEAD. Red cellire.

Walton's Wonder (Kenya)
TAG. Fine silver tinsel.
HACKLE. Bright blue hackle fibres.
BODY. Red floss silk.
RIB. Fine silver tinsel.
HACKLE. Black hen, or a few fibres of speckled guinea fowl.
WING. Barred teal flank feather, with strips of white duck wing quill over.

Winter's Selected (Kenya)
TAIL. Fibres of well marked guinea fowl hackle.
BODY. Bronze peacock herl.
THROAT HACKLE. Furnace hen.
WING. Summerduck feather fibres or substitute. These are the light brown barred feathers with no black bar.

MISCELLANEOUS FLIES

Cumilahue Special (Chile, S/America)
TAIL. Three fibres barred teal flank.
BODY. Orange floss all the way, covered with bronze peacock herl.
HACKLES (WET FLY). Two Cree saddle hackles. Dry fly—same colour stiff neck hackles.
HOOK. No. 8 L/Shank for wet fly, No. 10 16 for the dry fly.

Green Highlander (Tasmanian Trout Fly)
BODY. Bronze Peacock herl.
TAG AND RIB. Fine oval gold tinsel.

HACKLE. Black hen's hackle.
WING. Barred teal flank feather, dyed "Green Highlander" green.

Jassids (Tasmania and America)
HOOK. No. 14 wide gape down eye.
BODY. Clipped scarlet chenille.
HACKLE. Black cock.
WING. Fibres of white flecked guinea fowl tied on flat. Sometimes the tip of a small jungle cock feather replaces the guinea fowl, and a black body (silk) is an alternative.

INDEX

Abbreviations

Dap.	Dapping Flies	S.J.	"Slim Jim" Flies
Fl.	Fluorescent Flies	T.	Trout Flies
S.	Salmon Flies	Tan.	Tandem Hook Lures

Tube—Tube Flies

Patterns in **bold type** are illustrated in colour